FLORIDA STATE
UNIVERSITY LIBRARIES

DEC 8 1999

TALLAHASSEE, FLORIDA

THE LI DYNASTY

THE LI DYNASTY
HONG KONG ARISTOCRATS

FRANK CHING

HONG KONG
OXFORD UNIVERSITY PRESS
OXFORD NEW YORK
1999

OXFORD
UNIVERSITY PRESS

Oxford University Press is a department of the University of Oxford.
It furthers the University's objective of excellence in research, scholarship,
and education by publishing worldwide in

Oxford New York

Athens Auckland Bangkok Bogotá Buenos Aires Calcutta
Cape Town Chennai Dar es Salaam Delhi Florence Hong Kong Istanbul
Karachi Kuala Lumpur Madrid Melbourne Mexico City Mumbai
Nairobi Paris São Paulo Singapore Taipei Tokyo Toronto Warsaw

with associated companies in Berlin Ibadan

Oxford is a registered trade mark of Oxford University Press

Published in the United States
by Oxford University Press Inc. New York

© Oxford University Press 1999

First edition 1999
This impression (lowest digit)
1 3 5 7 9 10 8 6 4 2

All rights reserved. No part of this publication may be reproduced,
stored in a retrieval system, or transmitted, in any form or by any means,
without the prior permission in writing of Oxford University Press,
or as expressly permitted by Law, or under terms agreed with the appropriate
reprographics rights organization. Enquiries concerning reproduction
outside the scope of the above should be sent to the Rights Department,
Oxford University Press, at the address below

You must not circulate this book in any other binding or cover
and you must impose the same condition on any acquirer

British Library Cataloguing in Publication Data
available

Library of Congress Cataloguing-in-Publication Data
available

ISBN 0-19-590904-6

Printed in Hong Kong
Published by Oxford University Press (China) Ltd
18th Floor Warwick House East, Taikoo Place, 979 King's Road, Quarry Bay
Hong Kong

**To my wife Anna
and our son Jonathan**

ACKNOWLEDGEMENTS

This book would never have been written—or finished—without the patient support and encouragement of my wife, Anna. It would also not have been written if the members of the Li family themselves had not cooperated over a period of almost a decade by making themselves available for numerous interviews, sometimes to the point where their privacy was in danger of being invaded. Many colleagues and friends of Li family members also made themselves available for interviews.

But I would like to acknowledge the help, first and foremost, of David Li. He paved the way for me to meet his father, F. S., as well as his uncles and other members of his large and distinguished family. The member of the Li family with whom I have spent the most time over the span of a decade is Simon Li, who, over the years, has become a personal friend.

I was privileged to interview Li Chok-lai, the last surviving member of the elder generation, as well as Mrs Li Lan-sang, Leung Suk-ying. I also wish to acknowledge the contribution of other members of Simon's generation: F. S. and Daisy Li, Fook-hing and June Li, Ronald Li, Doris Li, Aubrey and Laura Li, Henry and Vivian Li, Fook-kow and Edith Li, Eric Li, Alan Li, Cornel Li, and Helena Li.

Alas, because this project has been so many years in the making, some of those who contributed substantially to the book died before its publication, including Mr F. S. Li, Dr Henry Li, Mrs Edith Li, and Mr Li Chok-lai.

As for the younger generation, I am particularly indebted to David Li, Arthur Li, Gladys Li, Andrew Li, Donald Li, Aubrey Li Jr. and Elizabeth Li, Alfred Li, Lawrence Li, Erica Li, Stephen Li, Simon Li Jr. and June Li, Dominique Li, and Didier Li. Other members of the family who were of help included Paula Li, whose childhood memories were of enormous value, Stanley Li, who provided insight into the life of Chok-chung, his father, Li Fook-kay, Li Fook-hoi, Li Kwok-ho, Edwin Li, Albert Li, Grace Li, Carol Li, Patricia Li, and Raymond Chow.

Outside the immediate Li family, I am also grateful to many of their friends and associates, including David MacDougall, Sir Kenneth Fung, Lawrence Fung, Sir Y. K. Kan, Michael Kan and Tom Kan, Raymond Pih, Sir Jack Cater, Sir David Akers-Jones, T. C. Cheng, Steve Tsang, Augustine Chui, Elizabeth Wong, Michael Cartland, Billy Lam, Thomas Sin, John Banigan, Fung Man-yet, Woo Jan-ya, Lau Kaai, Joyce Symons, Wang Gungwu, and Leo Goodstadt.

In addition, for various acts of kindness and assistance, I am grateful to Edward K. Y. Chen, Elizabeth Sinn, Steve Tsang, Anthony Dicks, Wei Pei Ti, the late Brother Brendan Dunne of St Joseph's College, George Ho, J. S. Lee, Raphael Chan, James Hayes, Brook Bernacchi, and Peter Vines.

I am most grateful to Carl Smith for sharing the information on Hong Kong's history he has accumulated over the years, as well as making available his voluminous files. I am also grateful to Robert Lloyd George for providing access to the archives of the former Banque de l'Indochine, now Banque Indosuez, in Paris.

I have made use of the Public Records Office in Hong Kong, as well as the Public Records Office in London, records kept at Lloyd's Register of Shipping, and archives of old Chinese-language newspapers published in Saigon that are now kept in Versailles. In addition to personal interviews, much information was also gleaned from newspaper accounts and records of births, deaths, marriages, and other major events.

In addition, I owe my sister, Priscilla Chung, and her husband, Peter Dobson, a big debt for the helpful comments they made on the manuscript at various stages.

CONTENTS

Acknowledgements   vii

Introduction   xi

The Early Years

1. The Sojourner: Li Ka-shing (1808-1868)   1
2. Li Shek-pang (1863-1916): The Patriarch as a Youth   9
3. Li Shek-pang Becomes a British Citizen   18
4. 1910: Sued by his Nephew   25
5. Li Koon-chun (1887-1966): The Patriarch's Successor   32
6. 1918: A Bank is Born   39

The Pre-War Era

7. 1924: Battle with the Foreign Office   47
8. The 1920s: Turmoil in the Shipping Business   58
9. 1933: A Double Wedding Binds Three Families   65
10. Shek-pang's Sons Grow Up   74
11. Li Tse-fong: Banker, Horse-Owner, Politician   85

War and Enemy Occupation

12. Li Lan-sang (1900-1969): Racing Continues as War Approaches   97
13. 1941: Hong Kong Surrenders to Japan   104
14. 1943-1945: Life Under Enemy Occupation   115

In the War's Aftermath

15 Charges of Collaboration: Tse-fong's Final Days (1945–1953)   123
16 The 1950s: After the War—A Changed Existence   129
17 F. S. Li: Man on a Hit List—The Cultural Revolution Strikes   136

Modern Hong Kong

18 Simon Li: First Chinese High Court Judge   149
19 Aubrey Li: Negotiating Hong Kong's Future (1982–1984)   162
20 David Li: Banker and Politician   174
21 Ronald Li: Father of the Stock Exchange   186
22 The Fall of Ronald Li   198
23 Li Fook-kow: A Very Senior Civil Servant   207

Into the Twenty-First Century

24 Simon Li: Drafting Hong Kong's Constitution (1985–1990)   219
25 Gladys Li: Chairman of the Bar   226
26 Arthur Li: Doctor and Educator   236
27 One Family, Four Nationalities   243
28 Andrew Li: The First Chief Justice   248

Conclusion   265

The Li Family Tree   268

INTRODUCTION

This is the true story of a Chinese family in Hong Kong—not an average family, but a very special one with great wealth and power. This family is unique because its members have been prominent for five generations as businessmen, bankers, senior government officials, legislators, and advisors to the British governor—and, in recent years, as advisors to the Chinese government. During the transition from British to Chinese sovereignty, members of this one family became important players on both the British and Chinese sides.

Though at various times others have surpassed it in terms of wealth or power, this family is unmatched in its staying power, from generation to generation. This book is a chronicle of that special family—the Li family of Hong Kong—arguably the most outstanding aristocrats in the British crown colony and, very possibly, the first aristocrats in China's first Special Administrative Region.

In the history of this one family, its tragedies and its triumphs, lies the history of Hong Kong itself. Members of the Li family have been in Hong Kong from its earliest days, experiencing the rough and tumble of life in what then was a frontier region. They are still here today, when the vibrant, pulsating city, whose very existence affirms the capitalist way of life, is launching itself into a new era of uncertainty as a Special Administrative Region of the People's Republic of China after 1 July 1997.

The Lis always thought of themselves as Chinese. Even when sons were sent to England to study and rub elbows with upper-class British boys, care was taken to tutor them regularly in Chinese.

Respectability was the hallmark of the family. They have been likened to the Rockefellers in terms of wealth and to the

Kennedys in terms of political influence. Until Ronald Li, former chairman of the Stock Exchange of Hong Kong, with personal wealth estimated at over US$1 billion was convicted on corruption charges, there was never a whiff of scandal associated with the family. The family has long been associated with the prestigious Royal Hong Kong Jockey Club (now the Hong Kong Jockey Club). Today, the club's chairman, Alan F. S. Li, is a member of this elite family. In addition, three of the eighteen honorary stewards are Lis.

The Li family's involvement with Hong Kong goes back to the earliest days of the British colony. The first Li to seek his fortune in Hong Kong was Li Ka-shing, a native of Heshan, in Guangdong Province, who probably arrived in the 1850s, part of a wave of relatively well-off Chinese who sought refuge in the British colony from the turmoil of the Taiping Rebellion.

His youngest son, Li Shek-pang, is revered today as the founder of the clan in Hong Kong. His father died when he was only five years old, so Shek-pang was largely a self-made man. He enrolled himself in a Roman Catholic missionary school and acquired a smattering of English, enough to enable him to get by when he needed to deal with colonial officials or Western businessmen. At a time when trade was the colony's raison d'être, he went into the shipping business, buying second-hand cargo vessels to ply between Saigon and Hong Kong. His fortunes were considerably enhanced by the First World War, when his rusty vessels, which escaped requisitioning for four years, enjoyed a near monopoly. He was also a major importer of rice from Annam (currently part of Vietnam) and operated his own rice-milling operations.

A shrewd businessman, he eschewed politics though he was among the group of prominent Chinese who were consulted by the colonial rulers on major issues. This included a law to make the fashionable Peak district a Caucasian preserve, a move to which the Chinese grudgingly acquiesced.

INTRODUCTION

By the time of Li Shek-pang's death in 1916, he left a fortune of such dimensions that it was enough to make each of his six sons (born of one wife and two concubines) independently wealthy. Some of his sons squandered their wealth, and one even fell into poverty so abject—after dissipating his patrimony on gambling and women—that he had his mother's remains exhumed so as to sell her burial plot.

But the other sons prospered mightily, both through developing their father's various businesses and by starting ventures of their own, in particular by founding the Bank of East Asia in 1918, together with several other prominent Hong Kong families. Their progeny were so numerous that, at the death of Li Shek-pang's last surviving widow in 1965, at the age of eighty-four, his living descendants numbered well over a hundred, with four sons and a daughter, twenty-four grandsons and twenty granddaughters, thirty-four great grandsons and thirty great granddaughters, and two great-great grandsons and one great-great granddaugther.

By the time of World War II, the Li family was prominent in politics as well as business, serving as advisors to the British colonial government. Two brothers also served the Japanese occupation authorities, one of whom had to face a British investigation on suspicion of collaboration after the Allied victory.

Hong Kong was a much smaller community in the pre-war days, and the children of the families associated with the Bank of East Asia grew up together, played together, and married each other. Three of the main families were linked through one pivotal wedding ceremony in 1933, in which twin sons of the Fung family married daughters of the Li and Kan families. For decades, the families were bound together by the ties of marriage and business. But, over time, family interests diverged. For years at a time, members of one family would not speak to members of another family. Perhaps because the ties that bound them together were so deep and all-encompassing, the wounds inflicted when those ties were ripped apart were that much deeper.

The Bank of East Asia is now the largest local bank in Hong Kong. The chairman of the board and chief executive is David Li, great-grandson of Li Shek-pang. When the bank celebrated its eightieth birthday in January 1999, six of the thirteen board members were from the Li family. The oldest was the eighty-two-year-old Aubrey Li, David's predecessor as chairman, and the youngest was his son, Aubrey Jr., the forty-eight-year-old managing director of N. M. Rothschild & Sons (Hong Kong) Ltd. Only a single descendant of one of the other founding families remains on the board: all have yielded pride of place to the Lis.

Many of Li Shek-pang's descendants, well-educated, sophisticated, and able to operate in either a Chinese or Western milieu, made their mark on Hong Kong. One was the first local boy to become a chartered accountant, one became the highest-ranking Chinese civil servant of his day, and one was a pioneer who established a stock exchange. Converted to Christianity during the ordeal of the Japanese occupation, many became active in church affairs. One was a deacon in a church in Los Angeles' Chinatown and met his death at the hands of a crazed gunman who shot down several people before he was killed himself. (This was not the only instance of death by violence. Another Li was killed on New Year's Day, 1983, in a murder that remains unsolved.)

During the communist-inspired riots of 1967, the name of Li Fook-shu, better known as F. S. Li, oldest grandson of Li Shek-pang, appeared on a death list of six prominent Chinese deemed to be traitors to the motherland. The Chinese government abrogated a contract to sell rice to the family's rice importing company. The riots drove a number of Li family members—as well as other Hong Kong people—to emigrate, primarily to the United States, though some returned when the threat receded.

Introduction

When the Communist takeover in 1997 became a certainty, some members of the Li family again prepared to pack their bags to leave. But, ironically, others enjoyed the confidence of the Communist Party. And now, the Chinese government is itself a part owner of the Bank of East Asia. And David Li, whose father's name had appeared on a communist death list, is one of China's trusted advisors.

The Li family for generations was held together by common reverence for its patriarch but, as the family branched out, the old traditions began dying out. Today, the family is so numerous that relatives pass each other on the street without knowing that they are related. As the curtain comes down on one era of Hong Kong history and rises on another, some Lis are ebullient while others apprehensively adopt a wait-and-see attitude. In their mixed feelings, members of this aristocratic family reflect the emotions of their fellow Hong Kongers.

The Early Years

Chapter 1

The Sojourner: Li Ka-shing (1808–1868)

In the pre-dawn darkness of 23 November 1988, a Toyota Crown sedan pulled out of the deluxe White Swan Hotel on Shamian Island. Following the contours of the Pearl River, it came to Zhongshan Road, where it took a sharp left to cross the Pearl River Bridge. Then it wound in a south-westerly direction through the streets of Guangzhou, formerly known to the West as Canton.

Inside were three passengers. One was Simon Li, recently retired as vice president of the Court of Appeal in Hong Kong, a distinguished man with thinning grey hair and a receding hairline; he wore a conservative dark jacket and red tie over a crisp white shirt. His wife, Lillian, a quiet, private woman in her sixties, wore a grey Western jacket over a striped blouse and slacks. The third passenger was an official from Heshan County, south of Guangzhou, who had gone to the provincial capital the day before to escort the couple back to Heshan (Hokshan in Cantonese).

The former judge, sixty-six years old, was in the southern Chinese city for a meeting of the Basic Law Drafting Committee. He had a free day between sessions and decided to take the opportunity to travel to Heshan, his family's ancestral home, which he had never visited.

During his youth, the family had maintained tenuous ties with the ancestral village. Twice a year, on traditional festivals, all male members of the family in Hong Kong received roast pork sent by relatives in Heshan. But by the time it arrived, the meat was so rotten it had to be thrown away. After the triumph of the communists in China's civil war in 1949, these ties were severed. In fact, the local authorities in Heshan denounced the Li family as 'wealthy merchants'.

Heshan today is one of six counties that make up Jiangmen municipality, in the western Pearl River Delta, along the lower reaches of the West River. It has a population of over 300,000 people. Jiangmen, like the rest of the Pearl River Delta, benefited from the economic boom of the late 1980s, brought about by China's Open Door policy and the resulting flood of investment from Hong Kong. Waitun, the Li ancestral village, lies in the county's north-eastern corner, almost surrounded by the waters of the West River and its tributaries. It is now home to 13,000 people.

Despite the early hour, the streets of Guangzhou and the surrounding countryside were clogged with trucks, bicycles, and three-wheeled rickshaws, turning the eighty-kilometre journey to Heshan into a two-hour crawl.

As the car approached the county seat, thousands of people thronged the streets in welcome. Streamers honouring the visitors were tied between trees. Local officials greeted the visitors, while young students in uniform clapped and chanted in unison: 'Welcome! Welcome! Warmly Welcome!' Schoolgirls placed garlands around the visitors' necks. Firecrackers crackled. A lion dance was performed to the music of drums and cymbals.

The Early Years

A sign prominently displayed outside the main office building proclaimed in golden letters set against a red background: 'Warmly welcome the glorious return to their hometown of Mr and Mrs Li Fook-sean.' It was signed 'The People's Government of the County of Heshan'. Throughout the festivities Simon Li and his wife maintained a subdued demeanour, characteristic—perhaps—of a judge.

Virtually the entire leadership of the county turned out. These included the county's party secretary, its vice governor, the director of the Overseas Chinese Affairs Commission, the chairman of the Overseas Chinese Association, the vice chief of the Reception Centre, the head of the United Front Department, and the township party secretary.

After lunch came a tour of Heshan, which underlined the Li family's roots in the area. Two bridges and a hall in the local high school bore the name of Li Shek-pang, Simon Li's grandfather.

The tour included a visit to Waitun village, where Simon was taken to view ancestral property, complete with a cluster of new-looking houses. Originally built by his great-grandfather, the structures had been recently rebuilt, the old ones having been torn down in a political campaign against landlords and capitalists. So meticulous were the local leaders in their restoration that eight mango trees, planted by Simon's great-grandfather and subsequently cut down, had also been replaced.

When the communists took over in 1949, part of the Li properties were flooded and uncared for. The family by then spent very little time in Heshan, having made Hong Kong their home. Houses stood empty. Because the Li family was classified as 'rich merchants', Simon Li's father had received a letter from Heshan after the communist takeover. It accused him of corrupting the youth of Heshan because he had financed the establishment of a primary school before the war. His acts of charity—sending of rice to relieve food shortages during bad times—were interpreted as attempts to bribe and win the support of gullible villagers.

But all that was in the past. By the early 1980s, the communist authorities were eager for foreign investment, and established Hong Kong families, like that of Simon Li, were sedulously wooed. In 1986, the old Li family houses were rebuilt and put on display.

The tour ended in the late afternoon on the outskirts of the village. A ninety-year-old man whose gnarled face was framed by grey hair and a grey stubbly beard led Simon and his wife to a mound overgrown with grass on White Silver Hill. That, the old man said, was the grave of Li Ka-shing, the judge's great-grandfather, who had died in 1868. Sitting on a rock, the ancient told the visitors that, as children, he and his friends used to play in the vicinity.

Simon and Lillian removed the garlands around their necks and placed them gently on the mound. Devout Catholics both, they bowed their heads and said a silent prayer before the unmarked grave.

The nonagenarian, referring to the widely held Chinese belief in *feng shui* (literally, 'wind and water'), or geomancy, said that the grave site was extremely auspicious, and was known locally as 'Five Ghosts Transporting Treasure'. The later success of Li Ka-shing's progeny convinced many that the site was truly auspicious. And so, over the years, many others were buried nearby in the hope that their descendants, too, would share in some of the good fortune that fate had seen fit to bestow on the Li family in such abundance.

✻   ✻   ✻

The Early Years

Li Ka-shing was born in 1808, in Waitun Village of Twin Bridges District, in the north-easternmost sector of Heshan county. In the north, far away in the capital of Peking (Beijing), the forty-eight-year-old Jiaqing emperor was on China's Dragon Throne, the fifth in the line of Manchu emperors. On the surface, the empire was at peace, and the population had grown to about 300 million. In fact, the population had increased so rapidly that the country was finding it difficult to feed all its people. In southern China, provinces such as Guangdong (Kwangtung), where Heshan was situated, were often the victims of pirates.

Li Ka-shing's family had lived in the area for generations. Lis had lived in or near Heshan since before 1732, when Heshan was made a county. (The name means 'Crane Hill', an allusion to a nearby hill that was thought to resemble a crane.) At that time, ten per cent of the population of the seven districts that comprised Heshan were surnamed Li. In Twin Bridges District alone there were fifteen separate Li families. But, according to the official county history, the Lis of Waitun were not indigenous to Heshan. They had moved there from Nanhai County, just across the West River. Before that, they had lived further north, in northern Guangdong, near Jiangxi Province.

Little is known about Li Ka-shing's childhood, though oral tradition has it that his family was not wealthy; his father and grandfather were both farmers. As was customary at the time, his family arranged for him to take a wife at a young age, a local girl from the Lu family. By the time she produced a son, Ying-choi, Li Ka-shing was twenty-six years old. Later, he took a concubine, one of his own choosing, surnamed Fung. She gave him two more sons, whom he named Kin-choi and Pui-choi, born in 1859 and 1863 respectively. (The youngest son, Pui-choi, was also known as Shek-pang.) Li Ka-shing also fathered four daughters, some of whom died in infancy. Nothing is known about them, not even their names.

The Li Dynasty

By the time Li Ka-shing was a teenager, the smoking of opium was an increasingly serious problem. The import, sale, and consumption of opium had been banned in China since the eighteenth century. However, widespread corruption among customs officials meant the trade was conducted more or less openly. The hub of this traffic was Guangzhou, barely eighty kilometres from Heshan.

When the Opium War broke out in 1839—the war that led to the cession of Hong Kong Island to the British in 1842—Li Ka-shing was in his thirties. He did not own land, but had to rent it from a landlord. Like others in Heshan, he supplemented his income from crop planting by raising fish.

By the early 1850s, southern China was in the grip of civil unrest. An uprising, known as the Taiping Rebellion, started in Guangxi and spread east towards Guangdong, as well as north. The leader of the revolt, Hong Xiuquan, claimed to be the brother of Jesus Christ. The movement's pseudo-Christian origins caused the countries of the West to consider, albeit only briefly, giving support to the rebels. The uprising was of such scope and intensity that the Qing Dynasty was almost overthrown.

As the Taiping rebels headed north, they inspired a series of uprisings in Guangdong. The fall of Foshan, the siege of Guangzhou, and the general unrest in Guangdong caused an exodus of the wealthier classes to Hong Kong in the 1850s. It is likely that Li Ka-shing was part of this wave of people who flooded into Hong Kong.

For the most part, new arrivals such as Li Ka-shing were sojourners, not immigrants. They sought refuge in Hong Kong, but intended to return eventually to their native villages. Some stayed in Hong Kong because of the business opportunities but, like Li Ka-shing, they kept close ties with their homes in China. In this, the Chinese were no different from their Western counterparts. Hong Kong, unlike other colonies, was a trading post where the residents, Chinese and Europeans alike, were not settlers.

What little we know about Li Ka-shing's business emerged more than forty years after his death, when one of his grandsons took an uncle to court in a dispute over family property. Li Ka-shing was associated with a firm known as Sui Shing, which was in the ship chartering business. His connection with the firm must have been substantial since, after his death, two of his sons also worked for the company.

We know that, while he lived and worked in Hong Kong, his wife and concubine remained in Heshan. All of his children were born there, not in Hong Kong, and he made trips home to see his family.

As Li Ka-shing became more successful, he built a complex of houses in Waitun for himself, his wife and concubine, and their children. He allotted separate houses to each of his three sons. A manager was in charge of running the family's affairs. Servants bought food in the market each day for the various households within the family, and the food was hung outside each doorway, to be prepared by members of that household.

Like many who achieved limited financial success, Li Ka-shing sought to raise his social status by purchasing an imperial Chinese title, that of *deng-shi lang*, or Court Gentleman for Promoted Service. This was equivalent in rank to the lowest civil service grade, but for someone who had little formal schooling, it was a breakthrough into the elite circle of scholars and officials. Moreover, he lavished funds on his eldest son so that the young man had the means to obtain a classical Chinese education and become a real scholar.

In 1868, on one of his trips back to Heshan, Li Ka-shing became ill and died at the age of sixty. He was survived by his wife and concubine, as well as his three sons. The funeral was enormous. The mourning ceremony was conducted in the street, since no local building was large enough to hold all the mourners. A temporary bridge of wood and bamboo was erected over a river to allow the funeral procession to reach the burial plot. The grave was located on White Silver Hill; at that time, no other graves existed nearby.

Chapter 2

Li Shek-pang (1863–1916): The Patriarch as a Youth

The death of Li Ka-shing left his three sons fatherless. While the eldest was already thirty-four years old, the two others were mere children. Nine-year-old Kin-choi and Shek-pang (Pui-choi), who was only five, were sent to Hong Kong to be brought up by relatives and friends. Kin-choi died at twenty-nine, but Shek-pang went on to become one of the British colony's wealthiest men.

The boy was apprenticed to the Sui Shing shipping firm in 1878, at the age of fifteen, joining his brother Kin-choi, who had already worked there for three years by then and was, at the tender age of eighteen, the firm's manager and cashier. Shek-pang remained with the firm for over a decade. The company's offices were at 96 Bonham Strand, in the heart of the Chinese business district, to the west of Victoria, the Central District, where British, American, and European companies were located.

Bonham Strand was a narrow street that wound gently along the former shoreline. In the 1870s, the road no longer fronted the sea, thanks to massive reclamation projects to increase

Hong Kong Island's usable land area. Bonham Strand was lined with Chinese herbalists and importers and exporters of such popular Chinese commodities as beans, teas, wines, medicines, and fertilisers. The tiny area encompassed by Bonham Strand, Bonham Strand West, and Wing Lok Street (dubbed 'Rice Street' because of its many rice merchants), gave birth to many Chinese tycoons who rose from humble origins. Many more would-be tycoons, of course, lived and died in obscurity.

Shek-pang worked on the ground floor of a three-storey building, which, like the other houses on Bonham Strand, was relatively new. The area had been rebuilt after a destructive fire in the 1850s.

The Sui Shing office was conveniently situated. If Shek-pang needed flour he would go next door to the shop on the right, while on the left was a grocer. Across the street was Cheung Fat, the barber, and Tai Fung, a store that sold baskets and bamboo furniture. Number 96 was the next-to-last house before the Western Market, which each day saw a hubbub of activity. There the young man could buy fresh vegetables, live chickens squeezed together in wicker baskets, and fish, which were kept alive in basins of water. Hawkers would pluck a chicken for their customers, slit the bird's throat, and drain its blood into a bowl. Fish would be unceremoniously scooped from a basin and immediately gutted.

Much of the late 1860s and early 1870s was a period of depression for the shipping industry, but by the time that Shek-pang started work, it had emerged from the doldrums. The number of vessels using the colony's harbour in 1878 reached 29,369, weighing well over two million tonnes.

Sui Shing was one of seven Chinese-owned ship charterers in the colony. It specialized in running cargo ships between Hong Kong and Saigon, in what was then known as Annam, a Chinese vassal state that was increasingly coming under French influence. This route was shared by other Chinese charterers, such as Tung Kee and Lee Wing. Chinese-owned chartering companies tended to confine their rusty, second-hand coastal steamers to shorter routes. The major shipping routes, those to London, New York, or San Francisco, were the preserve of larger, well-established Western companies.

The late 1870s and early 1880s, when Shek-pang worked as an apprentice, saw a gradual transformation of the colony. A census taken in 1881, compared with one taken in December 1876, illustrated the progress made in just five years. The number of Chinese trading companies increased from 215 to 395; Chinese brokers from 142 to 455. And, while there were no Chinese bankers in 1876, by 1881 there were fifty-five. Even the number of fortune tellers rose from 341 to 2,562. These were signs of increasing prosperity.

But the most spectacular transformation Hong Kong was undergoing lay in the gradual transfer of ownership of land from Europeans to Chinese. The total value of properties bought by Chinese from Westerners was HK$1.7 million, a hundred times more than what Westerners were buying from Chinese. Similarly, Chinese were buying three times as much land as Westerners.

The colony's growing prosperity and increasing business opportunities were evident to young Shek-pang. He realized, however, that he would make little headway within the Western-dominated Hong Kong business community unless he could speak English.

With this in mind, the youth enrolled himself in St Joseph's College, a boys' school with a reputation for turning out graduates who worked in the colony's businesses and government offices. St Joseph's was run by Roman Catholic missionaries known as the Christian Brothers, an order of educators that ran schools in Egypt, Burma, Malaya, Singapore, Britain, and even the United States.

The Christian Brothers first arrived in Hong Kong in 1875. In the early years, the students at St Joseph's were largely Portuguese. Chinese boys were not accepted.

Only in 1880 was an Anglo-Chinese division set up for Chinese students. Li Shek-pang, then aged seventeen, was one of the first thirty Chinese students; he studied such subjects as reading, writing, arithmetic, grammar, geography, and history. All teaching was done in English.

After finishing at St Joseph's, Shek-pang returned to work full time at Sui Shing. He was no longer an apprentice. While he did not receive a salary, he took an active part in the firm's business and earned commissions. He became quite well travelled, since the ships sailed to such places as Guangzhou, Singapore, and Saigon.

Shek-pang discovered that there were two ways of doing business. When dealing with Westerners, every detail of the agreement had to be written down, vetted by lawyers, and signed. But when Chinese dealt with each other, a word or a handshake was enough to seal a deal. Neither party would dream of going back on an agreement just because it was not written down in black and white. A contract was considered not only unnecessary but insulting, since it implied that the other party could not be trusted to keep his word. More deals were done in opium dens and tea houses than in offices.

By this time, Shek-pang was ready to start a family. Or rather, his mother felt that he should take a wife. Through a matchmaker, the old lady in Heshan arranged for her son to marry a girl from a respectable family who was the same age as he, named Hau Yung-chuang.

Like most girls, the bride was illiterate. But she was from a family where girls were not expected to work. As proof of that, her mother had her feet bound when she was a little girl—an extremely painful process—so that they would never grow to a normal size. Tiny feet were valued as a mark of great beauty. Women whose feet were bound also walked with a slightly swaying gait, which accentuated their femininity.

The Early Years

Shek-pang and Hau Yung-chuang moved into an apartment at 190 Queen's Road Central, not far from the Sui Shing office. They lived on the second floor, above a large store that sold imported European goods. From his window, Shek-pang could hear carousing sailors in the evening on their way to the many taverns, or 'grog shops', that dotted the area. They bore such names as 'New York Tavern', 'Empire Tavern', and 'Nemises Tavern'. The area was the contemporary equivalent of Wanchai, which became famous for its Suzie Wong bars during the Vietnam war.

From his home, Li Shek-pang was able to walk to work. Rough stone steps that led down to a narrow lane known as Mercer Street offered a shortcut to Bonham Strand. Enterprising Chinese merchants filled this lane, which was home to such small businesses as egg dealers, box makers, a firewood seller, and a blacksmith.

On his way to work, Shek-pang would smell the sweet aroma drifting from Chinese herbal stores, as well as the more pungent odours that emanated from dealers of salted fish, dried squid, and preserved vegetables. He would also pass such establishments as banks, goldsmiths, pawnbrokers, and ship chandlers.

In 1887, at the age of twenty-four, Shek-pang became a father. His first-born, Koon-chun, was delivered at home, with the help of a midwife. It was a joyous event. Infant mortality was a serious problem at the time, and Shek-pang was lucky that his first-born was healthy. As was the custom, when the baby was one month old and hence likely to survive, Shek-pang celebrated by giving a banquet to which he invited all his relatives and friends.

Shek-pang's wife presented him with children at regular intervals. Not all were born in Hong Kong. Sometimes, when she was pregnant, she returned to Heshan to be with her own family, and had the baby there. Altogether, she gave birth to four sons and four daughters. Only three—all sons—survived.

Shek-pang retained close ties with his mother, uncles, and cousins in Heshan, whom he would see on visits home. He also had business interests in his native village, such as the raising of fish and silkworms, and preparation of special paper for rolling into cigarettes. In addition, he had an interest in a Chinese native bank called Nam Wing.

In 1888, he went to Heshan again, but this time it was not a journey of joy. Instead, it was to mourn the death of his brother Kin-choi, who had worked with him in the Sui Shing firm for over a decade. Kin-choi, only twenty-nine, left behind a widow, a concubine, and several small children. After the funeral, Shek-pang consoled the women and assured them that he would take care of them. For the next two decades, he sent money every month to support his brother's family.

Shek-pang also used this trip to build up his capital by selling what land he owned in Heshan. After returning to Hong Kong, he left the Sui Shing firm, which was then in dire financial straits, and in 1891 invested his money in another ship chartering company, called Nam Wo. He became its manager.

Nam Wo, like Sui Shing, specialized in running ships between Hong Kong and Saigon. But Nam Wo did not own the ships and, when not under charter to Nam Wo, the owners would charter them out to other people for other purposes, such as taking part in the coolie traffic, sending labourers from China to work overseas on plantations and building railroads.

Shek-pang worked hard to make his fortune, making the most exacting demands on himself, to the detriment of his health. Moreover, he enlisted the help of his oldest son, Koon-chun, from the age of thirteen. As a result, the boy received little formal education. After working all day, Koon-chun studied in the evenings at the home of a scholar, Mok Lai-chee, often sleeping little more than three or four hours a night. He also received some lessons in English from an American ship broker, Edward Constant Ray, but he learned most of his English on his own, with the help of a dictionary.

In 1899, Li Shek-pang took a concubine. It was, in a sense, a mark of success for a man to have a concubine, since it showed he could afford more than one wife, as well as a large number of children. In fact, it was not unusual for a wife to pick a concubine for her husband.

Shek-pang's wife, Madam Hau, decided that her own maid, a plain, headstrong sixteen-year-old girl called Yam Sui-chee, twenty years younger than her, would be appropriate. The girl was a *mui tsai*, or slave girl, from Heshan, a distant relative from a poor family. It was common in those days for girls from poor families to be sold to wealthier families to work as servants for life. Those who were lucky became concubines.

The young woman had worked for the Li household ever since she was a little girl, serving Madam Hau by fanning her in the hot afternoons, pouring her tea, and giving her massages. After she became Shek-pang's concubine, she and the wife continued to have an amicable relationship. To show the respect she had for the older woman, the concubine always addressed the wife as 'Elder Sister'.

Madam Hau instructed her children to treat the concubine with respect, since she had helped to care for them when they were infants. To them, she was known as 'Second Mother'. The concubine, like other girls who were brought up to work as servants, had normal feet, usually referred to derisively as big feet. So, while Madam Hau had tiny 'lily feet', 'Second Mother' had large feet, which were considered unsightly.

Taking on a concubine meant expanding the household. Shek-pang found larger quarters at 115 Wing Lok Street East, not far from Bonham Strand. There, the Li family lived for the next six years. 'Second Mother' Yam the following year presented Shek-pang with a son, Lan-sang. This son was followed by a girl who, like all Shek-pang's other daughters, did not live long.

A few years later, Shek-pang took a second concubine, a beautiful dusky woman named Chou Shing-kam who, because of her dark complexion, was popularly known as Black Peony. This spouse was his own choice, not his wife's. She was referred to as 'Third Mother'. Another concubine meant another move, this time to 81 Wing Lok Street. This move was permanent; the property would remain in the hands of the family for generations.

Like his other spouses, this concubine was illiterate. Women at the time were not expected to be educated or to take an interest in public affairs or business, or even to appear unaccompanied in the streets. The traditional value system decreed that women should subordinate themselves to their fathers before marriage, to their husbands after marriage, and to their sons in old age. 'Ignorance in a woman is a virtue', ran the adage.

Shortly after Black Peony joined the household, tragedy befell the family. Li Shek-pang's mother, widowed for three-and-a-half decades, was dying. His father had died when he was only five, so she was the only parent he had ever known. In a desperate attempt to save her, he resorted to the traditional Cantonese concept of *tsung hay*, or 'suffusion of happiness', whereby it was believed that a critically ill person might recover because of a joyful event. He arranged for his oldest son, fifteen-year-old Koon-chun, to take a bride, a girl of the same age from Heshan.

This desperate manoeuvre did not achieve its purpose, for the old lady died not long after the wedding. But, because of this marriage, Koon-chun's older children were about the same age as his father's children by his second concubine. Black Peony presented Shek-pang with two sons, Chok-chung, born in 1906, and Chok-lai, born five years later. In all, between his wife and two concubines, Li Shek-pang fathered nine sons and six daughters. Six of the sons survived, but by the age of fifty,

Li Shek-pang had no living daughter. Although traditional Chinese families valued sons, Li Shek-pang desperately wanted a daughter.

Chapter 3

Li Shek-pang Becomes a British Citizen

Li Shek-pang's business was severely disrupted in the 1890s, when the scourge of bubonic plague hit Hong Kong. The shipping industry was especially affected, as foreign ports quarantined all vessels from Hong Kong. By the time the plague broke out in 1894, he had already been a partner with the Nam Wo shipping company for three years. The company had become quite successful over the years, and had even acquired one of the colony's first telephone listings. These were limited to government agencies, the police, newspapers, and a few prominent firms and individuals. Nam Wo's telephone number was five. It was to be Shek-pang's telephone number for the rest of his life.

The old man who was the principal owner of Nam Wo was very fond of Shek-pang and, at one time, had wanted the young man to marry his daughter. When the owner died, the business was run by his two sons, who squandered the capital on women, gambling, and alcohol. Creditors threatened the two young men with bankruptcy and imprisonment, since Hong Kong law provided prison terms for those who could not pay their debts. The two brothers turned to Shek-pang and asked him to bail the company out. Shek-pang declined, saying that it

The Early Years

would be wrong for him to take over. But when the two young men got down on their knees and begged him to help, he could not refuse.*

However, Shek-pang wanted to be the sole proprietor of his own shipping company. So he started a new company, Wo Fat Sing, which was initially housed within the Nam Wo premises. It used the Nam Wo telephone, shared Nam Wo ship charterers, and eventually took over the Nam Wo business.

The main cargo that Wo Fat Sing ships brought back from Saigon was rice. It did not take Li Shek-pang long to realize that, if it was profitable for others to charter his ships to carry rice, it would be even more profitable if he himself were in the rice business. So he started another company, Nam Wo Hong, to import rice from Annam.

He sent the newly married Koon-chun to Saigon to run his rice business. The young man proved himself fully up to the task. Koon-chun noticed that unhusked rice had to be milled in Saigon before it was put in sacks and placed aboard ships bound for Hong Kong. He decided that it made better business sense to own a mill, rather than giving that portion of the business to someone else, so he bought a large rice mill in Saigon. Eventually, Shek-pang was involved in all stages of the rice business, from the buying of paddies to milling and packing.

After Wo Fat Sing ships arrived in Hong Kong with cargoes of rice, they would return to Saigon laden with silks and Chinese medicines. Malaria was prevalent in Annam, and quinine was often carried as cargo on Wo Fat Sing's ships.

Shek-pang steadily expanded the scope of his business. With the help of friends and associates, he set up a series of companies in Guangzhou. These were engaged in related businesses, such as importing and selling rice, silks, and fabrics. Still, Li Shek-pang was not content. He dreamed of one day owning his own ships. Before he could do so, however, he had to spend several years laying the groundwork for such a bold

---

* Account provided by F. S. Li, Shek-pang's grandson.

venture. Since the passage of the British Merchant Shipping Act of 1894, only British subjects could own British ships.

Anyone born in Hong Kong was automatically a British subject but, since he was born in Heshan, Li Shek-pang was still a Chinese citizen, in spite of having lived for more than thirty years in the colony. He began to think of applying for naturalization. There were many who had preceded him in such a move, mainly businessmen who believed that their new status would be helpful in business ventures and who also wanted British consular protection while in China.

At first, Parliament in London had to approve each case. In 1880, the Hong Kong Legislative Council began to confer British nationality by passing individual ordinances each time. Most of those who applied were prominent in business, and it was almost a prerequisite for them to own property in Hong Kong, an indication that they were men of substance with a commitment to the colony. Accordingly, in 1900, Li Shek-pang became a property owner.

The first piece of property he acquired was purchased from Un Lai-chuen, a merchant who owned one of the ships Shek-pang chartered. He paid HK$14,000 for the waterfront property. In the next few years, he gradually built up his stable of properties, mainly buildings along busy thoroughfares, such as Wellington Street, Queen's Road West, and Connaught Road West.

Naturalization was a long and difficult process. It involved filling in of forms and a personal interview. Fortunately for Li Shek-pang, he applied for naturalization in 1903, shortly after the passing of a nationality ordinance that made naturalization an administrative rather than a legislative procedure. He was among the first to be naturalized under the new law. The official who interviewed him was a young man named Cecil Clementi, who in later years rose to become governor.

After becoming legally British, Li Shek-pang set about the

business of becoming a shipowner. He bought the *Telemachus*, which he had been chartering for years. That vessel, along with the *Pheumpenh* and the *Laertes*, all British-built, became the workhorses of his shipping empire. To limit his liabilities, Li Shek-pang set up one company for each ship. Thus, the *Telemachus* was put under the Lai Hing Shipping Company Ltd., the *Laertes* the Hung Hing Shipping Company Ltd., and the *Pheumpenh* the Luen Hing Shipping Company Ltd. All these companies were housed at 81 Wing Lok Street, and all the ships were managed by Wo Fat Sing.

Since the Hong Kong business community was relatively small, Li Shek-pang often found himself dealing with the same individuals in his different businesses.

In 1904, Li Shek-pang acted as guarantor for the Bangkok compradore of the Banque de l'Indochine, the French bank that played a quasi-official role in Indochina, including the issuing of currency. The compradore's job in Asia was to deal with the local business community on behalf of Western companies. Since the economy of Southeast Asia was dominated by Chinese businessmen, virtually all compradores were Chinese. The compradore for a bank was responsible for all dealings with the Chinese community. He hired and fired Chinese employees and paid them out of his own salary and commissions. Each Western company had to have a compradore. So important was this position that, at the Banque de l'Indochine, it was not unusual for the compradore to generate at least half of the bank's business. Because so much money was involved, banks were very selective about whom they employed as compradore. To protect themselves, they demanded collateral or a guarantor or both.

The compradore for the French bank in Bangkok was Sam Hing-hi. His guarantor had died and a new one was needed. Li Shek-pang agreed to act as the guarantor and deposited with the Banque de l'Indochine title deeds to property valued in excess of HK$50,000, the amount guaranteed. In return, he stood to receive a share of the compradore's commissions.

Li Shek-pang's ties with the Banque de l'Indochine were strengthened two years later when his friend, Kwok Siu-lau, the bank's first compradore in Hong Kong, a bespectacled man with close-cropped hair and a mole to the left of his mouth, resigned after having served in that post for over a decade. His successor was a young Cantonese named Ho Wing-tsun, a member of an old established local family, who had previously worked for the Hongkong and Shanghai Bank. The French bank required security of HK$100,000, and Kwok and Li each put up half of that amount. It was unusual for the same person to act as guarantor for compradores in two different cities, and the fact that Li Shek-pang performed this dual role testified to his wealth and standing at the time.

The early years of the twentieth century saw Li Shek-pang expand his investment in real estate and financing. Hong Kong's teeming population caused it to expand lengthwise along the coast, both east and west of the city centre. The construction of a tramway in 1904 paved the way for the creation of population centres as far east as Shaukeiwan.

Shek-pang also became active as a moneylender, accepting mortgages against loans. Western-style banks were still uncommon, and private moneylenders were in great demand. As with all creditors, he sometimes had difficulty getting his money back, and he had to resort to legal action. Although Li Shek-pang had studied English at St Joseph's, it was still necessary for each document he signed to stipulate that the contents had been explained to him in Chinese.

Like many Hong Kong businessmen, Li Shek-pang recruited men from his native village to work for him. Many of them, in fact, were relatives from Heshan less fortunate than he. These included his wife's younger brother, Hau Sau-nam. One day his brother-in-law decided to start his own business, leaving

The Early Years

abruptly and taking with him several key members of Wo Fat Sing's small staff. His defection precipitated a crisis for Wo Fat Sing, and for several difficult years Li Shek-pang had to work extremely hard to keep the business going.

He was ably assisted by his oldest son, Koon-chun. Over the years, Li Shek-pang had been a hard taskmaster, demanding as much of his son as he demanded of himself. Once, when Koon-chun was given a bowl of congee (soupy rice) to eat, he set it down and waited for it to cool. His father said: 'Work while you're waiting. It will cool on its own!' Such discipline paid off. Koon-chun's duties ranged from writing out manifests to walking up and down the waterfront, carrying a sandwich board that said 'Fast ship to Saigon'. It was with his help that Li Shek-pang's business prospered, and the older man came to rely more and more on him.

Because of the long years of unremitting toil, Li Shek-pang's health suffered. He contracted tuberculosis, which at the time was prevalent in the colony. He also suffered from diabetes.

In 1907, when Li Koon-chun was only nineteen years old, his father formally gave him power of attorney to act on his behalf in all business transactions. The older man had full confidence in this son, who displayed keen business acumen and sound judgment. From then on, it was Li Koon-chun's signature that graced many of the agreements signed on behalf of the older man.

With wealth came the desire for honour, and Li Shek-pang, like many others in his position, purchased an official title from the Chinese government. He did not hold any government office, and the title purchased did not bring with it any real power. But it did entitle him to wear special robes during festivals, the most important of which was the Lunar New Year. It was customary for businessmen to call on each other during the holidays, wishing each other a most prosperous new year. Li Shek-pang would receive these visitors at his office at 81 Wing

Lok Street. He would entertain both Westerners and Chinese—shipowners, charterers, brokers, insurers, and rice merchants—in the front, while his children and grandchildren remained in the back, eating and drinking with the staff.

Chapter 4

1910: Sued by his Nephew

About this time, Li Shek-pang encountered a threat that was more serious than any he had faced before. This one came from within his family.

For a long time, the widow and children of his brother Kin-choi had pressed him for money, accusing him of having taken over his late brother's assets. The death of Li Shek-pang's mother removed the last restraining influence. His sister-in-law became more insistent, claiming that Shek-pang had appropriated her husband's business interests, and his brother's daughter and son joined in this effort. In 1906, the nephew, a brash young man named Li Chok-hung, arrived in Hong Kong for the specific purpose, as he saw it, of claiming his rightful inheritance. After his arrival the nephew hounded the older man, asking him to give a rendering of accounts of his father's estate.

In 1908, twenty years after the death of his father Kin-choi, the young man started legal action, suing as the representative of his step-mother (his father's formal wife). He asked for an accounting of the assets of his deceased father and for the payment of such amounts as might be found due. Before the case went to court, however, his step-mother died, aborting the action.

The next year, the nephew commenced a new action, in which he widened the scope of the case. Li Chok-hung now claimed to be the administrator not only of his father's estate, but also that of his grandfather. He claimed that some of the assets controlled by Li Shek-pang belonged to his father, Li Kin-choi, while others belonged to his grandfather, Li Ka-shing who, he declared, had been a partner in the Sui Shing shipping company.

In January 1910, the case finally reached the courts. The stakes were high. If Li Shek-pang lost, he was liable to lose the bulk of his assets, estimated at over a million Hong Kong dollars, a phenomenal sum in those days. The nephew filed a writ of *lis pendens*, enjoining his uncle from disposing of any of his properties.

Because so much was at stake, both sides spared no expense. Chok-hung's team of lawyers consisted of three barristers and two solicitors. The barristers were led by Sir Henry Berkeley, a King's Counsel (a title accorded only to the most senior barristers), Dr Ho Kai, then serving his twentieth year as a legislative councillor, and Eldon Potter. Shek-pang's legal team was led by barristers Marcus Warre Slade and C.G. Alabaster. Together, they constituted Hong Kong's most prominent barristers. The case was heard by Acting Chief Justice William Rees Davies in the Supreme Court building, an imposing nineteenth-century structure topped by a classical dome right in the heart of the city.

From the beginning, it was clear that the case would make legal history. It exemplified the difficulties of trying to reconcile conflicts of the legal systems of China and Britain, as well as their wholly different cultures. To this day, Chinese customary law continues to be honoured in Hong Kong. Up to the 1960s, polygamy was legal in Hong Kong, with a man entitled to a wife and an unlimited number of concubines, even though the practice had been outlawed both in mainland China and on Taiwan.

The Early Years

One of the main characteristics of Chinese culture was the extended family. Frequently, when the head of a household died, the property would not be divided, since division would imply the breaking up of the family. This situation might persist for generations, with the property being considered the common property of the family, or, more precisely, of its male members.

When the case of Li Chok-hung v. Li Pui-choi (Li Shek-pang's formal name) opened in court, Sir Henry Berkeley, acting for the plaintiff, asserted that Li Shek-pang had used money his brother had invested in the Sui Cheung rice firm, as well as money invested by his father in the Sui Shing shipping company, to buy shares, property, and steamships. The defence rejected all these allegations, contending instead that Kin-choi had died insolvent, indebted to his brother and others, and that Li Shek-pang had paid off his brother's debts as well as his funeral expenses, and had gone so far as to remit money monthly for the maintenance of his brother's family.

After that, the case plodded on, with days lengthening into weeks. On Friday 11 March, with the trial in its third month, the case took a dramatic turn. Sir Henry Berkeley asserted that the defendant, when he applied for naturalization in 1903, had claimed that his father, Li Ka-shing, had been a partner in the Sui Shing shipping company, a claim he now denied. Sir Henry said Li Shek-pang had told the assistant registrar general, Cecil Clementi, that he had come to Hong Kong at the age of five to study English and had lived on a ship, the *Charteris*, which belonged to the Sui Shing shipping firm, of which his father had been a partner. He summoned Mr Clementi, now Assistant Colonial Secretary, as a witness.

Once Clementi was on the witness stand, he confirmed that in 1903 he had interviewed Li Shek-pang. In the course of the interview, he said, Li Shek-pang made 'a certain statement'. Clementi said he did not remember if Li Shek-pang had mentioned his father's name, but the government official said he had at the time made a note of the statement. Asked to produce the note or to refresh his memory by referring to it, the Assistant Colonial Secretary refused.

'I have been instructed by the Colonial Secretary to inform the Court that the statement was made to me in confidence,' he said, 'and the head of my department instructs me also to say that the production of the document would be injurious to the public service, and that the disclosure of its contents would be equally injurious.'

The tenacious Sir Henry, however, persisted, and Clementi was asked to find out from the government if there were any objections to answering questions the lawyer put in writing. When court resumed in the afternoon, Sir Henry asked: 'Have you made an enquiry?'

Clementi answered, 'Yes'.

Sir Henry: 'And the answer?'

Witness: 'I am instructed not to answer.'

Thus was foiled the attempt to catch Li Shek-pang in a lie. If it was true that Li Ka-shing had been a partner in the Sui Shing shipping firm, then presumably he would have left assets to be equally shared by his three sons. By this time, Shek-pang was the only son still living, and he would have had to give an accounting to his nephews. It will never be known what the government documents involved contained.

The court adjourned for the Easter recess on 24 March, reconvening the following week. The hearing of evidence did not conclude until 3 May, and the barristers for the two sides then began to make their concluding arguments. They were interrupted by the sudden death of King Edward on 6 May. When the news reached Hong Kong, all legal proceedings were halted. Hearings did not resume until after George V was proclaimed King of Great Britain and Ireland and Emperor of India.

That week, the case drew to a close. On Friday, 13 May,

after fifty-two days of hearings (the longest-running case in Hong Kong history at the time), the trial concluded. Judgment was delivered on 6 June. It took two hours. The judge split his judgment, finding in favour of the defendant where Li Kin-choi's assets were concerned, but for the plaintiff where Li Ka-shing's assets were concerned. He ordered Li Shek-pang to give an accounting on the assets of Li Ka-shing and said the case had 'cast serious and well-founded suspicions against the bona fides of the defendant'.

Both parties appealed. In November, the case was heard by the Court of Appeal. During the proceedings, Li Chok-hung withdrew his appeal, but his uncle persevered. Judgment was given on 22 December. The chief justice, giving the decision of the full court, reversed the original judgment, totally vindicating Li Shek-pang. While the final outcome undoubtedly provided a great sense of relief, the prolonged trial had sapped Shek-pang's energies.

By that time, Li Shek-pang was already a grandfather many times over. His first three sons were all married to women introduced by matchmakers. Wherever possible, the matchmakers tried to find women from Heshan for Heshan men. This was not easy, since the womenfolk tended to remain in Heshan while the men went to seek their fortunes in Hong Kong. In 1897, for example, there were 3,012 Heshan males but only 511 Heshan females in the colony.

Li Shek-pang's oldest son, Koon-chun, had two daughters and a son. Shek-pang's second son, Siu-pang, was married while still a student in Guangzhou to a Heshan woman named Luk Lai-seung, and was already the father of two boys who enjoyed teasing and bullying their girl cousins.

The third son, Tse-fong, was married to Tang Sau-hing, whose father was compradore of the Mercantile Bank of India. She was his only child, born in Hong Kong. She had been brought up in the traditional way, with bound feet. During the wedding ceremony, she wore a red veil over her entire face. Kneeling to offer tea to the senior members of the family, her veil obscured her vision. When she was supposed to offer tea to Tse-fong, she mistakenly offered it to his brother Siu-pang instead. For a long time, the family joked that she had accidentally married the wrong man.

She and Tse-fong soon had a baby girl, who died in an unfortunate accident when only a few months old. She was being carried by a servant on the street when the woman stumbled and dropped the baby. The infant died instantly. The grieving mother had a dream in which the dead girl appeared and said she was lonely and asked for permission to marry. To ensure her happiness in the netherworld, a ceremony was held whereby her spirit was betrothed to that of a boy who had also died in childhood.

Shek-pang lived on Castle Road, a steep winding street in the fashionable Mid-levels area above the Central business district. The living room was lined with red mahogany furniture. Shek-pang eschewed soft Western beds, preferring the hard Chinese variety. Under the bed, he kept a bulging cloth bag. One day, when his first grandson, Fook-shu, was three years old, the old man asked him to pull the bag out. He untied the bag and the child saw that it was full of gold coins.

Shortly after the court case with his nephew was settled, Li Shek-pang took action to ensure his family's financial security. He was so fond of his youngest concubine and her two infant sons that he gave them extensive properties and made her their trustee. The sons, he stipulated, would take possession of their property upon reaching the age of twenty-one.

Next, he provided for the son of 'Second Mother', setting aside three pieces of property to be held by her in trust until the twelve-year-old boy, Lan-sang, reached the age of twenty-one.

Having set up trusts for his three minor sons, Li Shek-pang then made provision for his grown children (Li Koon-chun, twenty-five, Li Siu-pang, twenty-four, and Li Tse-fong, twenty-two), bestowing gifts of property on them.

He by no means gave away all his properties. One building he retained in his own name was the headquarters of Wo Fat Sing at 81 Wing Lok Street. Shipping remained his main business, and the *Telemachus* remained the pride of his small fleet.

Chapter 5

Li Koon-chun (1887–1966): The Patriarch's Successor

World War I turned out to be a blessing in disguise for Li Shek-pang. The shipping industry was severely hit, more so than any other sector of the economy. German and Austrian vessels stopped arriving altogether. Some of the largest and finest vessels of the British merchant marine were requisitioned by the British government to carry munitions and other commodities. As a result, the value of ships not requisitioned, such as those of Wo Fat Sing, was enhanced. As the American consul in Hong Kong at the time, George E. Anderson, said: 'Ship owners are enjoying a harvest.'

While Li Shek-pang's business prospered, his health declined. In mid-1916, after returning from a trip to Annam, he discovered that his pulmonary tuberculosis had become acute. He had very little time left. On 4 July, Li Shek-pang took an unusual step for a Chinese; he drew up a will. His father had died intestate, which led to the bitter legal battle with Li Chok-hung, and he was determined to spare his children such an experience. Two days after signing the will he died at home.

Eldest son Koon-chun made the funeral arrangements, placed an announcement in the newspapers, and reported the death of his father to the registrar. Koon-chun also approached St Joseph's College and made a donation of HK$12,000 in his father's memory. In turn, the school named its main hall after Shek-pang.

After the funeral service, Shek-pang's body was kept in a 'coffin home' operated by the Tung Wah Hospital to await burial in China. Return of a body to China for burial was a common practice that reflected the attitude of many Chinese who, regardless of how long they had lived in Hong Kong, thought of China as their homeland.

In his will, Li Shek-pang designated Koon-chun his sole executor. 'I direct that all the existing businesses of the firms established by me in this colony and various ports and also the business of the Compradore Department of the Banque de l'Indochine in this colony shall be carried on as heretofore,' he instructed. He designated all his sons as equal heirs. He stipulated that the property was not to be divided until his youngest son had reached the age of twenty-one. Since Chok-lai was only four at the time, he and his brothers had to wait seventeen years before getting their full inheritance. In the meantime, the will stipulated, each son would be entitled to draw up to half his inheritance if money was needed for business or education.

Li Shek-pang bequeathed to his wife, Madam Hau Yung-chuang, HK$50,000, to his first concubine, Yam Sui-chee, HK$15,000, and to his second concubine, Chou Shing-kam, HK$30,000. His wife had to be accorded a bequest that reflected her more exalted status. Clearly Chou, the youngest of the three women, was especially favoured, certainly more so than Yam.

The will said the money was not to be given to the concubines immediately. Li Shek-pang stipulated two conditions: They must continue to live with the wife, and would only receive the money if, by the age of forty, they had not remarried. For Concubine Yam, this meant a wait of five years; for

Concubine Chou, eight years. In the meantime, they were allowed to collect interest at the rate of 6 per cent a year.

He also gave instructions that HK$30,000 be set aside as the dowry of his infant daughter, Yuet-seung, the daughter he had longed for but who did not arrive until his own time had almost run out.

Ironically, 'Third Mother', or 'Black Peony', the youthful concubine of whom he was so fond, who had produced for him not only two more sons but also the only daughter to survive him, outlived Li Shek-pang by only four years. A heavy smoker, she died of consumption at the age of thirty-six. In a will drawn up the day of her death, she named Koon-chun the executor of her estate. Her children then moved in with Madam Hau, the principal wife. But that lady, too, was in failing health, being afflicted, like her husband, with diabetes. She died in 1923 at the age of sixty-one.

But his first concubine, least favoured and given the smallest inheritance, survived him for forty-nine years and became the family's matriarch. She turned into a domineering woman, who lived with her only son and his family, ruling the household with an iron hand.

'Second Mother' became an institution. It was around her that the family gathered every year to celebrate Chinese New Year, and it was to her that each member of the Li family annually performed the ritual kowtow. Koon-chun, her step-son, was only a few years younger than she, yet each year, on New Year's Day and on her birthday, he would pay his respects and, in the presence of the whole family, kneel down on a cushion and touch his head to the floor to pay her homage. After this, the entire family would do likewise, one couple at a time, generation by generation, while she sat on a chair beside the family altar. On the wall hung portraits of Li Shek-pang and his three spouses. Strings of firecrackers were set off as part of the celebrations, stretching from the fourth-storey rooftop to the street below. The noise they made lasted for half an hour, and could be heard several blocks away. After this the whole family, sometimes numbering over a hundred, would sit down to a meal.

Yam Sui-chee died in 1965, at the age of eighty-four, having outlived two of her step-sons. At that time, Li Shek-pang's living descendants numbered over 100, including four sons and one daughter, twenty-four grandsons and twenty-two granddaughters, thirty-four great-grandsons and thirty-six great-granddaughters, and two great-great-grandsons and a great-great-granddaughter.

The death of Li Shek-pang made Koon-chun the head of the family. The young man's life had already been marked by tragedy. Even before his father's death he had lost his wife of ten years and become a widower at the age of twenty-five. His wife gave him two daughters, Yue-chu, born in 1907 when he was barely twenty years old, and Wai-chun (later known as Fanny), two years later, before presenting him with a son, Fook-shu. Shortly after giving birth to her third child, she caught pneumonia and went to Guangzhou for treatment, dying in that city before the baby boy was a month old. While pregnant, she had consulted a fortune teller about the sex of the baby. He told her, 'Madam, after having given birth to two daughters, you have now conceived a son. But I cannot offer you my congratulations because I fear you may not live for long after giving birth.'

After her death, the bereaved Koon-chun realized he needed someone to take care of his children and so remarried. This wife was named Tam Doy-hing, from a respectable family from Zhongshan, in Guangdong Province. Her father had died young and her mother sent her to Hong Kong to live with an aunt, who had married a very wealthy man, Woo Hay-tong. The idea was that she, too, would find a good man to marry. Tam Doy-hing became a devoted wife. She quickly presented Koon-chun with more children; three girls arrived in succession, followed by a son.

Although Li Shek-pang had stipulated in his will that his arrangement with the compradore department of the Banque de l'Indochine was to remain unchanged, his wishes were frustrated. As soon as his death was known, the director of the bank's Hong Kong branch sent a special advisory to its Paris headquarters. In it, he estimated Shek-pang's estate at HK$5 million, almost a ninefold increase from 1906, when the compradore agreement had been entered into. According to the agreement, Li Shek-pang's liability would continue until three months beyond the date when his executor formally told the bank of his death, including transactions taking place subsequent to his death.

Li Shek-pang had named Koon-chun as his executor, and evidently intended his son to continue his role as guarantor of the compradore. Perhaps for that reason, Koon-chun did not submit official notification to the bank of his father's death. But this seriously worried the other parties involved: Kwok Siu-lau, the other guarantor, and Ho Wing-tsun, the compradore.

Because the 1906 agreement had provided that its terms would continue until three months after official notice of death had been received, the absence of notification meant that the agreement would continue indefinitely. However, for some unknown reason, both the compradore and his other guarantor, while happy to do business with Shek-pang, were quite unhappy at the thought of doing the same business with his son.

On 21 July, a letter was sent to the bank's director in Hong Kong by the solicitors' firm of Johnson, Stokes and Master (still one of the leading firms in Hong Kong today) informing him that Koon-chun 'is not a man who is agreeable' to Kwok Siu-lau and Ho Wing-tsun, who suspected that Koon-chun was deliberately withholding official notice of his father's death 'with the object of remaining associated with the bank and receiving his father's share of the compradore's commission'.

The lawyers went on to say 'it appears to be useless to call upon Mr Li Shek-pang's son to give notice, and to be impossible (as the compradore agreement stands) to get rid of him by notice either on the part of the bank or on the part of the compradore'.

As a way out of this dilemma, Ho Wing-tsun suggested that the bank fire him as compradore—an act that would automatically terminate the old compradore agreement. If the bank refused to take this step, the compradore said, he would offer his resignation, which would bring about the same result. The bank did as he suggested, after which they promptly rehired him with new guarantor arrangements that excluded Li Koon-chun.

In another area, too, the terms of Shek-pang's will were not fully observed. He had stipulated that his three widows should all live under the same roof after his death. Each woman, however, preferred to live with her own children. Thus, his wife spent ten days of every month with each of her three sons. She travelled from son to son in a sedan chair, accompanied by her personal maid. Actually, there was not much travelling involved, because her eldest son, Koon-chun, lived on Caine Road and her second and third sons lived in adjacent houses on nearby Seymour Road.

Like his father, Koon-chun was totally uninterested in politics. He had ample opportunity to join the Hong Kong government's various advisory bodies but declined, devoting himself wholeheartedly to business. Because he had to go to French Indochina to look after the family's business interests there, two brothers pitched in. Tse-fong helped run the Wo Fat Sing shipping company and Siu-pang became secretary of the rice importing company. While Wo Fat Sing was known within shipping circles, it was not a household name. (This was reflected in a newspaper account of a funeral service, when a list of people who sent wreaths ended with the words 'and Mr. Wo Fat Sing'.)

The lucrative war years were followed by an immediate, sharp decline in the shipping industry. During this period, Koon-chun temporarily veered away from the shipping business and turned Wo Fat Sing into an investment company, making loans and in return accepting land as security. The company also obtained a five-year lease on new premises at 2 Queen's Road Central from the China and Japan Telephone and Electric Company, which operated the telephone monopoly. Interestingly, in view of later developments, the agreement specified that the premises could be used as a private residence, for business offices, or 'as a bank'.

Chapter 6

1918: A Bank is Born

In May 1911, just months after Li Shek-pang's triumph in the lawsuit against his nephew, his third son Tse-fong was enjoying a triumph of his own. The governor, Sir Frederick Lugard, went to Queen's College to present badges to the school's first prefects. The occasion was the birthday of Queen Victoria, celebrated as Empire Day. One of the fourteen recipients was Li Tse-fong.

The Second Master, a Mr Ralphs, delivered a speech in which he sought to impress on his young charges the magnificence of the British Empire, of which they were fortunate enough to be a part. 'When Hong Kong is wrapped in the darkness of night, some other part of our Empire is enjoying the midday sun,' he said. 'We might go further and say that there are very few hours of the day or night here when it is not noonday in some British land . . . On this territory dwell 410 millions of people, more than one-fifth of all the world's inhabitants, people of every race and clime, of every colour and every religion, speaking innumerable tongues and living in various degrees of civilisation.'

This was the second time in four months that the nineteen-year-old Li Tse-fong had received an award at the hands of the governor. The previous February, at the school's annual Prize Day, the lad was the recipient of the Ho Tung Scholarship for having distinguished himself in hygiene, geography, and translation. The prize money was HK$100.

Nineteen-eleven was the eve of the Republican Revolution in China and the young man, like his fellow students, still wore a long, white Chinese-style robe and cloth shoes. The front of his head was shaved and his hair was combed to the back of his head and dressed into a long queue, the official hairstyle of the Qing Dynasty. (The following year, the students would don Western-style suits as Chinese cut off their queues to signify the end of 267 years of subjugation by the Manchus.)

Most of the boys were from well-to-do families, and competition to enter the school was stiff; often 40 per cent of the applicants were denied a place. In the classrooms, boys were cramped together, sitting six to a bench, chanting their English lessons. While boys of all races were accepted, the vast majority of the students were Chinese, since a separate school for British children had been set up in 1902.

Tse-fong was older than the average student because he had been sent to Guangzhou to receive his early education in Chinese literature. After returning to Hong Kong, he was tutored at home for several years before enrolling in Queen's College.

In fact, when he received the gilt badge from the hands of the governor, he was already married and, that year, his wife gave birth to their first child (who died in infancy). Married students were not a rarity, and in earlier years used to be quite common. The principal felt that married boys could not concentrate on their class work and would 'invariably lose position in class'. But Tse-fong proved an exception; he was a consistently high achiever, obtaining many distinctions and scholarships.

The Early Years

Two months before the Empire Day celebrations, the Legislative Council passed an ordinance to set up a university in Hong Kong. The university was formally opened in March 1912, but it was not until September that the first undergraduates were admitted. Among the first students enrolled was Li Tse-fong.

When the University of Hong Kong opened its doors, Tse-fong found himself one of only fifty-five students, twenty-two of whom were from Queen's College. They were housed in the Main Building, one of only a handful of buildings on the campus. In addition to the faculty of medicine, there was a faculty of engineering and a faculty of arts. Tse-fong enrolled in the faculty of arts, which did not have a full-time professor but did feature five lecturers who taught courses in English language and literature, modern history, economics and political science, Chinese literature, and Chinese history. Commercial subjects were given special emphasis.

Tse-fong threw himself enthusiastically into the affairs of the university. He was elected to the council of the University Union. The government granted the union land for a recreation ground, and the council worked to raise the HK$18,200 needed for a club house. The zeal with which Tse-fong tackled academic and extra-curricular affairs was perhaps surprising, since domestic affairs, too, claimed much of his time and attention. His wife gave birth to two sons during his four years at the university.

He graduated in December 1916, but the joy of being part of the first graduating class was dimmed by the death of his father five months earlier. Twenty-three graduates received degrees, eight in medicine, twelve in engineering, and only three, one of whom was Li Tse-fong, in arts.

Tse-fong had originally wanted to go to England to study law, but after his father's death he decided to remain in Hong Kong and to help Koon-chun and his brother Siu-pang. (To

41

consolidate the family's rice-related assets in Indochina, Koon-chun created a new company, Sam Hing. The name was a play on words; Sam Hing meant 'three prosperities', but it was also a homonym for 'three brothers'. Koon-chun, Siu-pang, and Tse-fong were the directors of the company.)

While Tse-fong's involvement with Wo Fat Sing and Nam Wo Hong was to continue throughout his life, his main business interest lay in banking. Tse-fong had studied the theory of banking at university and learned much about its practical aspects from his family's connection with the Banque de l'Indochine and his father-in-law's connection with the Mercantile Bank of India.

At this time, the Li brothers met a man who had just returned from Japan after working for the Yokohama Specie Bank and the National City Bank of New York. His name was Kan Tong-po. His family, too, was from Heshan and he, like Tse-fong, was also a graduate of Queen's College. He wanted to set up a Western-style bank in Hong Kong, using Chinese capital, to serve Chinese in the colony and overseas.

At the time, Western-style banks were not common in Hong Kong. Modern Western banks, such as the Hongkong and Shanghai Banking Corporation, primarily served the needs of Western corporations, working with Chinese businesses through their compradores. Many Chinese companies and individuals continued to do business with Chinese native banks, known as *ngan hao*, or 'money shops'. These used methods sanctioned since time immemorial and were increasingly unsuited for modern times, since their resources were generally limited to those of one family or sometimes two or three. They did their business in secret, published no figures, and charged high interest rates.

The two Li brothers decided to join forces with Kan Tong-po and a number of like-minded businessmen to found a new bank. By and large, it was a young group. Kan Tong-po was thirty-six, Li Koon-chun was thirty-one, and Tse-fong was only twenty-nine. Chow Shou-son, at fifty-nine, was one of the oldest. A short, slightly stooping man with bushy eyebrows and a protruding forehead, he would assume leadership of the bank in later years.

On 14 November 1918, the Bank of East Asia was officially incorporated with an initial capital of HK$2 million and a staff of twenty. The initial capital was divided into 20,000 shares of HK$100 each. The nine founders each agreed to put up HK$200,000 with the remaining 2,000 shares offered to the public.

Pong Wai-ting was elected chairman. The board appointed Kan Tong-po chief manager and Li Tse-fong as his deputy. The bank's articles of association were later amended to make Kan Tong-po chief manager for life, and to make Li Tse-fong manager for life.

The board fixed the monthly salary of Kan Tong-po at HK$600 and that of Li Tse-fong at HK$500, adequate but not overly generous, reflecting the conservative nature of the bank. On 4 January 1919, the bank officially commenced business.

Soon, the board made plans to set up agencies and representative offices around the world. The first country to occupy the directors' attention was Vietnam. It was decided to use two Li family companies, Wo Hing in Saigon and Nam Shing in Cholon, as the bank's agents.

The bank's early days in Saigon were marred by an unfortunate incident. On the day of the grand opening of the Saigon branch, the bank's accountant, Yum Man-chee, boarded a train from Saigon to Cholon. He handed a twenty-cent note to the conductor, an Indian, to buy a ticket. The conductor noticed that the note was forged. Yum then produced a HK$20 note and a HK$5 note, but the conductor said he had no change. The accountant then reached in his pocket and pulled out a handful of twenty-cent notes, asking the conductor to choose one. The Indian examined them and found them all to be forged. As soon as the train arrived at the station, Yum was taken into custody.

The police searched the premises of the bank and found more forged twenty-cent notes, amounting to less than HK$10. As a result, they arrested two more men, Li Chak-nien, the financial controller, and Cheng Lin-chi, the cashier. Finally, it was determined that the forged notes had been sent to the Bank of East Asia by another bank, along with genuine notes, to enable the new bank staff to differentiate between them. All three men had mistakenly used the forgeries, and were acquitted.

In addition to its branch in Vietnam, the bank set up a network of banking relations in Europe, Japan, and North America. Agencies and correspondents abroad included Midland Bank in England, the First National City Bank in New York, American Express, the Royal Bank of Canada, and Sumitomo Bank in Japan.

Shanghai, China's financial centre, was considered so important that the bank decided to set up a full branch there, to be followed by another branch in Guangzhou.

The bank's first annual meeting was held on 7 February 1920, presided over by Chairman Pong. He announced that the results of the first year were 'most satisfactory', with net profits standing at HK$370,268. The directors proposed that a dividend of 6 per cent be declared and that an additional HK$37,540 be paid in bonuses to directors, holders of founders' shares, and staff.

'Though the amount of profit would justify the declaration of a higher dividend,' Chairman Pong said, 'yet in order to place the bank on a more solid basis, the directors propose to create out of the profit a reserve fund of HK$200,000, which I trust will have the wholehearted support of the shareholders.'

The Early Years

With both Li brothers in attendance, the chairman also announced the acquisition of a new site for the bank: 'The directors have recently acquired premises next to the Netherlands India Commercial Bank, known as Number 10 and 10A Des Voeux Road Central, for the accommodation of the head office.' The bank's permanent address would be 10 Des Voeux Road Central.

Attention now focused on the opening of a Shanghai office. Spacious premises on the Bund, Shanghai's banking district, were procured and the branch opened for business on 1 April 1920. The bank was situated in the International Settlement in Shanghai, which meant that businesses and residents there would be governed by English law. This offered a large measure of protection against the tumultuous political changes sweeping China and the arbitrary rule of Chinese officials.

Four members of the board, Chow Shou-son, Mok Ching-kong, Chan Ching-shek, and Fung Ping-shan, went to Shanghai to attend the opening ceremony. Li Tse-fong was named the branch manager. Although he was concurrently deputy chief of the head office, he spent most of the next two years in Shanghai, with his family remaining in Hong Kong. By this time he had six children, the youngest of whom was his fourth son, an infant known as Fook-kuen, or Henry.

With the opening of the Shanghai branch, the bank turned its attention to spreading its net in China. A branch in Guangzhou was important, since much business was conducted between that city and Shanghai. But the bank hesitated to open a Guangzhou branch, although it had a site, because of political risk.

The Pre-War Era

Chapter 7

1924: Battle with the Foreign Office

On 2 January 1922, Chow Shou-son and Fung Ping-shan boarded a ferry for Guangzhou to attend the opening ceremony of the Bank of East Asia's latest branch. While still apprehensive of political instability in the city, the bank decided that Guangzhou was too important for it not to have a branch there. Messrs Chow and Fung went a day earlier than the other directors because they wanted to pay a courtesy call on the British consulate in Guangzhou, located on the island of Shamian, in the hope of getting the consulate's help to secure the bank's Guangzhou assets.

Shamian was separarated from the rest of Guangzhou by a canal. In fact, Shamian is an artificial island, reclaimed from a sandbar in the Pearl River by the British and French during their occupation of the city from 1857–1861, during the Second Opium War. It is so small that a person can walk around its perimeter in less than an hour. The island was important because it was administered not by the Chinese authorities but by the British and the French, and was maintained as a European enclave exempt from Chinese law.

No Chinese was allowed to own property there, and the only Chinese allowed to live on the island were servants. Every night, at ten o'clock, the two bridges, one guarded by the French and the other by the British, would close and Shamian would be cut off from the rest of China until the next morning. In such an environment, the Bank of East Asia thought, its clients' money would be safe from marauding Chinese soldiers and local bandits.

It was no accident that these two men were designated by the bank for this mission. They were the most socially prominent members of the bank's board. The Hong Kong government had its eye on Chow Shou-son, who was already a justice of the peace, and was planning to appoint him to much more senior posts. Fung Ping-shan, also a justice of the peace, had served in the two most prestigious posts within the Chinese community: chairman of the Tung Wah Hospital and of the Po Leung Kuk, a charitable organization that cared for orphan girls. More importantly, both men were British subjects.

During their courtesy call, Chow Shou-son, Fung Ping-shan, and the British officials exchanged pleasantries but discussed nothing of substance. The bank was unsure how the British consulate would react to its acquiring land on Shamian.

The following year (1923), however, an appropriate property on Shamian was identified by the bank, a house owned by a British Parsee firm headed by a man named F. P. Vasania. Chow Shou-son, then a member of the Legislative Council, returned to Guangzhou to consult the British consul general, Sir James Jamieson, on the matter. Chow explained that 'owing to the disturbances in Canton, the directors wished to know whether they could get protection by establishing themselves in Canton under British protection'.

Jamieson said that, given the situation in China and the attitude the Chinese authorities were taking regarding persons of Chinese descent, he could not effectively give protection. He said that, even if he agreed to give protection, he could always be asked by Chinese officials to explain why he assumed jurisdiction over a Chinese, or at least a person of Chinese race.

Chow Shou-son, however, was not so easily put off. He said that his father and grandfather both lived in Hong Kong and were British subjects, while he himself was a natural-born British subject, having been born in the British colony. He pressed the diplomat to see what could be done. The consul general again expressed his regret and terminated the discussion. That, he thought, was the end of the matter.

But it was not. The bank decided to go ahead and, in January 1924, the consul general received a letter from the bank's lawyers, the firm of Deacon, Harston & Shenton. The letter reaffirmed the bank's intention of 'acquiring property on the Shameen [Shamian] for the purpose of opening up a branch of their banking business, and have in fact a particular property in view'. After pointing out that seven of the bank's twelve directors were British subjects, the letter asked the consul general 'whether there is any objection to our clients carrying out their proposal'.

The consulate replied, stating that Sir James 'regrets that he is unable to consent to the proposed acquisition of property on the British Concession here by your clients the Bank of East Asia Limited'.

The bank, however, was undeterred. Its lawyers pointed out that 32,268 of 50,000 shares in the bank were held by 'British Chinese', such as 'the Hon. Chow Shou-son, Li Koon-chun, Li Tse-fong and P. K. Kwok'. The lawyers asked 'whether there would be any objection to the property in question being purchased under one of the above four names and then rented out to the Bank of East Asia Limited'.

This proposal, too, was rebuffed. The consulate said Jamieson was 'not prepared to reconsider his decision regarding the acquisition of property on the British Concession here more especially when it appears that British Chinese only hold a little more than half the shares in the bank'. With that exchange of correspondence, the British consul general thought, 'the question had been finally disposed of'.

Again he was mistaken. On 10 August 1924, a Hong Kong lawyer named H. C. Macnamara appeared in person at the consulate and asked to register a deed under which Vasania, on 4 August, had assigned to the bank his Crown lease of his lot on Shamian. The vice consul, Frank Arnold Wallis, refused.

On 5 October, Sir James received a formal application in writing asking for the transfer of ownership to be registered, together with a threat of legal proceedings if the request should be refused. The fledgling Bank of East Asia was jousting with the British Consul General and, through him, the British government.

Jamieson did two things. He confirmed his refusal to register, and also sent a telegramme to his superior, the British Minister in Beijing, that said: 'I have refused to register assignment by a British subject of a lot on Shameen to Bank of East Asia, a Chinese company registered in Hongkong, and am in consequence threatened with legal proceedings which I am prepared to face. If the principle that such companies can acquire land on the island be conceded, it will lead to others following suit which from every point of view would be undesirable.'

The Beijing Legation cabled the Foreign Office in London about the matter, and echoed Jamieson's view that 'if principle that Chinese controlled companies can acquire land on Shameen be conceded it will lead to others following suit which from every point of view would be most undesirable both locally and at other concession ports'. The minister urged the secretary of state to instruct the consul general to refuse to register the Bank of East Asia as tenant of any part of the British Concession at Shamian and that British protection not be accorded to the bank.

The trial, which lasted four days, began on 28 October 1924 in the Shanghai Supreme Court, which was presided over by Judge Sir Skinner Turner. The bank had engaged a distinguished barrister in Hong Kong, Eldon Potter, to argue its case. The defence was handled by Crown Advocate H. P. Wilkinson.

In his opening argument, Potter said the issue was important but simple: Was a Hong Kong limited company, on becoming the assignee of land at Shamian, entitled to registration? And could any minister of His Majesty's government, no matter how highly placed, deprive an assignee of land of the right given him by public statute to become the registered owner of that property?

In response, the defence argued that the Bank of East Asia was not a British bank, but a Chinese concern. And Shamian land regulations stipulated no 'native of China' could own land there.

The judge interposed, saying, '"Native of China" must be a natural person, it cannot be an artificial one [such as a company].'

'Yes,' Potter responded, 'a natural person. In no possible circumstances of law can an English company be a "native of China" although for the purposes of argument we may assume an individual shareholder to be a native of China in the fullest sense of the term. But you cannot bring a Hong Kong limited company within the meaning of that phrase. It could not at one and the same time be in law a British company and also "a native of China".'

Li Tse-fong was the first witness. He stated the business of the bank was directed from Hong Kong, site of its head office. 'The books and correspondence are all kept in English,' he said.

'Most of the directors are British subjects, and British subjects hold about 60 per cent of the shares.'

Asked why the bank was not a member of the Foreign Bankers Association, Tse-fong said the bank had applied for membership but had been refused. He said he did not know why the application had been rejected. Tse-fong pointed out that the Guangzhou branch of the bank had, from the beginning, exhibited a signboard announcing that it was an English bank.

After Li Tse-fong left the witness stand, Potter called Macnamara, the lawyer who had attempted to register the bank's deed at the consulate. The transaction was genuine, Macnamara testified, and the bank had paid for the property. But it could neither sell nor mortgage the property because the title was not good until the transfer was completed by registration at the consulate.

Next, Sir James Jamieson testified that originally only people who had business on Shamian were allowed on the island. As time went by, however, this rule was departed from and the number of Chinese coming became 'so great an impediment to the good government of the island that restrictions had to be enforced'.

Asked if the presence on the island of Chinese who could not be protected would add to the difficulties of the situation, he replied: 'Very considerably. No purely Chinese institution, no association of Chinese, can at the present day dissociate itself from politics, and in the course of the various political disturbances that arise one can never be sure which particular party may want to persecute another particular party, and at no time can one be certain what steps a man's enemies may take to arrest him or assassinate him; and were Chinese, or British subjects of Chinese descent, to reside on the island there would be danger of attempts being made against them on political grounds, and thus the government would be hampered and the inhabitants involved in trouble.'

Wilkinson asked: 'Do you think the presence of this bank, as now constituted, on Shameen for the purpose of business would be open to objection?'

Jamieson responded: 'Yes, I have reason to think so, because the nature of the bank's business differs from that of other banks, such as the Hongkong and Shanghai Bank, the Chartered Bank, the International Bank or any purely foreign bank. They do a purely Chinese business and their clients are purely Chinese, and if I am correctly informed they are associated with the opium trade.'

As soon as Jamieson made this allegation, Potter objected vigorously and asserted that the Bank of East Asia was run on entirely the same lines as the Hongkong Bank. But Jamieson repeated his allegation, saying he had every reason to believe his information was correct.

The Bank of East Asia did not allow the allegation to go unchallenged. It publicly asserted that Jamieson's allegation was 'wholly unfounded and grossly improper'. The bank denied that it had any connection with the opium trade, 'even to the extent that such trade is legal', and challenged Jamieson 'to produce any evidence whatsoever in support of his calumny'. The bank pointed out that, if there were any truth in the allegation, 'it is curious that the information has not, ere this, been placed at the disposal of the Hong Kong Government so that proceedings might be instituted against the bank.'

When hearings resumed, Eldon Potter brought the matter up again. The judge said he regretted the fact that the statement had been reported in the press, and said that there was 'no suggestion that the bank was not conducted in all respects as a perfectly proper banking business'.

Before judgment was pronounced, Li Tse-fong returned to Hong Kong where, at a meeting of the board of directors, he gave an account of the trial, and of his testimony. He told the other directors that Potter's view was that the consul general's case was weak, and the only reason why Jamieson might win was his contention that he represented the Crown. The other directors were cheered by this assessment.

Judgment was pronounced on 5 December 1924. Sir Skinner Turner found in favour of the bank. He unequivocally rejected the view that the consul general could refrain from carrying out his official duty of registering a land transaction, even if ordered to do so by his superiors.

As to whether a British bank could be construed as a 'native of China', Sir Skinner said: 'I entirely fail to see how it can be contended that this British bank can come within the clause "native of China" merely because some of its shareholders and/or directors may not be or even are not subject to British jurisdiction in China. Such a doctrine would affect many other companies. What is to be done with companies who have Americans, Frenchmen, Germans, Russians or Australians on their share registers? Nor do I know how to ascertain the proportion of shares which will turn a British entity into a "native of China". Is it one-third, one-half, five-eighths or what? And how is one to deal with the constantly fluctuating character of a share register? I do not know about the plaintiff bank, but I know bank shares in England are constantly changing hands, and the nationality of the shareholders in any limited company may, and no doubt does, vary from day to day.'

Copies of the judgment were immediately despatched to London. Separately, Wilkinson sent a telegram: 'Judgment today for plaintiffs with costs on ground that statutory duty to register assignment to bank which as British company not within exceptions in lease or Shameen Regulations. Judgment on narrow grounds logical and might be upheld.'

Even while he feared that any appeal would be futile, Wilkinson kept his options open and on 22 December applied for leave to appeal to the Privy Council in London. He explained the great public importance of the case, and asked for judgment to be suspended pending outcome of the appeal. Despite the protestations of the other side, the judge granted both requests.

Back in Hong Kong, the directors of the bank met once again. Li Tse-fong briefed his fellow directors, telling them about the Crown's plan to appeal the ruling to the Privy Council. 'The bank is prepared for this move and has already retained a distinguished lawyer in London,' he said. 'Potter feels it is extremely unlikely that the appeal will succeed.' Again, the directors had to bide their time before starting their operations on Shamian.

Meanwhile, the British government moved into high gear. In addition to pursuing the appeal, consideration was being given to changing the law. W. Leitch, an official of the Office of Works, which was responsible for the handling of Shamian, proposed in a letter to the Foreign Office that 'steps should be taken at once to make the recurrence of such an incident impossible, and we assume that you are considering the suggestion of an amendment of the China (Companies) Orders in Council... I may add that although we cannot now prevent the Bank of East Asia from being lotholders, we can refuse to renew their lease under the new scheme, and this will have to be seriously considered.'

By January 1925, the Foreign Office had decided to deal with the matter by amending the Shamian land regulations as the fastest and easiest solution.

In Hong Kong, the directors of the bank were jubilant when they heard that the appeal had been dropped. They had taken on the British government in court and won. Now, they could finally expand their business operations into Shamian and enjoy full British consular protection. Or so they thought.

During a discussion of the situation on 9 June, Li Tse-fong told the other directors that the Shamian premises had been rented out to a Japanese concern, and the lease would expire on 1 September. However, he said, the lease provided for an option to renew for an additional five years. The bank's lawyer warned them to abide strictly by the law in all their dealings so as to avoid problems with the British consulate. Li Koon-chun agreed.

'We must stick closely to the law to avoid trouble with the consulate,' he said. 'The first step is to register. The second step is to ask the consulate whether we can operate our business there. After getting a reply, we can start to move in. Once we move in we can consider sending people to live there.' Chairman Pong and all the other directors agreed with this plan of action.

Unknown to them, on 25 July, the Foreign Office sent formal notification to the British minister in Beijing approving the text of new King's Regulations entitled 'The Shameen Land Regulations (Amendment) Regulations'. The regulations were duly issued on 3 October and posted at the consulate general in Guangzhou on 17 October.

Under the new regulations, any corporation holding a lease of property within the British concession that becomes 'a corporation controlled by persons of Chinese race' shall, at the direction of 'His Britannic Majesty's Minister', become void. Furthermore, a 'corporation controlled by persons of Chinese race' was defined as one:

(a) in which the majority of its directors, or persons occupying the position of directors by whatever name called, are persons of Chinese race; or
(b) in which the majority of the voting power is in the hands of persons of Chinese race or of persons who exercise their voting powers directly or indirectly on behalf of persons of Chinese race; or
(c) in which the control is by any other means whatever in the hands of persons of Chinese race.

The Pre-War Era

The new regulations effectively closed the door on any further encroachments by Chinese-owned Hong Kong companies into Shamian. However, since the Bank of East Asia transaction had preceded the promulgation of these regulations, the bank's title to its property was unaffected. The Foreign Office decided not to seek a forfeiture.

This is not to say that the Foreign Office was content to allow the Bank of East Asia to operate in Shamian. In 1925, the Foreign Office asked the British minister in Beijing to determine if the Bank of East Asia was likely to apply for a renewal of its Crown lease on Shamian and, if so, whether such an application should be entertained. Sir Ronald Macleay sought the views of the acting consul general at Guangzhou, J. F. Brennan. That gentleman said the objections that Sir James Jamieson had to the Bank of East Asia being allowed to establish a branch on Shamian 'continue in full force, and I am strongly of the opinion that an application by the bank to renew the existing lease, or to acquire further property in the British concession, should be refused'.

Opposition to the bank on the part of British officialdom remained as strong as ever. Because of this implacable British opposition, the bank never did open its branch in Shamian.

Today, seventy-five years after the events narrated here occurred, and more than half a century after it reverted to Chinese rule, Shamian is still a cosmopolitan island in an overwhelmingly Chinese city. It has been designated by China as a protected historical area. The straight, tree-lined streets with wide sidewalks on each side reflect the slower-paced lifestyle of an earlier age. And European-style architecture, featuring arched windows and doorways, as well as balustrades, testify to the island's Western origins.

Chapter 8

The 1920s: Turmoil in the Shipping Business

The 1920s was a difficult period for Hong Kong, as the economy at times came to a virtual standstill because of a crippling seaman's strike, followed by the overflow of political turbulence in China that led to a protracted trade boycott. These events seriously affected the main businesses in which the Li family was involved: shipping, banking, and real estate.

The strike by the Chinese Seamen's Union was the first example of modern trade union action in Hong Kong. Up until then, trade unions had made little impact and, perhaps for this reason, demands by the fledgling Chinese Seamen's Union in late 1921 were ignored by shipowners, Chinese as well as Western.

The union was formed in the autumn of 1920, in response to attempts by shipowners to make seamen responsible for paying fines imposed by the United States government for smuggling Chinese into the country. The reasoning, presumably, was that the seamen were involved in such smuggling. From its earliest days, the union had a close association with the Kuomintang (KMT or Nationalist Party) of Dr Sun Yat-sen.

When it was inaugurated in Hong Kong, Dr Sun sent a representative to attend the ceremony.

The union's first priority was an across-the-board wage increase. In August 1921, it sent a letter to shipowners requesting this. The demand was ignored. A second letter was sent in November, couched in stronger terms, demanding specific increases for various classes of seamen. This, too, was ignored. Then the union asked for a meeting with representatives of the shipowners.

On 1 January 1922, Li Koon-chun and other Chinese shipowners, who controlled about a quarter of all tonnage and whose seamen were among the worst paid, held a meeting to discuss the situation. They unanimously resolved not to deal with the Seamen's Union on the ground that it did not represent the men it claimed to represent. Western companies by and large followed suit.

On 12 January, the union delivered an ultimatum to all shipowners:

> We beg to inform you that we have received no answer to our letters of 25 November and 23 December, except from Messrs. Jardine Matheson and Co. Ltd., and Messrs. Butterfield and Swire, at whose request the representatives of this Union attended a meeting with the representatives of Messrs. Jardine Matheson and Co. Ltd. and Messrs. Butterfield and Swire on Monday last at the office of the Secretary for Chinese Affairs, which meeting unfortunately proved fruitless. Under the circumstances, we have to inform you that the members of the Union have reluctantly but unanimously resolved to declare a general strike unless some satisfactory answer to our demands is received before 10am on Friday next, the 13th instant.

The ultimatum finally got the attention of the shipowners. That day Chinese and Western shipowners held a joint meeting and decided that each company would sound out its own crew members 'in order to rectify any grievances which may exist'. If the owners had taken this step earlier, it might have been acceptable to the union. Announcing such a move at the eleventh hour looked like an attempt to split the union by offering to negotiate separately with the crew of each vessel.

The Hong Kong government, not wishing to see the colony crippled, attempted to mediate. The Secretary for Chinese Affairs met with union officials, but to no avail.

The following day, Friday the 13th, the seamen struck. At 10am, Chinese seamen working on ships in port walked off their jobs, about 1,500 men working on fifty ships. The union issued them with train tickets for Guangzhou, where the seamen would be provided with food and accommodation. Sending them to Guangzhou reduced the chances of violence. It also removed them from the jurisdiction of the Hong Kong government. Another, not unimportant, factor was the lower cost of living in Guangzhou, which would enable the union to stretch its resources further.

Some ships, such as Japanese steamers with few Chinese seamen, were not seriously affected. Others, however, including the British companies, which relied on Chinese to work as seamen, cooks, pilots, and stewards, found it difficult to function. The ships of Wo Fat Sing had British officers but their crews were all Chinese.

Wo Fat Sing was one of the companies first affected. On 14 January, the first full day of the strike, the *Pheumpenh* was one of four ships that came into port. The following week, its sister ships, the recently acquired 2,790-tonne *Apoey* and the *Telemachus,* arrived. Their crews walked off their jobs and climbed onto trains to join their striking brethren in Guangzhou. All three Wo Fat Sing ships were idled. Chinese shipowners, such as Li Koon-chun, were in a difficult position. They did not command the resources of the major British or American companies, and, having all-Chinese crews, were more vulnerable to pressure.

Two leaders of the Chinese community, Lau Chu-pak and Chow Shou-son, met with a representative of the Seamen's Union and told him that the Chinese shipping companies wished the Chinese Chamber of Commerce to effect a settlement. Chinese shipowners apparently urged the seamen, as fellow Chinese, to return to work on their ships first, pledging to meet any increases later agreed to by the foreign owners. The proposal was rebuffed.

When the seamen did not return to work on Monday, the Hong Kong government proclaimed martial law. It placed armed military and naval guards at important points to preserve order and to demand passes of those going in and out of the territory. That day, seven representatives of Chinese shipowners and seven representatives of Western shipowners held discussions. They proposed pay raises ranging from 7.5 per cent to 25 per cent. This compared with a union demand for increases of 30–40 per cent. The offer was rejected by the seamen.

The effects of the strike quickly became obvious as shipping was the lifeblood of the colony, one of the busiest ports in the Far East. Within less than two weeks, food prices had soared. The government sent ships to Guangzhou to buy food but failed to procure supplies.

On 26 January, the seamen proposed the setting up of an arbitration board at Guangzhou that would include representatives of the Guangzhou government, the Hong Kong government, the British consul general, the European shipowners, the Chinese shipowners, and the seamen. They also proposed that, to end exploitation by labour contractors and recruiting agents, all seamen should be employed through the union.

Hong Kong's governor, Sir Edward Stubbs, responded that the proposal that seamen should only be employed through the union 'makes any discussion useless'. He also rejected the proposal to hold the arbitration in Guangzhou.

By the end of January, the strike had spread, with other workers joining the seamen in sympathy strikes. As of 27 January, Chinese New Year, 30,000 people had walked off their jobs. To prevent the strike from spreading further, the Hong Kong government declared the Seamen's Union an unlawful society, along with three others that had struck in sympathy. Union premises were raided by the police.

By 1 February, 166 steamers were tied up in Hong Kong harbour. Foodstuffs rotted in the holds of unloaded ships.

On 12 February, delegates arrived from Guangzhou and, the next day, held a meeting at the Tung Wah Hospital. However, talks centred not on ending the strike but on reopening the Seamen's Union. The government said the union could only be recognised again if it furnished proof of 'freedom from unlawfulness'. Such proof was to consist of the return to work of all strikers. The government said that if the seamen returned to work first on the conditions offered by the shipowners, and awaited the decision of the arbitrators, the proclamation closing the union would be lifted. Several rounds of talks were held, with the delegates shuttling back and forth between Hong Kong and Guangzhou, but no real progress was made.

Toward the end of February, the government invoked emergency regulations empowering it to requisition private property and force individuals to work. Military units were sent to requisition food stores. Policemen went to seamen's hostels and offered their occupants the option of work or imprisonment. To prevent the strikers from leaving, the government stopped rail service to Guangzhou and required all Chinese to obtain passes before they could leave Hong Kong. Military detachments were stationed at the frontier to prevent people from leaving.

While the Hong Kong government was tightening control, the Guangzhou government again offered its good offices, proposing that representatives of both governments as well as the British consulate attend negotiations between union and owners. As the situation had become critical, the Hong Kong government accepted the new proposal with alacrity.

The order forbidding people to leave Hong Kong led to the most violent incident of the strike. Several thousand Chinese who were walking toward the border were confronted by policemen and soldiers near Shatin, in the New Territories. When the marchers refused to halt, troops fired into the crowd, killing three people and wounding eight.

The killings fuelled anti-government sentiment. The strike took on strong anti-British overtones. More groups joined the walkouts. Public transportation was halted and most offices were shut. Garbage accumulated on the streets. Food had to be rationed. At this critical juncture, serious negotiations finally took place.

On 3 March, Chinese shipowners met to nominate their negotiators, who would be vested with full powers. Nine men were chosen, one of whom was Li Koon-chun. These men joined the four representatives of Western shipping companies the next day, when negotiations began. In addition to the shipowners and representatives of the seamen, those present included Jamieson, the British consul general, as well as senior Hong Kong officials.

The talks proceeded smoothly, and agreement was reached the first day on all issues except that of strike pay. A full accord was arrived at the following evening. As part of the agreement, the government rescinded the order that declared the Seamen's Union an unlawful society. Emergency regulations were repealed, and all those arrested for being union members were released. As for wages, the owners agreed to increases ranging from 15 to 30 per cent, depending on the route and type of vessel.

Ships were sent to Guangzhou to ferry workers back to Hong Kong, free of charge. This difficult task took many days as, by this time, the number of strikers had reached 120,000, out of a total population of 600,000. A fifth of the entire population had taken part, though only 23,000 were actually seamen.

With the end of the strike, the port emerged from its long, enforced idleness. On 8 March, the *Pheumpenh* received clearance for Saigon. The next day, the *Apoey* was cleared for Swatow. And, three days after that, the *Telemachus* sailed for Saigon. Koon-chun heaved a sigh of relief that Wo Fat Sing, like the rest of Hong Kong, was back in business.

This was a period of emotional stress for Koon-chun at home as well. His wife, Doy-hing, who had given birth to three daughters and a son, was pregnant again. Her infant son had died shortly before she was due, and she was hoping for another boy. Koon-chun was at work when the new child was born. Koon-chun's mother teased him by sending a messenger to say the baby was a girl. When he got home in the evening, his mother placed the naked baby in his arms and he was pleasantly surprised to find that he had at last fathered a healthy son.

From then on this child, who grew up to become Judge Simon Fook-sean Li, was nicknamed 'Ah Mui', or 'Little Sister', a nickname that stuck with the boy during his childhood years, to his great embarrassment. His mother called him 'Number Eight', since he was his father's eighth child.

Chapter 9

1933: A Double Wedding Binds Three Families

While the shipping business was periodically paralyzed, a building boom helped the colony recover from the economic doldrums. New technology enabled architects to build taller, steel-framed buildings, precursors of the multi-storey office towers and residential buildings that dot Hong Kong's skyline today.

The Li brothers, Koon-chu and Tse-fong, capitalized on this building boom by working closely with the other directors of the Bank of East Asia on numerous property deals, buying and selling property and jointly developing real estate. They became such close friends that they built houses next to each other, established weekend residences together, started companies together and, in some cases, linked the families together through marriage.

A core group centring on Chow Shou-son, Koon-chun, and Kan Tong-po formed a syndicate to buy and sell real estate, develop properties and establish companies. In the aftermath of World War I, land fever spread throughout Hong Kong with such frenzy that property development became a natural business to go into in the early 1920s. The Li brothers were involved in developing sites in the newly reclaimed areas of Wanchai, as well as in the Mid-Levels. One of their biggest property projects was on Robinson Road, a narrow, winding street halfway up the Peak. The Lis purchased the main site for HK$343,000 in April 1923 in conjunction with eight other buyers. These included Kan Tong-po, the bank's chief manager; Chow Shou-son, the bank's chairman, and his cousin, Chow Chi-nam, the chief cashier; Peter Kingson Kwok, another director; Wah Man-cheng, the chief accountant; and Ling Man-lai, deputy accountant. The only man in this syndicate not associated with the bank was Wang Kam, a wealthy property owner. The property was purchased from the executors of the estate of an Indian named Belilios, whose wealth stemmed from the opium trade. The shrewd purchasers mortgaged the property back to the original owners for HK$240,000 the same day the deed of purchase was registered. This meant that they only had to put up capital of little over HK$100,000.

At the same time, an even more valuable piece of Belilios property, situated directly above Kennedy Road, overlooking the harbour, was bought by a second syndicate, of which the Li brothers were a part, for HK$565,000. Belilios had constructed a large building, which he named Kingsclere, on part of the site. Eight of the ten men in this syndicate were involved in the earlier purchase. Again, a back-to-back mortgage was arranged. This arrangement not only reduced the amount of capital the purchasers had to put up but also provided the Belilios estate with a steady source of interest income.

The Robinson Road site was primarily an investment, but the Kennedy Road site differed in that many of the purchasers intended to build houses there for their own families. Because the vast plot of land was on an incline, a huge retaining wall was built, dividing the site into two sections, each at a different level. The side that faced Kennedy Road became known as Kennedy Terrace. It was there that Koon-chun built two houses, side by side, for his growing family. They were Numbers 6 and

The Pre-War Era

8 Kennedy Terrace. Sir Shouson Chow (as he was known after being knighted in 1926) later moved in next door, at Number 10. Kan Tong-po built Number 12 but never moved in. Number 14 was owned by Sir Shouson's cousin, Chow Chi-nam, while Number 16 was the house of Wong Yun-tong, another bank founder. Peter Kingson Kwok built a house on the site for his family, as did his nephew.

Koon-chun moved his family into the new premises on Kennedy Road after the four-storey houses were completed. There, the rest of his children were born. In the 1930s, Koon-chun converted a garage in front of the houses into a bungalow, with a game room for his children and a carport for his two Chevrolets.

With plans for the building of residences well in hand, the group of friends and business associates turned to the construction of country homes. Shouson Chow approached the government, pointing out that his family had lived in Hong Kong for 200 years and that he himself had been born near the fishing village of Aberdeen. He asked to be allowed to take over a tract of land on the south side of Hong Kong Island, near Deep Water Bay, where he could build a temple and an ancestral hall in honour of his forefathers and where he and his business associates could build western-style weekend villas, rose gardens, and tennis courts. The area at the time was far beyond the city boundary, with few inhabitants.

One government official, in considering the proposal, described the people involved as 'gentlemen of standing and of means' who were not engaged in speculation. The government, eager to encourage new development and provide a better living environment for Chinese entrepreneurs, agreed to sell the land to the group without opening it up to a public auction.

For most of the people involved, it was a chance to build recreational homes. But for Shouson Chow, it was a chance to leave his name to posterity. Today the area, known as Shouson

Hill, is one of the more prestigious addresses in Hong Kong.

Sometimes Koon-chun and Kan Tong-po accepted mortgages jointly. Kan Tong-po saw Koon-chun as a kindred spirit, a quiet, reserved but shrewd businessman who shunned the limelight.

Not only did the Lis and their banking partners do business together, they also played and traveled together. On one of these occasions, Tse-fong experienced at first hand the great Japanese earthquake of 1923, which levelled Tokyo and Yokohama.

Tse-fong and Mok Ching-kong, another director of the bank, went on holiday to Japan with two other friends, Wong Kam-pui and Liang Lai-sang. Tse-fong knew the other men well. Mok, in particular, was a founder of the bank and soon to become a relative. (Tse-fong's younger brother, Chok-chung, was engaged to Mok's daughter.)

On 24 August, the four men boarded the luxury liner *Empress of Australia*, which was bound for Vancouver by way of Shanghai, Kobe, and Yokohama. The 24,000-tonne vessel arrived at Kobe on the 29th, and the four friends spent two days there, seeing the sights. On the 31st, the *Empress of Australia* continued on its voyage, arriving at Yokohama early on the morning of 1 September, a Saturday.

The four friends disembarked in high spirits, ready to continue their Japanese adventure. They were planning to stay at the towering Fairmount Hotel but, through a mixup, ended up at a much smaller hotel with a similar name.

Not wanting to waste their first morning, they had only a cup of tea before beginning their sightseeing. People at the hotel suggested that they drive to Kamakura, a coastal village twenty kilometres from Yokohama. The village is of great natural beauty, renowned for its swimming beaches and many historical remains, including a colossal bronze statue known as Daibutsu, or the Great Buddha, dating from the thirteenth century.

The Pre-War Era

The four men hired a car and driver and drove southwards. After going through five or six tunnels, they drove along the seafront. It was then that they had the first inkling that something was wrong. The waves were enormous and, even though they remained inside the car, they became thoroughly soaked. Before getting to Kamakura, they had a flat tyre, which took the driver twenty minutes to change.

When they eventually got to Kamakura, they went immediately to see the Great Buddha. The four men admired the splendour of the statue, its head bowed in sorrow for the sins and sufferings of the world, in the midst of a ruined temple. They also visited other famous sites in the vicinity. After sightseeing, while on their way back to Yokohama, disaster struck.

Just after crossing a stone bridge, they suddenly felt the earth shake. The car rocked so much that they felt as if they were in a boat being tossed about on a stormy sea. They saw the ground heaving up and down, forming fissures through which jets of water shot up. Luckily, they had crossed the bridge, which collapsed behind them with a loud roar, and fortunately they were now in an open area. If not for the flat tyre, they would have been back in Yokohama, caught in the midst of falling buildings, including the Fairmount Hotel, which collapsed like a house of cards within thirty seconds of the gigantic earthquake. And, if they had dallied any longer in Kamakura, they would have been caught in the tidal wave that swept over the area, leaving 1,000 people dead.

Because the road was impassable, they left the car to make their way back on foot. After walking a short distance, the road vanished. The earthquake had caused two hills to collapse onto it. To reach Yokohama, they would have to climb over the hills. At that point, Mok developed cramps in his legs and could not walk. Li Tse-fong and the two others persuaded some peasants to sell them a cart. Unable to hire any labourers, the three men put Mok in the cart and took turns pushing.

When they finally got to the top of the hill, they saw that Yokohama was on fire. Great oil drums on the hillside above the Yokohama naval station had exploded, and rivers of oil swept down upon the city, turning it into a flaming sea. Flames licked the dark red sky. Knowing it was futile to press on, they climbed higher up the hill and finally found a small, sturdily built house that had not collapsed. It was late, and rain was coming down. The four friends, wet, cold, and miserable, begged the occupants of the house for assistance. They were offered shelter and passed the night sleeping on piles of hay. The vacation of their dreams had turned into a nightmare.

The next morning, they again thought of returning to Yokohama. They worried about their safety because each man was carrying a large sum of money, and the earthquake had probably precipitated a breakdown in law and order. The local villagers, however, persuaded them not to go, saying that Yokohama was still burning. Though their village, too, had been hit by the earthquake, the wooden houses had survived the shocks in good condition.

The Hong Kong visitors soon discovered that their fears of being waylaid were valid. The earthquake had brought down the walls of Nogishi prison, freeing 5,000 inmates, many of whom were Koreans. The prisoners went on a rampage, killing any Japanese who happened to cross their path.

At noon, the Koreans arrived at the village where the four men were staying, their arrival heralded by loud voices and gunshots. The women and children of the village ran to hide in the hills and the men stayed behind to fight. The Koreans were finally defeated, but, during the battle, the four friends had numerous narrow escapes. First the Koreans mistook them for Japanese, then the Japanese mistook them for Koreans. That night, the four were so fearful that they dared not sleep.

When Tse-fong and his friends, weary and apprehensive, eventually returned to Yokohama, they found a city in ruins.

Eighty per cent of the houses had collapsed or were burned to the ground, and casualties ran into the hundreds of thousands. Corpses lay everywhere. The sight of several ocean liners in the harbour cheered them, but soon they discovered that the ships were turning people away. Japanese ships were refusing to take foreigners, while the foreign liners would take only Westerners.

Fortunately, the four had bought return tickets, but to get out to a liner, they needed to hire a sampan. The four friends had to pay an exorbitant 150 taels of silver before a sampan owner agreed to take them out to the harbour. On the way, the sampan was buffeted by strong winds, and waves tossed the tiny vessel two metres into the air, but at last the friends managed to board a ship bound for Kobe.

Once in Kobe, they were able to communicate with their families in Hong Kong. Tse-fong sent a telegram to the Bank of East Asia, telling his colleagues that he was safe. The earthquake had severed all ties between him and his family and friends in Hong Kong for five days. In Kobe, the four friends transferred to the Peninsular and Oriental Steamship Navigation Company steamer *Dongola*, which took them back to Hong Kong by way of Shanghai.

Meanwhile, in Hong Kong, Tse-fong's family had been trying desperately to reach him ever since news arrived of the destruction of Yokohama. His colleagues cabled Kobe for news of Tse-fong, only to be told that he and his friends had already left for Yokohama—the worst hit of all cities—the day before the earthquake.

Tse-fong returned to Hong Kong on 21 September, but his relief at getting home safe and sound was short-lived, as he found out his mother had died two weeks previously, the very day he reached safety in Kobe.

The Lis not only worked and played with their business partners, they also matched their children in marriage. Aside from the marriage between Li Chok-chung and the daughter of Mok

Ching-kong, another wedding that linked two of the bank's main families was that arranged by Koon-chun for his eldest daughter, Yue-chu, a shy teenager who graduated from St Paul's Girls College in 1924. She was affianced to Chow Hau-leung, a young man of an athletic bent who loved to swim and play soccer. He was the grandson of Chow Chi-nam, the bank's chief cashier.

After the engagement, young Hau-leung frequently visited the Li residence to pay his respects, but tradition dictated that the young couple could not meet. He was allowed to take Yue-chu's younger brothers and sisters out for meals, but not her. Still, there were occasions when Yue-chu caught a glimpse of him in the house—the man with whom she was to spend the rest of her life, a man she hardly knew, but who had been chosen for her by her parents.

The marriage between Yue-chu and Hau-leung linked the Li and Chow families. But the wedding that really cemented three of the bank's leading families occurred a few years later, in 1933, when the twin sons of Fung Ping-shan (d. 1931) were married in a double wedding. One son, Kenneth Fung Ping-fan (later to become Sir Kenneth Fung) married Ivy, the eldest daughter of Kan Tong-po, while the other son, Fung Ping-wah, married Wai-yin, the eldest daughter of Li Tse-fong. According to old Chinese beliefs, twins should be married on the same day, and these two were. Both were alumni of the University of Hong Kong. Fung Ping-wah succeeded to his father's seat on the board of the bank a few years later but emigrated to the United States before World War II. Kenneth held the seat after the war.

Wai-yin, who later assumed the name Doris, became the first member of her family to pick her own husband, or, as she put it in a letter to the author, to be 'married in modern ceremony'. Until then, all marriages, including those of her father and uncles, had been arranged by matchmakers.

The rare double wedding was celebrated on the afternoon of 13 December at the China Emporium, of which both Tsefong and Kan Tong-po were directors. Y. K. Kan, son of Kan Tong-po, was the best man to Kenneth Fung. The two brides dressed alike, since they were marrying twins. Their gowns were of silver satin, empire style, with pretty draped sleeves and a long train lined with georgette and trimmed with pearls. A silver embroidered veil draped with pearls and orange blossoms finished off the charming dresses. The young women carried bouquets of white roses and gladioli with asparagus fern. The wedding was the social event of the season. It was accompanied by a lavish reception, attended by 1,000 guests, many of whom were prominent bankers or businessmen.

The head of the University of Hong Kong, in proposing a toast, said, 'This afternoon we are doubly cementing an alliance between the great trading house of Fung and the Bank of East Asia, an arrangement full of happy augury. A double cord is not easily broken.'

In 1933, and indeed for a long time afterwards, the Lis, the Kans and the Fungs were indeed inseparable. These lifelong friends, and their families, had been linked unto the next generation. Events in later decades would test the firmness of those bonds.

Chapter 10

Shek-pang's Sons Grow Up

In August 1932, Shek-pang's youngest son, Chok-lai, marked his twenty-first birthday. There was much to celebrate, not only for him but for all his brothers, for their father's will had stipulated that his estate would be divided when his youngest son attained the age of twenty-one.

Nine months later, on 27 May 1933, all the brothers trooped into the office of Deacons, a leading firm of solicitors, where each signed legal documents that formally distributed the family assets. Koon-chun had managed his father's businesses so well that the family fortune in 1933 was considerably larger than that bequeathed by Shek-pang in 1916.

The six brothers maintained a close relationship, even though they were the offspring of three different spouses. In appearance, the first three sons, children of the formal wife, had more in common, being big and tall, like northern Chinese. Koon-chun and Tse-fong had long, clean-shaven faces, while Siu-pang's square face sported a moustache. Lan-sang, the only son of 'Second Mother', was shorter and heavyset, while the two sons of 'Third Mother', Chok-chung and Chok-lai, were smaller in stature.

The Pre-War Era

Siu-pang and Tse-fong bought a piece of property on Seymour Road, where they built houses for their families. They were next-door neighbours all their lives, at Numbers 9 and 9A. Later, Lan-sang and Chok-chung also bought a large plot down the road on which they built adjacent houses, sharing one gate.

Koon-chun was careful not to liquidate all of Shek-pang's properties. A number were retained as the six brothers' common assets, with the same status as the rice and shipping companies. These were rented out, and Wo Fat Sing was responsible for collecting the rent every month. From time to time, he would use profits from the family businesses for philanthropic purposes, especially in their home town, Heshan, making donations in memory of his father. Emergency relief of clothes and rice was also provided during natural calamities. In fact, so close was the family's connection with Heshan that when Koon-chun's mother died, twenty students of the Shek-Pang Charitable School traveled to Hong Kong to attend the memorial service, led by their teacher. Some of the graduates of the school ended up working for Koon-chun.

The division of assets made each of the brothers rich. Siu-pang quickly prepared his own will the following month, and eighteen years later became the first of the brothers to die. By then, he had spent much of his inheritance, having lived as a gentleman of leisure, while maintaining a stable of horses and supporting a wife, three concubines, and twelve children. He left an estate of HK$1.6 million, to be shared by members of his large family.

Their sister Yuet-seung, known as Sylvia, did not share in the inheritance, being a female. She attended excellent schools in Hong Kong (Diocesan Girls School and St Paul's Girls College, from which she graduated in 1933) before going to Europe, where she studied in London, Paris, and Switzerland, becoming a scholar of French and German literature. She blossomed into a beautiful young woman. In September 1937, after returning from Europe, she married L. P. Kwok, son of Philip Gockchin, an entrepreneur who had made his mark in the department store business in Hong Kong and Shanghai.

Of the brothers, Koon-chun had the shrewdest business mind. A charismatic man who was quick to grasp the details of a particular situation and to act on them, he had little patience with tardy or incompetent people. Once, he ended a thirty-year business relationship because the person concerned kept him waiting for twenty minutes. As early as the 1920s, Koon-chun and his brother Tse-fong were so prominent, the governor regularly invited them to attend receptions on such occasions as the king's birthday. They were also the only two brothers whose English was good enough for them to be put on the jury list. Considering that Koon-chun's English was largely self-taught, this was quite an achievement.

Like many wealthy men, Koon-chun was frugal in his habits. His clothes were often old and worn, and he did not mind wearing darned socks. He would often have lunch at his office, sometimes eating only two pieces of buttered toast, coffee, and milk. Once he gave the office boy ten cents to pay for lunch and got three cents back in change. The coffee cost two cents, milk two cents, and the bread three cents. 'That's very cheap,' he said. 'Did this come from a street-side stall?' The boy nodded. 'Is it clean?' he asked. When assured that it was, Koon-chun proceeded to eat his simple meal with satisfaction.

Koon-chun always dressed in the Chinese style, unlike his brother Tse-fong who, because of his university education, wore Western suits and ties. Koon-chun normally wore a skull cap, a Chinese tunic, and loose-fitting trousers with cuffs secured under his feet by a cloth band. He and his wife were the last generation of traditional Chinese. Their sons would be free to choose their own wives, their daughters free to let their feet grow normally.

On occasion, his wife, Doy-hing, would come to the office

at the end of the day and take him home. The employees, all of whom were from Heshan, addressed her as 'First Master's Wife', since Koon-chun was Shek-pang's oldest son. Those who were distant relatives called her 'Aunt'.

Though Wo Fat Sing and Nam Wo Hong operated in close conjunction and were located on the same street, the employees were quite different. Those at the Wo Fat Sing shipping company had to understand English, since they dealt with Westerners, while the Nam Wo Hong rice company only had Chinese customers. Koon-chun was upset when one of his employees referred to a Western woman as a *gwaipor* or 'devil woman', a commonly used term. 'Next time someone like that calls,' he ordered, 'she is to be referred to as 'sai fu' ['Western lady'], 'gwailo' ['foreign devil'] must never be used.' Nam Wo Hong staff were taught one sentence of English. If anyone called looking for Koon-chun, they were instructed to say 'Please call 20005', the telephone number of Wo Fat Sing.

Koon-chun lived on Caine Road in a large, four-storey house, which had two basements. With him were his wife, Doy-hing, her mother, and their children, plus his youngest brother, Chok-lai, who was about the same age as his eldest son, F. S. The first basement served as living quarters for men-servants, while the second basement was used as a storeroom. There was a huge sitting room and study on the ground floor. Koon-chun and his wife lived upstairs, with their younger sons Fook-hing and Simon. The daughters shared the third floor, while F. S. and Chok-lai lived on the top floor. Each of the children had his or her own amah—sometimes a wet nurse—who slept in the same room, usually in the same bed, until the child was five or six years old.

A resident tutor also lived with the family. His job was to teach the children the Chinese classics. Rather than sending their children to school, wealthy families often relied on tutors until the children were well into their teens. Koon-chun believed a good grounding in the Chinese classics was more important than anything else in education. He himself had no such education, and he was determined that his children should. He often told them: 'Anything you own can be taken away from you, but not your knowledge. You can build a fortune in diamonds and property and it can be taken from you. But education is treasure inside your head that cannot be taken away.'

A child's education began at age five with a solemn ritual. Before daybreak, the child was awakened and dressed in formal Chinese attire, including a long gown and embroidered jacket. Only after worshipping the ancestral spirits, by kowtowing before wooden tablets on which his ancestors' names were engraved, would he receive his first lesson from the resident tutor.

Despite his emphasis on the importance of a classical education, Koon-chun was foresighted in giving both his sons and his daughters the best education that money could buy. All of his sons and three of his daughters were sent abroad for further education.

The resident tutor instructed F. S. and Chok-lai in the Chinese classics primarily. They were immersed in the subject, day after day. As a mark of respect to the tutor, F. S. ate his meals with him, while the rest of the family ate together upstairs. Koon-chun's oldest daughter was already married. His second daughter, Fanny, attended Diocesan Girls' School, where all the teaching was in English. Her nickname, in fact, was 'Lo Fan', or 'old barbarian', because while she could read and write very well in English, she could not do so in Chinese. Only after great effort did she later learn to write in Chinese.

When Koon-chun's later children—Margaret, Vivian, Simon, and Fook-hing—were old enough, they, too, were turned over to the tutor. He taught them to read and memorize such basic texts as the *Three Character Classic* and the *Primer* of a *Thousand Characters*. Only after six years or more of private tutoring at home were the children enrolled in school. Koon-chun was a strict disciplinarian who believed that a man's duty was to rule his home like a kingdom. He believed that children should read only uplifting books, such as those in the Confucian canon, or Tang-dynasty poetry. Popular books, read only for enjoyment, were banned. One day, he found a copy of *Dream of the Red Chamber* in his eldest son's room and immediately took a feather duster to him. Poor F. S. protested his innocence, shouting 'It wasn't me! It wasn't me!' as he ran round and round the dining table, with his father in pursuit. Only later did it turn out that Koon-chun's mother-in-law had been reading the proscribed book and had accidentally left it in F. S.'s room.

Work was Koon-chun's life. Every morning, before going to the office, he would call on his friend, Edward Ray, whose father had helped his father set up the shipping company, and discuss business opportunities. The two men were close friends and often cooperated in business deals.

At the Wo Fat Sing office, Koon-chun would see his brother Lan-sang, the company secretary. Each morning, they would have tea with their stockbroker, Rudy Choy, who called on regular clients by rickshaw to chat and exchange information. Koon-chun and his brothers were active in the stock market, concentrating on blue chip shares such as the Hongkong and Shanghai Bank, Hongkong Electric, Dairy Farm, the Star Ferry Company, and Kowloon Wharf.

The Wall Street crash of 1929 signalled a world-wide economic depression in the 1930s. Hong Kong, whose survival depended on trade between China and the West, was badly hit. Stock and property prices plummeted and property owners such as Koon-chun experienced a severe slump. So bad was the shipping business that Koon-chun had to put the *Telemachus* in mothballs for several years. He chartered out the

Lyeemoon for a year to be used in the coolie trade to Singapore and sold the *Halvard*. The Bank of East Asia, too, reported a steep decline in profits. The Hong Kong government in 1934 decided to appoint an economic commission to look into the situation and to recommend action.

The commission, headed by the postmaster general, M. J. Breen, had twelve other members, including three Chinese: T. N. Chau, a legislative councillor; William Thomas Tam, a lawyer, and Li Koon-chun. Their job was 'to enquire into the causes and effects of the present trade depression in Hong Kong and make recommendations for the amelioration of the existing position and for the improvement of the trade of the Colony.'

The commission deliberated for seven months, finally producing a report in February 1935 showing that Hong Kong was, generally speaking, not in control of its own fate. Eighty per cent of the colony's trade, the committee found, consisted of re-exports between southern China and the rest of the world. 'The volume of this trade between China and overseas has shrunk considerably in recent years,' it said. 'The existing depression in Hong Kong has its sole cause in external factors.' Fortunately for Hong Kong, the depression soon ended.

During this time, the Bank of East Asia showed an unshaken faith in the future. It invested considerable funds in the construction of a new headquarters—a modern eleven-storey edifice, the tallest completed structure in Hong Kong at the time. An outstanding feature was the special safe deposit vault, whose entrance was protected by a heavy steel circular door. The bank was the first to introduce the system of safe deposit boxes into the colony.

In addition to his other involvements, Koon-chun was also a major landlord, as were some of his siblings. He helped his younger brothers and his sister acquire properties, which they rented out to assure a regular income. Wo Fat Sing's cashier doubled as Koon-chun's rent collector.

The Pre-War Era

The large house on Caine Road became insufficient to accommodate Koon-chun's expanding family. When Koon-chun decided to move to Kennedy Terrace, he had two adjoining four-storey houses built. There, his youngest children, Catherine and Ronald, were born. By that time, age had mellowed Koon-chun; these two children enjoyed the love of a doting father, not the stern discipline that their older siblings had experienced. He was especially fond of Ronald and used to tell the young boy about the workings of the stock market and how to buy shares. Business was Koon-chun's life. It was an art to him; he told his children that doing business was like writing a poem.

A practical man, Koon-chun appreciated the need to learn English. When his eldest son F. S. was seventeen, Koon-chun decided it was time to send him to study English at St Joseph's. F. S., a freelance writer of essays for a Chinese newspaper under the pseudonym 'Rice Worm', resisted. His Chinese writing, both prose and poetry, was very accomplished, and he did not relish the idea of starting all over again in a new language. 'I'm already so tall,' he said, 'How can I go to school with boys who are seven or eight?'

'Think it over,' Koon-chun admonished.

A few days later, Koon-chun summoned his son again. 'Have you thought it over?' he asked. 'Yes,' his son replied. 'I'm sorry, but I'm not going.'

'Don't be stupid,' Koon-chun scolded him. 'I just want you to learn a few English words. After all, if I give you HK$1 million dollars, can you enjoy yourself? If you step on board an oceanliner and someone gives you a menu, you won't even know how to order. I want you to enjoy life. Hong Kong is only a tiny dot in the world. If you know English, you can go to Europe, America, Australia. . . anywhere you like.'

Because his son did not even know the alphabet, Koon-chun arranged for private tutoring for F. S. in English at home for half a year. After that, F. S. enrolled in class six, where he studied with boys aged eleven and twelve. He was first in his class. The next year, he was first again, and again the year after that.

At St Joseph's, he was also a member of the school's soccer team and played in matches against other schools. He was an avid swimmer, once swimming with two cousins across the harbour from Kowloon to Hong Kong, a distance of over over 1.6 kilometres. He graduated in December 1932 after four-and-a-half years and qualified for admission to the University of Hong Kong.

At the university, F. S. became friendly with another student, Daisy, daughter of a shipowner named Woo Hay-tong, whose step-mother was Simon's mother's aunt and whose sons had been at St Joseph's with F. S. The two were married in the spring of 1936, a year and a half before he graduated.

While Koon-chun and Tse-fong were serious businessmen, their brother Siu-pang lived the life of a gentleman of leisure with a propensity to speculate in gold and silver. His principal wife gave him three children, two sons and a daughter. He was something of a playboy, with three concubines who gave him seven more sons and two more daughters. Tragically, five of his sons died before him.

His brother's children found him an extremely generous uncle. He used to take his nephews swimming at Repulse Bay, where the sand was fine and white. After that, he invariably took them to a restaurant. He was a major horse-owner and loved going to the races.

Siu-pang dressed stylishly, sporting jade buttons on his clothes. He frequented private clubs for Chinese, which offered various games of chance. Gambling was in his blood. The clubs also afforded him a chance to be pampered by the numerous masseuses working there. He would lie down and be ministered to by three young women. One would fan him, one would massage his back, and one would massage his feet. In the clubs, he played mahjongg or *paikau*, a Chinese card game. He gambled for high stakes, and, when he won, he would give money to his children and his nephews and take them to a feast.

All the children looked forward to traditional festivals and birthdays, when their relatives would congregate. The biggest event of the year was the Chinese New Year. On New Year's day, the children would be taken by their parents to visit each of the uncles at their homes to wish them a happy new year; in return, they would receive *lai see*, or lucky money. They would also go to Wo Fat Sing to wish the employees a happy new year and sip champagne imported from Saigon. Koon-chun's business associates would call on him in his office, and while the grownups met out front, the children played in the back with the staff.

Later, in the 1940s, the family decided that, instead of everyone running around visiting everyone else, they would all gather at the home of Lan-sang, the only son of 'Second Mother', to celebrate New Year's; this was, after all, where Li Shek-pang's surviving widow lived. This ritual was known as *tuan pai* ('joint paying of respects'). They gathered at a time determined by consulting the Chinese almanac. The celebration was attended by all the descendants of Li Shek-pang and their spouses, usually sixty to seventy people.

'Second Mother' had fixed ideas on what was proper or improper. Thus, she was firm in not allowing Chok-chung's mistress, Ko Yuk-lien, or Madam Ko, to be treated like a *ping tsai*, or 'equal wife'. Since she herself was a concubine, she had no objection to Chok-chung taking one, but she was opposed to the idea of a concubine claiming equal status with the wife.

Actually, Chok-chung's marriage to Mok Yuk-yu had little passion from the beginning. She did become pregnant by him but, after marriage, the two did not live as husband and wife.

She lived in his house on Seymour Road, adjoining Lan-sang's home, while he moved out and lived with Madam Ko.

Chok-chung's efforts to have Madam Ko accepted by the family were frustrated time and again. 'Second Mother' refused to drink the ceremonial tea that was poured for her by Madam Ko. This adamant stance was maintained even after the lady had given Chok-chung eight children.

Largely because of 'Second Mother', Mok Yuk-yu for years continued to be recognized as the wife, and she and her son, Fook-hon, continued to attend family gatherings, while Madam Ko was barred. So dominant was 'Second Mother's' personality that, because of her opposition, no member of the family dared to meet Madam Ko socially. She was always referred to, not as sister-in-law or aunt, but simply as Madam Ko, to indicate that she was an outsider.

In addition to family get-togethers in Hong Kong, twice a year, during the Ching Ming and Chung Yeung festivals honouring the dead, the entire clan would journey to Guangzhou. There they would climb the hill where Li Shek-pang and his wife were buried, to pay their respects. Food would be brought as offerings to the dead, and, while the occasion was sombre, it was, especially for the children, almost like a picnic.

Chapter 11

Li Tse-fong: Banker, Horse-Owner, Politician

A jolly man who enjoyed travel, good food, fine wine, and racing his own horses, Tse-fong was more than a full-time banker. He also served on the boards of many major companies, including some of the colony's oldest concerns, established by British entrepreneurs in the nineteenth century. One was the Green Island Cement Company. Long before he won a seat on the board, Tse-fong took an interest in the company's activities. He joined the board in 1924 after helping to lead a shareholders' revolt.

In January of that year, a group of shareholders, feeling the board was too timid and lacking in vision, proposed a series of measures, including doubling the company's capital. But the directors rejected the proposal, denying there was any need for additional capital. Frustrated shareholders, primarily C. A. da Roza and Li Tse-fong, then obtained the signatures of thirty shareholders, representing about a third of all shares, and called for an extraordinary general meeting. At the meeting, they proposed that the company's authorized capital be doubled to HK$6 million. They also proposed that the board be enlarged from five to seven directors. C. A. da Roza and Li Tse-fong were proposed as the additional board members.

Instead of the sedate boardroom meetings typical of the time, an acrimonious exchange took place. The directors opposed the plan, but da Roza, speaking for the insurgent shareholders, charged that 'Green Island Cement Company has stood still' while, increasingly, foreign cement was being imported. He accused the company of pricing itself out of the market by use of old, inefficient, and worn-out machinery. Manufacturing costs, he said, could be brought down by importing modern equipment from Europe.

When the motion to increase the capital was put to a vote the chairman, Robert Shewan, abstained. The four other directors, including the distinguished Sir Paul Chater, opposed the measure; however, it was supported by a large majority of shareholders. As a result, the four directors resigned. The election of Tse-fong and da Roza carried easily, and the new board proceeded to replace kilns and other equipment in plants both in Hong Kong and Macau. The results were evident a year later as imports of foreign cement dropped markedly. The company's production could barely keep up with orders.

Tse-fong and da Roza were also involved in another business venture. They founded the insurance company China Underwriters in January 1924, together with Robert Shewan, Mok Ching-kong, and four others. Shewan, Tomes and Company agreed to act as general managers for China Underwriters, earning a commission on transactions. Businessman Robert Shewan (chairman of Green Island) had been in the colony for more than four decades.

A few months later, the agreement began to fail. The general managers made a commission from each deal, even when the insurance company itself suffered a net loss. Shewan, Tomes and Company agreed to cut its commissions in half, but even this was not enough. The founders then decided to assume control. The consulting committee, which included Tse-fong, transformed itself into a board of directors and replaced the general managers.

Hong Kong in 1924 was a small city, with a population of about 600,000. Its business community was also small, and a few prominent businessmen served on the boards of many different companies.

By 1926, barely ten years out of university, Tse-fong was on the board of the Bank of East Asia, Green Island, China Underwriters and the Hong Kong Tugboat and Lighter Company, another venture launched in 1924. Subsequently, he also served on the boards of two other established British companies, China Provident Loan and Mortgage Company, and the Hong Kong, Canton and Macao Steamboat Company.

Tse-fong had a long association with the steamboat company formed in 1865 to operate ferries between those three locations. In 1929, a rift developed between the Chinese members of the board—Li Tse-fong, Sir Robert Ho Tung, and M. K. Lo—and its European members. The issue was the company's policy of farming out part of its business (the carrying of Chinese passengers and freight) to an outsider, Woo Hay-tong, himself a shipowner. The three men pointed out that Woo's ships competed with the company's vessels.

'In the interests of the future of the company,' M. K. Lo said at a board meeting in November, on behalf of all three Chinese directors, 'it would be better to award the tender to an outsider rather than to the present farmer unless his tender shall be the highest.' The other directors insisted on Woo, who had been given this business for years, even if there were higher offers from others. Consequently, Sir Robert, Li Tse-fong, and M. K. Lo—who between them held more than a third of the company's shares—resigned from the board.

Then, in what was almost a repetition of the Green Island shareholder revolt of 1924, the three men obtained proxies from other shareholders for the annual general meeting in March 1930. M.K. Lo proposed a motion expressing strong disapproval of the directors. He said the company was using improper accounting methods and was misleading its shareholders. The company's steamers, he said, were being operated at a loss and the profits came from investments in the stock market and real estate. The motion of censure carried and Sir Robert, Li Tse-fong, and M.K. Lo were returned to the board of directors.

As soon as the annual general meeting concluded, an extraordinary general meeting took place. Sir Robert proposed the company stop farming out its Chinese business. The resolution, seconded by Tse-fong, was carried and control of the company passed into the hands of Tse-fong and his allies. The following year, the company announced that, by not farming out the Chinese business, the firm had realized substantial earnings on the Hong Kong–Guangzhou line but a drop in profits on the Hong Kong–Macao line. Overall, however, profits were well up over the previous year.

Tse-fong was also active socially. Unlike Koon-chun, who left his wife at home on major social occasions, Tse-fong's wife, Tang Sau-hing, often accompanied him. A frail, gentle person who was something of a socialite, her clothes were the height of fashion; she was also a founder member of the Chinese Women's Club and on one occasion was invited by St Paul's to be guest of honour on prize-giving day.

Tse-fong alone among the six brothers had only one spouse throughout his life. Together, they brought up nine children—six sons and three daughters. Tang Sau-hing used to drill into her children the importance of family unity, telling them that siblings should never fight among themselves. Even in her will, she exhorted: 'It is my desire that my sons and daughters should respect and love one another as brothers and sisters should do. They must act in cooperation and abstain from creating trouble.'

As he became more prominent in business and more active in social circles, Tse-fong caught the eye of the Hong Kong government. It was the practice of the government to pick individuals, usually successful businessmen, to serve on one or another of its advisory boards and committees. Tse-fong's first appointment came in 1929, when he was made a member of the Stamp Duties Committee because of his financial expertise. The only Chinese on the committee, Tse-fong, was chosen by Sir Shouson Chow, who was asked by the governor to recommend a 'suitable Chinese gentleman'. The government was considering imposing stiff stamp duties on share transactions in order to check the 'extravagant gambling in shares,' while simultaneously swelling the public coffers. The committee decided to amend the law to prevent evasion of the stamp duty on share transactions.

The following year, the Governor in Council (the Governor sitting with the Executive Council) decided to set up a Committee of Enquiry to look into the colony's currency situation. The Hong Kong currency was linked to silver, with the Mexican silver dollar set as the standard. The serious drop in the value of silver from the mid-1920s onwards badly damaged the colony's trading activities. The Executive Council asked Sir Shouson Chow to 'sound out' Li Koon-chun but he declined; Tse-fong was appointed instead.

The committee invited members of the public to express their views. Interestingly, when the Chinese Chamber of Commerce appeared before the committee, Li Koon-chun acted as spokesman, together with another chamber official, Li Hoi-tung. The Chinese Chamber urged, among other things, that the government take over the function of issuing banknotes. Hong Kong, then as now, relied on private banks, primarily the Hongkong and Shanghai Banking Corporation, to issue notes.

The committee decided to keep Hong Kong, like China, on

a silver standard, even though most of the world had switched to gold. 'Hong Kong is yoked to South China both geographically and commercially,' it said. Following the example set 'by Canada with regard to the United States,' it said, Hong Kong should adopt 'a monetary unit identical with that of our neighbours'.

In view of Tse-fong's services to the community, the government made him a justice of the peace. In England, a justice of the peace performs judicial functions of a relatively minor nature. In Hong Kong, however, considerable honour is attached to the title. Unlike British royal titles, such as the OBE (Officer of the Most Excellent Order of the British Empire), the Justice of the Peace title can be conferred by Hong Kong itself. Tse-fong's reaction, when offered this title, reflected the respect he had for his oldest brother. 'I shall be happy to accept,' he told the Colonial Secretary, 'if my brother Koon-chun were offered the same honour.' The Colonial Secretary acquiesced and, the following spring, both Tse-fong and Koon-chun joined the ranks of justices of the peace in Hong Kong, a group of the most powerful and influential individuals.

After that, ever more important appointments were offered to Tse-fong. In 1934, he was made a member of the Board of Education. In 1936, he was nominated to serve on the Court of the University of Hong Kong. About this time, he established several prizes to be awarded annually to students of St Joseph's College, his father Shek-pang's alma mater. He set up Li Tse-Fong Prizes for Chinese, Geography, and French, which were awarded along with the Li Shek-Pang Gold Medal for Chinese.

Because of his family's long association with St Joseph's, several of his sons studied there, including the four eldest: Fook-cheung, Fook-wo, Fook-tai, and Fook-kuen (Henry). The two youngest, Fook-kow and Fook-pui, attended another Catholic institution, the Jesuit Wah Yan College, while all three daughters, Wai-yin (Doris), Wai-kuen (Delia), and Wai-haan

(Nancy), went to St Stephen's College, an Anglican institution. Tse-fong did not send them to these schools because of any propensity towards Christianity. In fact, when Fook-kuen wanted to be baptized, his father forbade it. (Only the trauma of the Japanese occupation during World War II would change Tse-fong's and his wife Sau-hing's attitude towards Christianity.)

In the summer of 1935, Tse-fong, his wife, and their children Fook-cheung and Fook-wo undertook their first journey to the United States. Tse-fong decided to send the boys abroad to study, the first members of the Li family to do so. While most parents in Hong Kong sent their sons to England, Tse-fong chose the United States. Fook-cheung (Norman) went to the Massachusetts Institute of Technology, while Fook-wo (Aubrey), not quite seventeen, attended Boston University.

Meanwhile, Tse-fong's official role increased. In October 1937, he was part of the reception committee welcoming the new governor, Sir Geoffrey Northcote. At this time, the Japanese were pressing their war against China, which began with a clash between Japanese and Chinese troops on 7 July 1937 at the Marco Polo Bridge outside Beijing. By October, Japanese troops had captured Guangzhou and were encamped on Hong Kong's doorstep. Blackout drills were conducted to prepare the public for air raids, even though British Hong Kong was officially neutral in the Sino-Japanese war.

In July 1939, Tse-fong attained three highly significant positions. The least known, but perhaps most important, was membership on the District Watch Committee. This committee, formed originally in the 1860s, consisted of a dozen or more of the richest, most influential, and most powerful Chinese. It was likened to a 'Chinese Executive Council', the colony's highest policy-making body, which was dominated by Europeans. The District Watch Committee exercised control over a constabulary force of watchmen separate from the regular police who patrolled the Chinese sections of the colony. But its influence lay in its official recognition as a body that represented the Chinese population and thus had to be consulted on all major issues. Membership in this elite body required recommendation by the Secretary for Chinese Affairs and approval by other influential Chinese leaders before being submitted to the Governor in Council for endorsement. Other members of the committee at the time included such luminaries as Sir Shouson Chow, Sir Robert Kotewall, M. K. Lo, Dr Li Shu-fan, and Thomas Tam.

That same month, Tse-fong was temporarily appointed to the Legislative Council and the Urban Council. In the Legislative Council he filled in for Dr Li Shu-fan, a physician studying in Europe and the United States the latest methods developed for the treatment of tuberculosis. In the Urban Council, he replaced Thomas Tam. Later, as openings arose, Tse-fong was appointed in his own right.

While decisions on membership of the Urban Council could be made within Hong Kong, each member of the Legislative Council had to be formally approved by London. Governor Northcote reported Li Tse-fong's appointment to the secretary of state for the colonies, but neglected to provide any details on Tse-fong's background. A miffed official in the Colonial Office observed in his minutes: 'I would have thought that, as the appointment had to be reported, we were entitled to be told who Mr Li Tse-fong was: And if they throw an unexplained name at us again like this I think we might take the matter up. But let it go this time.'

World War II was about to break out when Tse-fong took his seat in the Legislative Council on 20 July, joining T. N. Chau and M. K. Lo as the three Chinese councillors who had a special task: to represent the interests of the Chinese community. After Tse-fong swore the oath of allegiance to the British Crown, Governor Northcote announced plans to set up a reserve force, to be known as the Hong Kong Defence Reserve, on which all male British subjects between the ages of eighteen and fifty-five would be liable to serve. The governor said the draft would be restricted to British subjects of European descent. Alluding to the three Chinese councillors, who were also British subjects, he said he hoped 'the many other British subjects in this colony will understand that this differentiation is being made solely on grounds of practicality'. He added that the government had a register of British citizens of European descent, and that a similar register of other British subjects could not be compiled easily.

No one objected to the governor's proposal. The traditions of the Legislative Council emphasized seniority and, as the most junior member present, it would have been totally inappropriate for Tse-fong to speak. But the difference Governor Northcote attached to British subjects of European descent and 'other' British subjects did not escape him.

The following month, as war clouds gathered in Europe and as the Japanese continued to make advances in China, a meeting was held of all Chinese justices of the peace, including Koon-chun and Tse-fong. The newly knighted Sir Robert Kotewall, who had succeeded Sir Shouson Chow in 1936 to the sole Chinese seat on the Executive Council, presided. The meeting passed a resolution pledging the wholehearted support and loyalty of the Chinese community to the British Crown.

On 3 September, even before this declaration of loyalty was received in London, Britain declared war on Germany.

Tse-fong made his maiden speech in the Legislative Council on 20 February 1941. In it, he strongly criticized the financial secretary's budget and ridiculed the policy of piling up large surpluses each year. He asserted that, with Hong Kong facing unprecedented perils, the time had come to spend the colony's reserves. Tse-fong endorsed the suggestion that two ships be purchased and presented to the British admiralty for war purposes, and said the rest of the money should be used for carrying on defensive works in the colony.

The Chinese members of the Legislative Council handled complaints from the public. These usually came from Chinese, but on rare occasions, a complaint came from a Westerner.

On 22 September, Tse-fong and his fellow councillors received a letter from W. V. Taylor, secretary and treasurer of the Evacuation Representation Committee, asking for an enquiry to find out who was responsible for the policy of evacuating British women and children from Hong Kong, and whether the evacuation was conducted impartially. London had ordered the evacuation of British women and children to Australia. While the order did not specific the racial origin of those to be evacuated, it turned out that only British subjects of 'pure' European background were affected. Those of Chinese origin were not to be evacuated.

The evacuation policy was highly unpopular. Those not in line for evacuation felt they were the victims of discrimination, while those who were evacuated blamed the government for forcibly separating their families. The Evacuation Representation Committee, an organisation of men whose wives and children had been sent away, was agitating for the return of their family members.

A joint response from M. K. Lo, Thomas Tam, and Li Tse-fong was sent to the committee. In it, the three men indicated their unhappiness with the British policy of differentiation between British subjects of European descent and those of Chinese origin.

> We are aware of the bitterness and dissatisfaction on the part of those affected by the evacuation, and the way in which it was carried out, and we have every sympathy for them,' the letter said. 'But we confess we cannot see how an inquiry at the present time can serve the interests of the public as a whole or, indeed, how such an enquiry can

promote the interests of those your committee represents, if their object is that of getting their families back to Hong Kong as soon as possible.

Then, in a telling passage, the three Chinese members of the Legislative Council said:

> We venture to plead for a greater measure of tolerance, forbearance and goodwill in dealing with this difficult and controversial subject. May we add that, as representatives of the Chinese, we, too, have very strong and bitter feelings in regard to the evacuation, but from a different angle. While we have always considered that the evacuation should never have been made compulsory as regards a small class of civilians, we have abstained from ventilating our feelings during these critical days, when it is so essential that nothing should be done to affect or impair the unity and war effort of the colony.

In May 1941, Governor Northcote left Hong Kong. His successor, Sir Mark Young, arrived in September, barely three months before the Japanese invaded and occupied Hong Kong. Ironically, that year the colony was celebrating a century of British rule. A rousing welcome was laid out for the new governor, who was attired in full traditional regalia, including a plumed hat, when he arrived at Queen's Pier. He was met by the top officials of the government, the senior military officer, the chief justice, and all the members of the Executive and Legislative Councils. Watching the ceremony, one would not have known that the British Empire was nearing its end.

War and Enemy Occupation

Chapter 12

Li Lan-sang (1900–1969): Racing Continues as War Approaches

The British merchants who came to Hong Kong in the mid-nineteenth century introduced horse racing, opium, the system of British justice, and the British civil service. The opium merchants, the captains of industry, and the big bankers brought their horses with them from Manila, Australia, South Africa, and the Middle East. The sport, like everything else, was dominated by expatriates. The stewards consisted of the colony's most important bankers and businessmen. A common saying declared that Hong Kong was run by the Jockey Club, Jardine Matheson (the biggest and oldest British trading company), the Hongkong Bank, and the governor—in that order.

The Chinese people in Hong Kong, like those in Shanghai and other coastal cities in China, quickly warmed to this new sport. To many, this was another form of gambling, more exciting than the various games of chance to which they were accustomed. Before long, hordes of Chinese flocked to the races.

The extent of Chinese interest—and interest by the Li family—in horse racing is reflected in a tragedy in 1918 when three-storey-high matsheds, used as grandstands, caught fire and collapsed. More than 600 Chinese were killed and many more injured. Three of the Li brothers, all avid race-goers, were present: Siu-pang, Tse-fong, and Lan-sang.

Like other European clubs of the time, the Hong Kong Jockey Club did not accept Chinese members. Chinese could not become jockeys and could not own horses, though they were allowed to place bets and watch.

The general strike of 1925 caused the Jockey Club to change its position. Leading members of the Chinese community had manned essential services and taken part in street patrol duties. A special police reserve had been set up. These acts, aimed at preserving Hong Kong's stability against China-directed agitation, made an impression on the conservative leaders of the Western business community. In 1926, amid this new atmosphere of trust in the local Chinese elite, the Jockey Club changed its rules. Within a decade, the Chinese accounted for more than half of all horses entered in the races.

The first member of the Li family to race horses was Tse-fong, who as early as 1928 entered a horse, Gold Medal, which did not win any races. Three years later, he made something of a splash with another horse, Gold Key. In the appropriately named Hopeful Stakes, where Gold Key was given only an outside chance, he galloped off with the first prize, with eighteen other horses at his heels.

Tse-fong was joined by his brothers, Siu-pang and Lan-sang, each of whom owned his own stable. While most of Tse-fong's horses had 'Gold' as part of their name, Siu-pang had a stable of 'Soldiers'. But it was Lan-sang, the only son of 'Second

Mother', who went into horse racing in a really big way. Most of Lan-sang's horses had names containing the word 'View', such as Sea View, Misty View, and Distant View.

Lan-sang, like his brothers, invested heavily in the Bank of East Asia and was on its board of directors until his death. On occasion he joined his brothers Koon-chun and Tse-fong when they invested in property developments. Like his older brothers, he also made loans on mortgages and invested in stocks. He was a conservative at heart and refrained from striking out on his own in pioneering investments. One exception was Kowloon Dairy, a company formed in 1940. He was a silent partner and did not involve himself much in the company's affairs, dropping by once in a while to assure himself that everything was going well.

Lan-sang was exceptionally devoted to his mother. Every day, upon returning to his spacious home on Seymour Road, he would dutifully go to his mother's room to offer greetings. Long after he was a grown man, she would berate him, sometimes for hours in the presence of the servants, and he would never contradict her or attempt to defend himself. Once she upbraided him at the dinner table; he sat silently until she finished before getting up, leaving his food untouched.

As was customary in such cases, Lan-sang addressed his own mother not as 'Mother', but as 'Sister', since in a household with a formal wife and concubines, the formal wife was recognized as mother of all the children, regardless of whether they were her own or not.

Lan-sang took a wife at the age of eighteen in an arranged marriage. His real love, however, was his concubine, a beautiful woman named Leung Suk-ying. Lan-sang's wife, Chan Tsz-chong, gave him three sons and a daughter: Fook-ling, Fook-lim, Wai-yuk, and Fook-kong. His concubine gave him an additional four children, again three sons and a daughter: Fook-chuen (Eric), Wai-ngan (Helena), Fook-kwan (Cornel), and Fook-sum (Alan).

'Second Mother' was partial to Lan-sang's wife, whom she had picked, and her children. She did not particularly like his concubine or her children, and ran the household with an iron hand, forcing her daughter-in-law to ask for permission before going to a movie or using the telephone. All major decisions were left up to her.

Lan-sang almost never displayed his emotions in public. Even at home, he did not directly discipline his children, leaving that up to their mother. While they were at school, he might walk by and say, in a low voice, 'Why aren't you studying? Aren't your exams coming up?' That would be enough to send them scurrying to their desks.

A mild, unassuming man who shunned publicity, Lan-Sang had a voracious appetite. He loved food and could consume great quantities of it. He also had a booming voice, and it was said that when he laughed in Hong Kong he could be heard in Kowloon. However, he rarely raised his voice. He was totally unambitious in the conventional sense and pursued neither power nor wealth, though he had plenty of the latter.

Before Lan-sang took up racing, he was addicted to mahjongg, staying up late to play the game. His stockbroker, Rudy Choy, convinced him that it was much healthier to race horses than to play mahjongg. With that, Lan-sang's lifestyle changed completely. He went to bed early so he could get up in the pre-dawn darkness to watch his horses exercising. Not a day went by that he did not visit his beloved horses, even in the worst weather. His other hobby was cars. He owned several cars and, though he had a chauffeur, he often preferred to drive himself.

Lan-sang had traditional views on the role of women. He would not allow his concubine, Leung Suk-ying, to drive, even though she had passed her driving test. When she returned home with her driver's licence, Lan-sang tore it up and she never drove again.

He also believed that women should not work. After his daughter Helena graduated from secondary school, she applied for an office job, since she knew shorthand and typing. But he prevailed on her to stay at home, saying a woman should not go out to work as long as she had parents who could take care of her. Helena did as she was told. After her brothers went abroad to study, she was the only child who remained in Hong Kong.

The Li brothers' participation in horse racing was part of a boom experienced by the Jockey Club in the late 1920s and early 1930s, a direct result of the admission of Chinese members. By 1934, Chinese owners predominated, accounting for 60 per cent of all ponies entered. The biggest stable belonged to Lan-sang, known in racing circles as 'Mr Lan'.

During the depression, attendance at the races fell markedly, but a hard core of enthusiasts never faltered. Their enthusiasm for racing extended beyond Hong Kong. For religious reasons, the Hong Kong Jockey Club did not conduct races on Sundays. However, the club in Macau had no such inhibitions, and Hong Kong race-goers customarily took a steamer to Macao on Sunday morning, returning the same night. The horses, of course, had to be shipped over a few days before the race.

The younger generation, too, became racing enthusiasts, including almost all of Siu-pang's family. His two sons by his formal wife, Fook-wing and Fook-fai, were both horse-owners; Fook-fai was also an amateur jockey. Even Siu-pang's third son, Fook-yim, who died at the age of nineteen, was a horse-owner. Koon-chun was not much of an enthusiast, but his son F. S. became a member of the Jockey Club at eighteen. Lan-sang's children, too, grew up with horse racing in their blood.

With the return of prosperity in the late 1930s, spirited Chinese crowds returned to the tracks. The end of the depression was signalled by the record crowd that attended the finale of the racing carnival in late February 1937.

And now, Chinese women flocked to the races as well. The womenfolk had previously considered it unseemly to be seen at the races. Now, they vied with each other to be seen and, during the racing season, would wear a new outfit each day. Tse-fong's wife, Tang Sau-hing, was often seen at the races in the company of her daughter, Doris Fung, and other relatives; all would be dressed in the latest fashion. On special children's days, Tse-fong's young sons would appear, dressed in the traditional British schoolboy's uniform: cap and tie with shorts and long socks.

The jockeys were all amateurs, and many of the prominent ones came from Shanghai. The Li brothers frequently obtained the services of S. Y. Liang, who was a leading jockey. Liang's career came to a tragic end in April 1937, in the only fatal racing accident in the Jockey Club's history up to that time. In the main event of the day, the mile-long Gin Drinkers Bay Plate, Liang was riding Tse-fong's Tabby Cat, third favourite, when the horse galloped onto the pony immediately ahead of him. The jockey was thrown onto the track. He was rushed to the hospital, but died thirteen days later.

With the demise of Liang, another popular jockey from Shanghai, Raymond Pih, was invited to don the Lan stable's colours: red, dark green, and black. Pih, who shared Lan-sang's passion for horses, became like a member of the family. Before dawn every morning, Lan-sang and Pih would go down to the tracks together to watch the horses in training. Training would start at five-thirty or six o'clock, and go on for one or two hours. Only after that would the two men have breakfast before going home. In the late afternoon, they would meet again to see the horses being walked back to the stable. Lan-sang personally fed fresh grass to all his horses.

Pih won a string of races for Lan-sang and his brothers. Once, Tse-fong had two horses in the same event, Racing Boy and High Speed. Pih was on Racing Boy and a Portuguese jockey rode High Speed. During the race, Pih's rein broke, and he had to hold on to the ring of the bit with his hand. He continued riding in this dangerous fashion, and both horses finished in a dead heat. Tse-fong led both his horses in to the winner's circle, a grin blanketing his face.

The Jockey Club was thrown into turmoil in the summer of 1937 as the Japanese mounted an all-out offensive against China. The eruption of war sent 600,000 Chinese refugees pouring into Hong Kong. Several thousand British citizens and other foreigners were also evacuated to Hong Kong. The government turned the Jockey Club into a refugee centre. Members' boxes, each with a toilet and running water, were turned into bedrooms, and many beds were put up in the pari-mutuel stands. Lines of laundry floated from the verandahs instead of colourful bunting. Fortunately, this occurred during the summer racing recess. The refugees were all moved out before racing resumed in mid-September.

Although World War II was raging in Europe, the Pacific War had not yet started and, in Hong Kong, the good life went on. Racing and betting continued unabated. The early months of 1941 were marked by continuous heavy rain, causing two postponements of the opening of the annual races. That year, Lan-sang's Distant View won the Austral Derby, one of three derbies that included the Hong Kong Derby and the Rooty-Hill Derby. The race itself was a tame affair, as there was never any doubt as to the ultimate winner. Distant View won so easily that the newspapers merely said he 'won by many lengths'.

By October 1941, Hong Kong was in the grip of war fever. Still, the racing went on. The last race meeting of 1941 was held on 6 December, just two days before the Japanese invaded Hong Kong. Both Lan-sang and Tse-fong entered horses. On 8 December, the Japanese attacked. During the fighting, panic-driven horses, some injured and dying, stampeded through the streets.

Chapter 13

1941: *Hong Kong Surrenders to Japan*

When the sirens went off on the morning of 8 December, Aubrey Li was shaving. Another air drill, he thought. But when he turned the radio on, he heard the ominous news: the Japanese were attacking.

From the window of his apartment on Conduit Road, where he and his wife, Laura, lived with three-month-old baby Ellen, Aubrey could see Kai Tak Airport and the Japanese warplanes wheeling over it, dropping bombs on the buildings and the handful of Royal Air Force planes, caught like sitting ducks on the ground. Within minutes, Hong Kong's air defences were gone.

The phone rang. It was Tse-fong. 'Come over and bring the baby,' he said. He wanted the whole family to be together at this hour of crisis. Aubrey took Laura and the baby to Seymour Road to be with his parents. His two unmarried sisters, Delia and Nancy, were already there.

The big house was looked after by twenty-two servants, including separate doorkeepers for the front and back door. Each member of the household had a personal maid, and there was even a cook to prepare meals for the other servants. In those days, food was not refrigerated; one went to market twice a day, accompanied by an assistant who carried a basket. When war broke out, it was the job of Tse-fong's wife, Tang Sau-hing, to feed everyone.

At Koon-chun's home on Kennedy Terrace, preparations were also being made for the war. As soon as the Japanese attack started, he gave instructions that a large number of rice bags be delivered to his house from Nam Wo Hong. The rice bags were stacked up against the windows on each floor to guard against splinters and broken glass. They were also piled up outside the house, in front of the basement door and all the windows. This was a mistake, for it attracted Japanese bomber pilots who thought the house was a military post. Two bombs hit the roof. They penetrated all the way down to the ceiling of the first floor. Fortunately, the whole family had gone down to the basement as soon as the air-raid alarm sounded.

From the ground floor, they could see the sky through the gaping hole. Frightened by the damage, the family moved out of the house to the Bank of East Asia, to live in the vault. Everyone was there: Koon-chun and his wife Tam Doy-hing; his eldest daughter Yue-chu and her husband, Chow Hau-leung, and their children; F. S. and Daisy and their children, Jeannette, David, and baby Jennifer; Fanny, Simon, Viola, Catherine, and Ronald. They were joined by Tse-fong and his family. Sir Shouson Chow and his family also took refuge in the bank, as did Kan Tong-po and his family. His son, Y. K. Kan, was a lawyer with a baby daughter: one of three babies in the vault. Counting relatives, friends, and servants, fifty or sixty people sought refuge in the bank.

In just over a week, the Japanese overran the New Territories and Kowloon, leaving Hong Kong Island, which they bombarded from across the harbour. Those huddled together in the bank could clearly hear the 'whee' of the shells whizzing by. There was no hope that Hong Kong Island could withstand the Japanese onslaught, and no possibility of relief from British or Allied reinforcements.

Still, Prime Minister Winston Churchill wanted to deny the use of Hong Kong harbour to the Japanese for as long as possible. On 18 December, Governor Mark Young received a telegram from London commending 'the stirring conduct of all defenders of the fortress' of Hong Kong. 'Hold on!' it said. The Governor replied: 'We are going to hold on.' On Christmas Day, the Governor issued his last message to the people. He said there was no reason why Hong Kong could not hold out indefinitely.

That afternoon, his military advisers told him they could no longer hold out. The Japanese crossed the harbour in rubber dinghies from Kowloon to North Point, on Hong Kong Island, and over the hills to Repulse Bay and Causeway Bay (the least expected and most difficult route). They killed a great many of the defenders and civilians. Governor Young went to Kowloon to offer his surrender. It was formally accepted the next day. On 27 December, Japanese troops marched into Central District and raised the Japanese flag. They marched to the Bank of China, then the Hongkong and Shanghai Bank, before heading for the Bank of East Asia. The little knot of people inside watched while Japanese soldiers pasted a strip of paper on the door of the bank, saying it was now a station of the Japanese gendarmerie.

One soldier entered the bank and gave everyone inside three hours to pack. Aubrey and Laura decided to stay with his parents. Laura, whom Aubrey had brought back to Hong Kong from the United States, burned her American passport and flushed it down the toilet. British passports, too, went up in flames. As long as the Japanese were around, it was safer to be Chinese.

Officially, the Japanese depicted themselves as fellow Asians who had liberated the Chinese in Hong Kong from the British imperialists. Thus, the *Hongkong News*, the English-language occupation newspaper, said on 31 December 1941, six days after the British surrender:

The million and more who comprise the Chinese population of Hong Kong, and who have been under British Imperialism for over 100 years, have now been released. The Japanese Army, by its courageous advance, has, in the shortest interval of time lifted the hundred years' oppression which the Chinese people have suffered. The Chinese must understand that the Far East fighting has but this aim—the overthrow of British and American Imperialism, to release the races of East Asia and establish a Far East Co-Prosperity Sphere.

Two days after the fall of Hong Kong, the Japanese gendarmerie rounded up leading Chinese citizens and took them to the Hong Kong Hotel for questioning. The Japanese wanted them to cooperate and help control the local population. These leading citizens, including Li Koon-chun and Li Tse-fong, were the ones who held high office under the British administration. Day after day they were subjected to questioning and pressure, and only allowed to go home late at night.

On 1 January, some senior members of the former British administration still at liberty (R. A. C. North, Secretary for Chinese Affairs, J. A. Fraser, Defence Secretary, and C. G. Alabaster, the Attorney General) called on Sir Robert Kotewall and Sir Shouson Chow. Attention focused on Kotewall, since Chow by this time was a stooping, grey-haired man of eighty-one. North asked the two men 'and their colleagues' to do what they could to reduce hardship by cooperating with the Japanese.

These instructions from senior British officials broke the deadlock between the leaders of the Chinese community and their new Japanese rulers. On 10 January, over 100 prominent Chinese, referred to as 'former Chinese Justices of the Peace and other distinguished leaders representing all sections of Chinese society', including both Li Tse-fong and Li Koon-chun, were invited to a lunch at the Peninsula Hotel by Lieutenant General Takashi Sakai, the Japanese commander who had led the conquest of Hong Kong. (After the war, General Sakai was convicted of war crimes and executed.)

Two days later, the Chinese Chamber of Commerce held a meeting and decided to accept the Japanese invitation to cooperate. There was little choice. A committee of nine called the Rehabilitation Committee was formed to be the voice of the Chinese community and to advise on the reconstruction of the territory. The committee was headed by Sir Robert Kotewall and Sir Shouson Chow. The two no longer used their British titles, of course, but became Mr Lo Kuk-wo and Mr Chow Shou-son.

The other members of the committee were Li Tse-fong, M. K. Lo, and Thomas Tam, the three Chinese members of the Legislative Council, as well as Li Koon-chun, Tung Chung-wei, chairman of the Chinese Chamber of Commerce, and two others of lesser prominence. They were received by the Japanese authorities on 14 January at the Peninsula Hotel.

Food was the most urgent problem. Li Koon-chun's position in the rice trade enhanced his importance to the occupation authorities. Before fighting broke out, he had cooperated with the Hong Kong government in putting together great stocks of rice. That rice was appropriated by the Japanese, who used Nam Wo Hong as an agency to sell rice at a fixed price. The Japanese used Koon-chun and his connections to restore stability to the rice trade, a crucial move, since rice was the main staple of the Chinese population. On 14 January, Koon-chun called a meeting to discuss how rice merchants could resume business. Only in April did the first shipment of grain arrive on a freighter from Thailand.

Members of the Rehabilitation Committee tried in different ways to help the common people. They proposed that women be searched by women rather than by male soldiers and police. They also tried to keep the price of rice low. But the committee had little power and its members were denied access to heads of departments, being limited to talking to interpreters. The Chinese of Hong Kong, taken aback by the British defeat, found they now had to pay obeisance to their new rulers. Each person had to bow every time he or she passed a Japanese sentry; failure to do so could result in death.

While the Chinese population, by and large, was not treated as enemy aliens (because they were considered citizens of the Japanese puppet administration in Nanjing), Westerners were rounded up and put in prison camps, Stanley for civilians and Shamshuipo Camp for military prisoners. Many friends of Tse-fong and Koon-chun were among those interned. One was Gilbert Harriman, a stockbroker and amateur jockey who used to ride Tse-fong's horses. They were close friends, and Harriman called Tse-fong 'Daddy'. Efforts to send food parcels to camp inmates proved difficult.

The Japanese gendarmerie took over the Bank of East Asia building only briefly. When they no longer needed it, it was returned to the bank and, as it was a Chinese bank, instructed to reopen its doors. Foreign banks, such as the Hongkong and Shanghai Bank, the Chartered Bank, and Chase, were not allowed to operate.

The Japanese soon appointed their own governor, Lieutenant General Rensuke Isogai. (In 1947, General Isogai was convicted of war crimes in Nanjing and sentenced to life imprisonment.) He arrived on 25 February 1942 at Queen's Pier, now called Military Wharf, and was greeted by top Japanese officials and Chinese representatives. Many of these leaders had greeted the arrival of Sir Mark Young, Hong Kong's governor, at this same pier only a few months earlier.

The installation of a Japanese governor signalled a return to relative normality. As a result, the Rehabilitation Committee was disbanded on 30 March, after holding fifty-nine meetings. In its place, the Japanese established two new organs, the Chinese

Representative Council and the Chinese Cooperative Council. All Rehabilitation Committee members were appointed to one of the two committees; they provided a link between the Japanese authorities and the Chinese community. The high-powered Representative Council consisted of politically influential people. It had only three members: Kotewall, Lau Tit-shing, a pro-Japanese businessman and president of the Chinese-Japanese Returned Students' Association, and Li Tse-fong. General Isogai received members of the two new councils on 31 March. The next day, the *Hongkong News* carried the photographs of Kotewall, Lau, and Tse-fong on the front page.

The members of the Chinese Cooperative Council were considered influential in their own sphere of activity. They were handpicked by the Representative Council. Chow Shou-son was designated its chairman, and Li Koon-chun its vice chairman. Its twenty other members were all leaders of various organizations. The purpose of the council was to secure the opinion of all sectors of the community, working under the leadership of the Representative Council. Tse-fong and other members of the Representative Council met on a daily basis. The Cooperative Council met twice a week.

Japan's three-year-and-eight-month occupation of Hong Kong was fraught with destruction and decay. Up until World War II, the Hong Kong economy had centred on the port, along with some light industry, such as knitting and weaving and the manufacture of flashlights and rubber footwear. The war ended the colony's normal trading and manufacturing activities.

In a move towards normalcy, the Japanese resumed the British custom of horse racing. A new organization, the Hong Kong Race Club, was set up. Isogai used the opportunity to show the Chinese population that their new rulers were different from the old ones. 'In the past, the British Government used wrong methods and means to conduct horse racing here,' he said. 'The British way lacked justice and gave enjoyment to only a special class of people to satisfy their own selfishness and for their own benefit.'

Under the British the Jockey Club was run by an all-European committee of stewards, but now the Japanese named a Chinese, Ho Kom-tong, as chairman. Li Tse-fong was appointed one of the stewards. Lan-sang was appointed to the executive committee. In a move to obliterate traces of Western culture, the Japanese demanded that all race horses be given Chinese names. English names, such as Gold Coin or Far View, had to be abandoned.

The abolition of English names extended also to streets and buildings. The Peninsula Hotel became the Toa and Queen's Road became Nakameiji-dori. But the Japanese, who were replacing the British as colonial masters, involved large numbers of Chinese people at all levels of the government in a way never attempted by the British.

Most private cars had been requisitioned by the British before Hong Kong fell. The Japanese shipped many of them back to Tokyo. Because of Tse-fong's official position, the Japanese assigned a chauffeur and a Morris Minor to drive him to and from work every day. But, because gasoline was rationed, the car could not be used for pleasure. His son Aubrey would often walk to the office from Seymour Road, wearing shorts or jeans and a short-sleeved shirt. There was no point in wearing business suits, as there was no business to be done.

Before returning to Hong Kong, Aubrey graduated from Boston University, spent time at Harvard Business School, and worked at the Chase Bank for twenty months. While at Chase he went to New York University in the evenings and earned a master's degree in commercial science. He had wanted to be an architect, but agreed to go into business in order to work with his father. Upon his return to Hong Kong, he was hired by the

Bank of East Asia as an assistant accountant.

The bank was open from ten in the morning to three in the afternoon, but only for cash transactions. There were no remittances and no international business. Every day Aubrey, Y. K. Kan, Thomas Tam, and George Sze played bridge in the boardroom. Y. K. and George Sze were both lawyers and did not work for the bank, but there was no law to practice. Instead, they played bridge until three o'clock, then went home.

The Bank of East Asia functioned under the supervision of the Yokohama Specie Bank. Everyone at the bank, from Chief Manager Kan down to the lowliest messenger, was paid the same paltry salary: eighty Japanese military yen a month. The exchange rate was fixed at HK$4 to one military yen.

Such a small salary meant that everyone had to be careful about spending money. Even the Li family had to stretch its food budget; at the beginning, Laura had to divide one egg into two meals for baby Ellen. Fortunately, many things in the house could be sold. Since no new clothes were available, old clothes became valuable. Tang Sau-hing sold trunks full of used garments. Tse-fong's stock of good brandy was also useful; one bottle would buy a sack of rice on the black market.

People like Kotewall, Tse-fong, and Koon-chun paid a price for maintaining a measure of stability in Hong Kong. The Japanese used their names for propaganda purposes. On 7 July 1942, the fifth anniversary of the Japanese attack on the Marco Polo Bridge, a mass meeting was held, not to condemn Japan's aggression, but to pass a resolution urging the Chinese government in Chongqing (Chungking) to stop fighting and to seek peace with Japan.

The resolution was proposed by Li Tse-fong and seconded by Chan Lim-pak. According to press reports, it was 'vociferously' approved by a mass gathering at the Yu Lok Theatre (formerly King's Theatre). All the members of the two councils had to sign the resolution.

The Japanese did not prevent people from leaving Hong Kong. In fact, they were encouraged to leave to reduce the number of mouths to feed. In the first six months of Japanese rule, the population declined by about half a million.

Simon was the first of Koon-chun's family to leave. Imbued with patriotic fervor, he wanted to go to Free China, where the Japanese held no sway. Koon-chun did not like the idea but finally consented. 'It's your life,' he told Simon. 'You go if you want.' Before Simon left, his father gave him HK$5,000 in cash.

Most of Tse-fong's children also left Hong Kong. Aubrey was the only son to stay behind. So he, Laura, and his two unmarried sisters, Delia and Nancy, lived with their parents on Seymour Road. They had no electricity—no air conditioning, no electric fans. They played bridge by candlelight and closed the french shutters to keep out prying eyes.

The first anniversary of Japanese occupation was marked by staged celebrations. The people of Hong Kong were asked to contribute to a fund to erect a monument in honour of Japanese soldiers killed in the assault on Hong Kong. A 'spontaneous' mass meeting of 20,000 people was organized at which a resolution was proposed by Li Tse-fong. It was seconded by Li Koon-chun and was then 'unanimously' adopted. It said:

> 1. We hereby decide to unite in support of the Greater East Asia War.
> 2. We hereby decide to use all our manpower and resources to support the Greater East Asia War.
> 3. We will spread the two East Asian principles of morality and spirit as a base to work for a closer relationship between Japan and China.
> 4. We hereby decide to send messages to the Japanese Prime Minister and to the Ministers of the Army and Navy, expressing our gratitude and to hope for a Japanese victory.

Most galling was that leading members of the two councils had to issue a statement to the people of Hong Kong on the first anniversary of the fall of Hong Kong. It was signed by Kotewall, Lau Tit-sing, Li Tse-fong, Chan Lim-pak, Chow Shou-son, and Li Koon-chun, and read:

> This is a day of commemoration, of resolution, and of hope. We are resolved to collaborate with Japan in her military, political, economic, and cultural efforts to create in Great East Asia a new order; and we are also resolved to support and cooperate with the Government of Hong Kong loyally and to the utmost of our endeavors in their beneficent work of economic, industrial, and social constructions. With knowledge of Japan's strength and unselfish purpose, and with a more intimate knowledge of Japan's benevolent rule in Hong Kong, we look to the future with implicit confidence.

The Li brothers were humiliated and embittered. But they had little choice. All they could do was play along with the Japanese, and wait.

Chapter 14

1943-1945: Life Under Enemy Occupation

On New Year's Day, 1943, Hong Kong began its second year of life under Japanese occupation. The Japanese-installed government issued a New Year's message stressing the important role that the one million Chinese in Hong Kong could play.

> If these Chinese truly understand and faithfully cooperate with the work of building a Greater East Asia, it is possible that through them they will be able to make other Chinese, who had wrongly placed their reliance on Britain and America, understand the same principles,' the message said. 'If these Chinese can be made to understand and cooperate with Japan they can make Chungking realize its past blunder, whereupon peace in China will soon be realized.

Early in 1943, the Chinese puppet administration in Nanjing declared war on Britain and the United States. In response, the two Japanese-installed councils in Hong Kong issued a joint statement:

> Now that the important decision has been made by the National Government of China, all Chinese must give their government full support to work for final victory in the War of Greater East Asia. The Chinese must help to win this war for the sake of Greater East Asia, and contribute all their energy and resources to work for better cooperation between Japan and China.'

Koon-chun and Tse-fong were two of the six men who made up the nucleus of the leadership of the Chinese community. The others were Robert Kotewall, Lau Tit-shing, Chan Lim-pak, and Chow Shou-son.

Those forced to cooperate with the Japanese by and large did so with reluctance and misgivings. Aside from a few pro-Japanese individuals, most of those who put their names to propaganda messages were forced to do so. Koon-chun tried to minimize his involvement by attending as few meetings as possible on the ground of poor health. He was, in fact, sick for several months and confined to bed. Occasionally he would go down to check on his office at Wo Fat Sing.

During one such visit, with his son F. S., Koon-chun encountered a gang of knife-wielding robbers. They wanted Koon-chun to open the safe, but he did not have the key with him. The robbers ransacked the premises and found some cash. Not satisfied, they demanded more. 'Kill the fat fellow first,' they said, referring to Koon-chun, who at the time was fairly corpulent. Fortunately, before violence occurred, an employee who happened to see the robbers returned from Nam Wo Hong with a large number of rice coolies, carrying bamboo poles and hooks. The robbers immediately fled. This frightening experience set off another bout of illness, and Koon-chun was bedridden again for several months.

Tse-fong's health, too, deteriorated during this time. He developed hypertension and was put on a special diet of bland food, primarily vegetables and steamed fish. He could no longer eat shark's fins and other delicacies of which he was so fond. Unable to get the medicine he needed, he wrote to his son Henry, who was studying medicine at St John's University in Shanghai. Henry managed to get medication from Germany for his father.

Allied bombing raids on Hong Kong increased in intensity as the war progressed. One Sunday, when Tse-fong and his family were spending a quiet afternoon at home, the silence was broken by the droning of aeroplanes, followed by the boom of exploding bombs. Instead of striking the dockyard, the intended target, the bombs fell on densely populated Wanchai, hitting the Oriental Theatre and the Ying King teahouse. The next morning, pedestrians on the street were dragooned by the Japanese to help remove the dozens of burned bodies. Allied bombing posed a greater threat to much of the population than the Japanese constabulary; the raids helped spur the exodus from Hong Kong.

All this time, Koon-chun was concerned about his ships. Once the Japanese took over Hong Kong, he had been cut off from communications with British officials and he worried about the ships' insurance. The marine insurance on all five vessels expired in February 1942.

In June 1943, he succeeded in getting a message to a representative of Wo Fat Sing in Portuguese-governed Macau. The representative approached Macau officials, who passed the message on to Lisbon, which then forwarded it to London. Koon-chun wanted to know what needed to be done to continue marine insurance for his ships.

Unknown to Koon-chun, one of his vessels, the *Shun Chih*, had been scuttled by the Hong Kong government in December 1941 during the fighting with the Japanese. Moreover, the

Apoey was captured by the Japanese during the fighting. The *Helikon* narrowly escaped capture, having left Hong Kong three days before the Japanese attack. The *Lyeemoon* and the *Haldis* were in Singapore loading supplies when Hong Kong fell. The former was carrying 2,000 tonnes of firewood, the latter a shipload of rice and cattle. They promptly sought refuge in Singapore and were requisitioned immediately by the British.

With the fall of Hong Kong, ships previously requisitioned by the Hong Kong government were taken over by the Ministry of War Transport in London. The ministry discovered that, of the three Wo Fat Sing ships in British hands in December 1942, only the *Haldis* and the *Helikon* were still afloat. The *Lyeemoon* became a total loss in the first week of January during a heavy gale in Benghazi harbour while on sea transport service in the Mediterranean. However, the ministry decided to withhold this information from Koon-chun for security reasons, since he was himself in enemy hands. The ministry merely said that marine and war risks were covered by the ministry and therefore 'it is not necessary for any market cover to be obtained on owners' behalf'.

During the Japanese occupation, Koon-chun and Tse-fong continued to act as trustees for their brother Chok-chung, managing his properties. These properties were reduced because Chok-chung, needing money, sold his houses on Woosung Street to his younger brother, Chok-lai. (Chok-chung, once one of the colony's wealthiest men, lost his fortunes and died in poverty. In the 1970s he even had his mother's remains removed from the Aberdeen Cemetery, where she had been buried more than fifty years before, to sell her burial plot. His death in 1983 was not announced in the newspapers. Even close relatives were not informed.)

The Japanese aggressively pursued their policy of reducing Hong Kong's population to relieve the pressure for food. Large numbers of people were deported to China or abandoned on uninhabited islands to fend for themselves. This policy was implemented by the gendarmerie, who often picked up people on the street who looked like vagrants and deported them without notifying their families or checking to see if they had jobs. Members of the two councils did what they could to alleviate hardship. At a meeting of the Chinese Cooperative Council on 16 August, Koon-chun voiced concern over the situation. In an indignant voice he declared:

> In recent days, we saw people being rounded up, placed on special vehicles and taken to a concentration point where they would wait for ships to take them to a designated place. It will be a great pity indeed if men and women who have both rice tickets and employment, and children who have rice tickets and older relatives, are subjected to this treatment. I consider that the attention of government ought to be drawn to this matter.

Koon-chun proposed that the General Charity Society, in conjunction with the Repatriation Office, be allowed to evacuate such people 'to their home village or places nearby so that they will not be left stranded and unable to find any food'. Those with jobs and rice coupons, he said, should be allowed to remain.

Koon-chun's proposal was sent to the Chinese Representative Council. Kotewall then brought the matter to the attention of Governor Isogai, who told him forcible evacuation was unavoidable because of food shortages. The governor said even those with rice coupons might be deported if they were unemployed. Koon-chun's protest did not result in any improvement.

The next year, 1944, saw a dramatic deterioration of living conditions, with inflation and acute food shortages. The government had to raise the salaries of Chinese civil servants. Li

Tse-fong, in an interview, suggested that workers in commercial and industrial enterprises should also be given a pay increase. He suggested that employees without board and lodging should be allowed a certain quantity of rice each month. Vegetables were so expensive that they were even beyond the reach of the wealthy. People were told to grow their own vegetables. Use of electric lights was limited to four hours a day, and later electricity was cut off altogether, only to be intermittently resumed.

In this time of stress and deprivation, a remarkable thing happened. The Li family turned towards Christianity for solace and guidance.

The situation began with an accident involving Tse-fong's sister, Sylvia, and her husband, L. P. Kwok, who was active with the Young Men's Christian Association. The two were on a ship, the Lingnan Maru, which sank while on the way to Macao. They were knocked unconscious but, almost miraculously, survived the ordeal. Afterwards, they gave a thanksgiving service and told their story, attributing their good fortune to divine intervention. From then on Sylvia worked on persuading her relatives to embrace Christianity.

Aubrey was the first to convert. When Aubrey married Laura Jee in a civil ceremony in 1940, he had promised that, at some unspecified time in the future, he would become a Christian. After Ellen and Mabel were born, Laura asked that they be baptized, and Aubrey agreed. Later, his two sisters, Nancy and Delia, asked if they, too, could be baptized. Aubrey then started receiving Bible lessons from a deacon, the Reverend George She. He was baptized at St Paul's Church, together with his sisters and daughters, on 2 April 1944.

Tse-fong and his wife Sau-hing became interested in converting. There were few Chinese-speaking ministers at the time but, as luck would have it, a Baptist church stood on Caine Road, only a fifteen-minute walk from Tse-fong's house. The minister there, Reverend Lau Yuet-sing, went to Seymour Road every other evening to talk about Christianity and explain the Bible. One of Tse-fong's main concerns was what to do with the wooden 'spirit tablets' kept on the family altar, which were believed to embody the spirits of his ancestors. He was told that they could still be kept, though no longer worshipped. On 5 March 1945, less than a year after Aubrey's conversion, both Tse-fong and Sau-hing were baptized. Tse-fong assumed the Christian name Peter and his wife was baptized as Ruth. Other members of their family converted shortly thereafter.

Sau-hing took Christianity seriously. Once baptized, she gave up consulting the Chinese almanac for auspicious dates to clean the house or wash her hair. She loved to sing hymns and read the Bible. Every now and then she would say, 'Let's have a thanksgiving.' She was grateful for everything that she had in life and actively worked to bring about the conversion of her whole family.

As a result of the conversions, Christian members of the family no longer performed the kowtow to their ancestors and to 'Second Mother' during family reunions. Instead, they stood at respectful attention and bowed three times.

As 1944 wore on, allied bombing intensified, making people extremely insecure. One day, Koon-chun took his son F. S. aside and said to him, 'Son, I'm getting old. It doesn't matter what happens to me, but I want you to go away to safety.' By this time, F. S. was the only son still in Hong Kong, and Koon-chun wanted him to go to Macau to join his siblings. But F. S. protested, 'How can I do that as your son? I want to be with you.' Ultimately, the two agreed that they would either leave Hong Kong together or stay together.

In September, Koon-chun and his whole family boarded a boat and headed for the sanctuary of neutral, Portuguese-governed Macao. After a perilous journey, during which passengers were asked to throw some of their belongings overboard to lighten the boat, they finally reached Macao and safety. Tse-fong remained in Hong Kong. Because of his prominence, he could not go; his family could leave, but they decided to stay with him. He continued to appear and speak on public occasions.

As the war continued, Hong Kong's situation worsened. Inflation put even basic necessities beyond the reach of many people, resulting in widespread starvation. Even the General Relief Association ran out of funds and had to curtail its activities. To the very end, the Japanese sought to maintain an image of invincibility. At the end of July 1945, less than three weeks before the Japanese surrender, the Japanese-installed governor of Guangdong visited Hong Kong and vowed that Japanese forces would crush 'any landing attempt which may be made by the enemy'. He also promised to send Hong Kong additional rice. In response, Tse-fong expressed the hope that the promises given would soon materialize 'for the benefit of the Chinese people'.

In the War's Aftermath

Chapter 15

Charges of Collaboration: Tse-fong's Final Days (1945–1953)

Forty-four months of Japanese occupation and sporadic Allied bombing left Hong Kong seedy and run-down. With the end of World War II, thousands of people, both former government officials and civilians, poured out of the Japanese internment camps. The emaciated survivors were little more than skin and bones, gaunt men and women who had seen many of their companions either executed or die of maltreatment. Feelings ran high and charges of collaboration with the enemy were hurled at those who had worked with the Japanese. High on the list of those accused of being collaborators were Sir Robert Kotewall and Li Tse-fong.

A British military administration was set up under Rear Admiral Sir Cecil Harcourt, with Brigadier David M. MacDougall as Chief Civil Affairs Officer. Upon their arrival, the British were distinctly embarrassed by the fact that all the men they had appointed to senior positions had cooperated with the Japanese. MacDougall, writing to his superiors in London a week after his arrival in September 1945, reported:

> . . . The next thing was Quislings. At the Admiral's direction, I informed Kotewall that he was to withdraw from public life immediately and await investigation. (He had been frequenting government offices unabashed since the Japs left.) He seemed quite impenitent and very sure of his defence. We will never convict him of anything, that is certain. What will happen will be that he will be allowed to fade quietly away, I imagine.

Tse-fong was investigated for his role during the Japanese occupation. Clearly, however, the British felt there was a difference between him and Kotewall. In November, when a dinner was given in honor of Admiral Harcourt, Kotewall was absent but Tse-fong was among the local leaders present, led by Sir Shouson Chow (once again sporting his knighthood).

When it came time to appoint Chinese to the Legislative Council, the British had a problem: most candidates under consideration had been tainted by collaboration with the Japanese. MacDougall rejected all former members except M. K. Lo. He explained: 'My recommendation of appointment of M. K. Lo has been made after giving full consideration to the question of propriety of his conduct during Japanese occupation.' He said that F. C. Gimson, the colonial secretary interned in Stanley Camp, and others testified that M. K. Lo had resisted the Japanese 'to the best of his ability and was, in fact, imprisoned by them for a short period. Further, he incurred risks by sending food parcels to both the prisoner of war and civil internment camps throughout the occupation.'

In the end, all political leaders who had cooperated with the Japanese were 'rehabilitated' by the British. In a personal letter to the author, MacDougall later recalled the atmosphere of the time:

> I knew both well [Kotewall and Li Tse-fong], the former as a prominent holder of high public office, the other an equally prominent and successful banker. Neither lacked friends but their very success had also inevitably provided them with enemies. They were consequently natural targets for the sort of accusations that flew thick and fast in the newly liberated colony in 1945.

What the colony needed, MacDougall felt, was to recover from the wounds of war, not to be plunged anew into bitter division and discord. He reminisced: 'Always the problem seemed the same: how to distinguish and identify the motives behind accusations of collaboration. Was it a genuine thirst for justice, or the result of personal rivalry or spite?'

Explaining why men like Tse-fong were not reappointed by the British after the war, MacDougall wrote:

> Hong Kong was set to make a fresh start, if such was possible. Li Tse-fong and Kotewall (and a few others) who in a real sense bore the burden and the heat of the Japanese occupation had thereby inevitably become controversial figures, innocent though they were of any taint of collaboration. Their re-appointment in the latter half of 1945 would have raised controversy which was what we most wished to avoid. Men penned up for three and a half years by a hostile power do not think rationally, and passions had not cooled. So we did not appoint the leading figures of the occupation period to the leading positions they had held prewar.

But Tse-fong did win appointment to some advisory bodies,

continued to be invited to major functions, and was given a position of honour. He was third in line among eighteen distinguished Chinese guests to greet the arrival of a new governor, Sir Alexander Grantham, in 1947. Still, for the remainder of his life, Tse-fong was a bitter and disappointed man, bitter against life itself, and angry that he had had to suffer intense humiliation. Anger and frustration eroded his health, and he developed a heart condition requiring daily doses of digitalis.

The war had chastened and changed the British. Gone was the zest for empire. Instead, the British turned inward and divested themselves of many of their colonies. Sir Mark Young became a reformist governor determined to bring about constitutional changes. Having been humbled by the Japanese, the British no longer felt justified in treating Chinese as second-class citizens. A new sense of egalitarianism was in the air.

In London, the secretary of state for the colonies announced that the age of racial discrimination was over. In Hong Kong the governor, proclaiming an end to inequality, repealed laws such as the one forbidding Chinese to live on the Peak. Everyone spoke of the coming of self-government to the colony. In the end, despite all the hoopla, Britain decided on an extremely curtailed form of 'self-government' for Hong Kong, with a colonial administration governing in conjunction with an appointed legislature. The difference was that the appointed members would outnumber the government officials in the legislature by a majority of one.

The advent of peace meant that people could resume their normal life. Tse-fong's eldest son, Norman, was married in Hong Kong in January 1946 to Muriel Koo. This was followed a few days later by the wedding of Tse-fong's son Fook-kow to Edith Kwong in San Francisco. The war changed the old order not only in the government but in other spheres as well. It broke down the strong hierarchical structure within the Li family and eroded the iron grip of 'Second Mother' on family matters. Tse-fong and Sau-hing felt that, since so many members of the family were Christians, it was necessary for all concerned to be more charitable to one another, especially to Chok-chung's common-law wife, Madam Ko. They spoke to 'Second Mother', arguing that times had changed, the children had all grown up, and the time had come for a reconciliation within the family. Eventually, 'Second Mother' acquiesced.

The formal acceptance of Madam Ko into the family occurred on 5 June 1947. That day, Tse-fong's fourth son, Henry, married Vivian Woo, the daughter of Dr Arthur Woo, a prominent physician. Madam Ko was allowed to attend the wedding, the first time she was admitted into a family gathering. Chok-chung's former wife was present, too. Henry and others of his generation signalled Madam Ko's acceptance into the family by addressing her as 'Seventh Aunt' (since Chok-chung was the seventh child).

In view of his poor health, Tse-fong decided to put his affairs in order. He formed a company, called the Perpetual Investment Company Limited, into which Tse-fong put most of his public shareholdings. Each son was given 500 shares.

These shares represented Tse-fong's gift to his sons to mark his own sixtieth birthday, a grand affair. His six sons and their spouses all attended the party. The men all wore white Western suits, while Sau-hing and the daughters-in-law wore formal Chinese regalia featuring colourful embroidered brocade jackets and gowns. A family portrait commemorated the occasion. The proud parents sat in the middle, with daughters-in-law on both sides in order of seniority, and each son standing behind his wife. The birthday celebrations took place in Tse-fong's new three-storey house on Victoria Road, in which he installed a lift because of his increasing difficulty in walking.

The following year, Tse-fong and Sau-hing travelled to the United States to see their daughters and to seek medical attention for him. His diabetes had become so severe that doctors recommended amputation of his left leg, and he hoped to see a specialist in San Francisco. Tse-fong travelled first to the East Coast to visit his daughters Delia and Nancy, then to Colorado Springs to see his oldest daughter Doris. There he took ill, apparently a result of the high altitude, and developed pneumonia. His physician son Henry immediately flew from Hong Kong to take care of him. Because Tse-fong was afraid of flying, they decided to go to San Francisco by train. On the way, his situation deteriorated and Henry had to take him off the train at a small town in Nevada called Winnemucca. There Tse-fong died on 5 September 1953, sixteen days before his sixty-second birthday.

Li Shek-pang, who arrived in Hong Kong at the age of five, became one of the colony's wealthiest men and the founder of the Li clan.

The three wives of Li Shek-pang: his formal wife, Madam Hau (centre), Second Mother (left), and his favourite, Black Peony, (right).

Prefects at Queen's College wearing Qing dynasty hairstyles and clothing before the fall of the Qing in 1911. Li Tse-fong is second from the left.

Li Lan-sang, who owned the largest stable in Hong Kong, triumphantly leading one of his winners after a major race.

The Li Lan-sang branch of the Li family, with Lan-sang seated in the middle surrounded by family members.

Executives of the Shanghai branch of The Bank of East Asia in the 1920s. Li Tse-fong is seated, left.

Double wedding of Kenneth Fung Ping-shan (later to become Sir Kenneth Fung) and his twin brother, Fung Ping-wah, to Ivy Kan, daughter of Kan Tong-po, and Doris Li, daughter of Li Tse-fong, respectively. The December 193 wedding cemented relations between The Bank of East Asia's three leading families, but events in later years would test the strength of those bonds

Aubrey Li and his wife, Laura, showing Queen Elizabeth II and Prince Philip the sights during their visit to Hong Kong in October 1986.

Prime Minister Margaret Thatcher meets with Hong Kong Governor Sir Edward Youde and his advisors. F.S. Li is first on the left.

Aubrey and Laura Li at a get-together of their branch of the Li family.

Ronald Li loses his temper at a press conference after the October 1987 crash. Asked if he had closed the exchange to protect his personal interests, Ronald exploded, pointing an accusing finger and demanding that the reporter be immediately hauled off to prison. Courtesy of the *South China Morning Post*.

The first Chief Justice of the Hong Kong Special Administrative Region, Andrew Kwok-nang Li, being sworn in in the early hours of 1 July 1997 by Chief Executive Tung Chee-hwa. Courtesy of the Hong Kong SAR Government.

David Li receiving an honorary doctorate.

Simon F.S. Li, in the wig and robes of a senior judge, was the first Chinese to become a vice president of the Court of Appeal.

Chapter 16

The 1950s: After the War, a Changed Existence

When Li Koon-chun returned to Hong Kong from Macao after the war, he was an old man of sixty-eight. Although the war was over, he found his enforced idleness was to be prolonged.

The rice business was no more; the government decided to operate a monopoly in the face of a world-wide shortage. As for his shipping business, only the *Helikon* was sound. After fifty years, Wo Fat Sing was back to where it had started, with only one ship. Koon-chun spent his limited energy on minor dealings.

While Koon-chun continued to run the family businesses, his two youngest brothers, Chok-chung and Chok-lai, increasingly desired to strike out on their own. Each set up his own investment company. Chok-chung named his the Wang Shun Investment Company, with paid-up capital of HK$650,000. (The company was named after his favourite son, Fook-wang who, like Chok-chung himself, was the seventh child in the family.) He and his common-law wife, Madam Ko, were permanent directors; their eight children were the other shareholders. His business was primarily involved in real estate and the share market.

However, the company lacked professional management and did not do well. Chok-chung was repeatedly chastised by the registrar of companies for failing to comply with the government's filing requirements. 'At no time since the incorporation of the company has an annual report been filed within the statutory period of twenty-eight days after the date of the general meeting, and on each occasion it has been necessary to send several reminders from this office,' the Registrar wrote in January 1953. Meanwhile, the company's liabilities mounted and, in 1954, Chok-chung put the company in voluntary liquidation, having lost substantially in ths venture.

Chok-Lai launched his company, C. L. Li Investment Company, with his wife as chairman, with HK$500,000. When the company's indebtedness rose to HK$300,000 in 1953, he, too, dissolved the company.

But while the two brothers were in their prime, they operated in style. They had a permanent table at a major Chinese restaurant, where anyone who wanted to talk business could go. Throughout the day, dozens of people would talk, eat, then leave, and the two brothers always picked up the bill. Many deals were made on these occasions, but the two brothers rarely found themselves any richer as a result.

Chok-chung was the picture of sartorial splendour. He sported well-cut Western suits and would insist on making alterations of as little as two millimetres. He also loved cars; among many, he owned a 1930 Duesenberg J Derham Tourister, dubbed the ultimate American car. It had the most extensive selection of instruments of any vehicle in automobile history—only eight were ever built.

Koon-chun could do little but look on as his brothers' substance was gradually reduced. Both brothers disposed of their shareholdings in the family businesses. Koon-chun bought Chok-chung's shares in the names of his sons and Chok-lai's shares in the names of his daughters.

In the War's Aftermath

Chok-chung and Chok-lai were not alone in their financial problems. Siu-pang, too, came under pressure from creditors. Already sick, he was able to satisfy these creditors, but soon had to be taken to the hospital. There, at the behest of his daughter Wai-chee, he was baptized as a Catholic before dying in March 1951 at the age of sixty-two.

Life for Koon-chun after the war was not the same. Before the war, in the late 1930s and early 1940s, he was in his prime, and everything seemed possible. After the war, he was tired, old, and often sick. The war had destroyed the old order, of which he was a part, and a new, unfamiliar order was emerging. Before the war, Koon-chun did business with cold cash; it was a disgrace to borrow money. After the war, establishing a good credit rating was the way to obtain financing.

Koon-chun maintained his interest in business but was much less active. He considered properties vastly overpriced compared to their pre-war value. Land on King's Road, for example, was only one or two cents per square foot before the war. Now the values jumped tenfold with the influx of entrepreneurs from Shanghai fleeing the communists, who brought with them capital and manufacturing know-how and who helped transform Hong Kong's economy in the 1950s and 1960s. Many of these immigrants settled in North Point, which became known as 'Little Shanghai'. When a property came on the market, Koon-chun would laugh and say he had turned down the same property at two cents per square foot, so why should he touch it at ten times as much. Everything, he felt, was overpriced. He did not realize that, before long, prices would jump again by 1,000 per cent. Yet he still had a very sizeable portfolio of investments, and his daughter Fanny, a teacher before the war, now accompanied him everywhere as his secretary.

All Koon-chun's children were grown up. The marriage of his youngest son, Ronald, in July 1951, signalled the maturation and growing independence of the next generation. He decided

131

to put his own affairs and those of the family in order.

Koon-chun set up the Hong Kong Investment Company, into which he put most of his assets. His four sons were shareholders; the daughters were not included. Koon-chun kept the Kennedy Terrace houses and some other properties in his own name.

Various loose ends remained, however. When Shek-pang's estate was divided up in 1933, Koon-chun had kept some assets as the common property of all six brothers. Now, he thought, it would be best to put all common property into one company and divide the shares among the brothers and their children. As a result, he formed the Hing Wai Investment Company. Into that company went all that was still undivided of Shek-pang's estate. Since Chok-chung and Chok-lai had sold their shares to Koon-chun's children, Koon-chun's branch of the family owned half of Hing Wai, with the rest belonging to members of Siu-pang's, Tse-fong's, and Lan-sang's families. One of the main properties was a prime site in the heart of the Central District, along Queen's Road Central. On this site the family erected the new Hing Wai Building. Another valuable piece of property on Des Voeux Road West was later developed into the Emerald Hotel.

Koon-chun's children, although grown up with families of their own, continued to live with their father. All four sons, after returning to Hong Kong, moved into 6 Kennedy Terrace with their families, with one son occupying each floor. His eldest daughter, Yue-chu, lived a few houses away with her family while Koon-chun, his wife, and his one unmarried daughter, Fanny, stayed at Number 8. It was unusual, even in Chinese society, for grown men to live under the same roof as their parents, but Koon-chun was the head of a very unusual family.

He instilled into his grandchildren the same discipline that he had drilled into his children, asking to see their school reports and rebuking them with a stern look if they did badly. But, if one of them did well, Koon-chun would reward him at the dinner table by handing him a drumstick. And, while he himself was a heavy smoker, he forbade his children to smoke in his presence, though he did encourage them to develop a taste for fine wines.

Meanwhile, the amicable relationships that had existed within the board of the Bank of East Asia came to an end. The two great friends, Kan Tong-po and Li Koon-chun, no longer saw eye to eye. Their differences were exacerbated by the emergence of the sons of the bank's founders and the subsequent rivalry among them for positions within the bank. Relations between Kan Tong-po and Li Koon-chun became so bad that, beginning in late 1947, Koon-chun boycotted all meetings of the bank's directors and refused to attend the annual meetings for shareholders. In 1949, the bank created three assistant managers, posts to be held by Kan Tong-po's son Y. H. Kan, the late Fung Ping-shan's son Kenneth Fung, and Tse-fong's son Aubrey. Another move followed in January 1951 when another son of Kan Tong-po, the lawyer Y. K. Kan, was invited to join the board. The next generation was in the wings, ready to take over. Could they work together? And which one of them would be chief?

Tse-fong's death in 1953 left a vacancy at the bank that was not filled for three years. Kan Tong-po prepared the way for his eldest son, Y. H. Kan, who had joined the bank in 1947 after working for the Bank of China in Liverpool, to succeed him. While Y. H. Kan, Kenneth Fung, and Aubrey Li were all designated assistant managers, Y. H. alone was promoted to deputy manager and, in 1956, began to act in his father's place when Kan Tong-po was away. Things came to a head on 4 December 1956. At a crucial board meeting, Kan Tong-po proposed appointing his son Y. H. as manager.

Kan Tong-po wanted his son, like himself, to be appointed for life. This would have meant dominance by the Kan family for another generation. Such a move was bitterly opposed by

F. S., who represented his father. In the ensuing argument Kan Tong-po, in a fit of anger, took out a revolver he kept in a drawer and banged it on the table. Sir Shouson Chow, the ninety-four-year-old chairman, was so agitated that he lost bladder control. Because the Kans had the support of a majority of directors, the proposal was carried and an extraordinary general meeting was scheduled to confirm this decision through a special resolution.

The Li family prepared for legal action against Kan Tong-po. A charge of assault was contemplated, since he had brandished his revolver. Solicitors and barristers were contacted, both in Hong Kong and in London. The Kans, too, gathered together their own legal forces. Eventually Peter Griffiths, a prominent solicitor, advised the Lis against legal action and said they should concentrate on defeating the special resolution, which required a three-quarters majority of all voting shares. With the help of an old friend, Noel Croucher, head of Commonwealth Investments Ltd., which controlled 10 per cent of the bank's shares, the Li family lined up enough votes to block Kan Tong-po's motion. The meeting to appoint Y. H. Kan as manager never took place.

Eventually, a reconciliation between Kan Tong-po and Li Koon-chun was effected by a mutual friend, Thomas Tam. He arranged a small party for Koon-chun and Kan Tong-po, attended by members of the Li and Kan families, at which the two old men shook hands.

On 4 April 1958, Y. K. Kan, at a directors' meeting, raised the question of Koon-chun's prolonged absence from the board. F. S., speaking for his father, said meetings were usually held in the afternoon, and Koon-chun needed to rest then. Y. K. Kan then proposed a motion, seconded by Sir Shouson Chow, that the board write a letter inviting Koon-chun to resume his seat and further proposed that future board meetings be held in the morning.

The next meeting was held at noon on 8 May. On that day, the seventy-one-year-old Koon-chun took part for the first time since 1947. The meeting reflected the behind-the-scenes compromise worked out between the various families. Five new directors were added to the board: Sir M. K. Lo, the bank's legal adviser, Wong Chung-man, the son of founder Wong Yun-tong, F. S. Li, Y. H. Kan and Aubrey Li. The ten-year split within the board was healed, but the old intimacy was never restored. A new balance was achieved among the main families represented. The manager's post still went unfilled. Instead, the work was divided among Y. H. Kan, Kenneth Fung, and Aubrey Li.

In early 1959, Sir Shouson Chow, who had served as bank chairman for more than thirty years, died at the age of ninety-seven. Wong Yun-tong proposed Kan Tong-po as the new chairman, a move seconded by Koon-chun. Kan Tong-po continued to serve simultaneously as chief manager.

Y. H. Kan, Kenneth Fung, and Aubrey Li, as joint managers controlled, respectively, domestic loans, administration, and international affairs, all working under Chief Manager Kan Tong-po. The bank's staff, too, was divided along pro-Kan, pro-Fung, and pro-Li lines, with the Kan faction enjoying the upper hand.

Chapter 17

F. S. Li: Man on a Hit List

Koon-chun's oldest son, F. S., had decided to become a chartered accountant because his father wanted him to look after the family business. The war prolonged a five-year apprenticeship to a decade and, by the time he returned to the colony (the first local boy to become a chartered accountant), he was a mature man of thirty-six, tall, slim, and outgoing, with a wry sense of humour.

A pioneer in the accounting field, he helped set up the Hong Kong Society of Accountants, an association he cherished. After his retirement, F. S. kept a brass plaque proclaiming his membership number: 001.

Hong Kong then was a tightly knit society. The same individuals were leaders in business, in politics, and in religion. F. S., active in Anglican affairs, was a member of the council of the Anglican cathedral. There, he served alongside government officials and captains of industry. Ever since F. S. and Daisy were baptized in 1945, they had taken their religion seriously. All their children—Jeanette, David, Jennifer, and Arthur—were baptized. F. S.'s sister Fanny, who was childless and unmarried, was godmother to them all.

In the War's Aftermath

The Hong Kong government, which had decided against moving towards democracy and self-government, nevertheless was on the lookout for promising people to appoint to various advisory bodies. F. S. was an obvious choice. In 1954, he was invited to join the newly established Housing Authority. F. S. accepted the appointment. In this regard, he differed from his father, who by and large shunned political involvement.

The establishment of the Housing Authority signalled a new direction in Hong Kong government policy. In the immediate post-war years, the population had shot up from less than 600,000 to 2.5 million, as those who had fled Hong Kong during the Japanese occupation returned, followed by hordes of refugees fleeing the civil war in China and, after 1949, the rule of the communists. Until the communist takeover, the border between Hong Kong and China was open, and people could come and go as they pleased. The vast majority of the new arrivals had no homes. They constructed flimsy huts from tar-paper, hoarding, and whatever materials they could find. Squatter huts failed to meet minimal standards of hygiene. Structures with no electricity, running water, or toilets sprang up and took over every available bit of space in the hills and valleys surrounding the urban areas. The government adopted an attitude of non-involvement, hoping that these people, who arrived like a tidal wave, would depart in the same manner.

On Christmas Day 1954, a fire broke out at Shek Kip Mei in Kowloon, site of the largest squatter settlement, covering forty-five acres. As a result, 60,000 refugees lost their homes. The disaster forced the government to reverse its position and create a programme to provide minimal housing for all squatters. A Resettlement Department was set up with funds to build seven-storey apartment blocks, with only the most basic of amenities, into which squatters could be resettled.

At the same time, the Housing Authority was created to provide an ambitious housing programme for people other than squatters in need of low-cost housing, estimated to number 600,000. It had authority to plan, construct, and manage housing estates. Since large amounts of money were involved, someone like F. S. was needed to oversee its finances. By the time F. S. left the Housing Authority ten years later, it had spent over HK$200 million..

In 1960, when he had made his mark in the business world, F. S. was appointed to the Urban Council. The faces he encountered there were all familiar to him, such as his wife Daisy's brothers, the lawyer P. C. Woo and the physician P. F. Woo, and his fellow director at the bank, Y. K. Kan. In his first address on the council floor, F. S. dwelt at length on the housing issue. He cited the proliferation of rooftop squatters and the problems they created for both landlords and tenants, and asked for urgent action to resettle them. The population explosion also exacerbated the question of sewage disposal, and F. S. warned against the pollution of beaches by 'the continuous discharge of sewage into the sea'. This was a problem of long standing. (The problem remains unresolved and has grown to horrifying proportions as torrents of sewage are pumped into Hong Kong's famous harbour every day.)

Because of his interest in public hygiene, F. S. was made chairman of the food and restaurant committee, which set the standards of food served in public places. He occasionally made personal checks to see that food was properly handled and that no one with any skin disease was allowed to prepare food.

The governor, Sir Robert Black, appreciated his performance and, in May 1961, F. S. was made a justice of the peace; the following month, he was appointed a member of the Legislative Council, along with Y. K. Kan, following in the footsteps of his uncle Tse-fong.

In January 1963, F. S.'s name appeared in the annual New Year's Honours List. He was made an OBE, and became one of the leading lights in society and performed such functions as inspecting auxiliary police parades.

While F. S. was busy with his professional and public duties, his wife, Daisy, was busy too. She had looked after the children during F. S.'s professional studies and, when they were old enough for school, she took them to England, spending most of the 1950s there. F. S. bought a house in England and arranged for a Chinese servant to look after his children when they came on holidays.

After Daisy returned to Hong Kong, she occupied herself with community work. In 1961 she joined the Hong Kong Red Cross and, the following year, became a deputy director. In 1965 she became the Red Cross's director, a position she held for three years, during which she performed such ceremonial functions as accepting public presentations of checks and distributing prizes in schools.

Soon, the children of Daisy and F. S. Li grew up. Their eldest daughter Jeanette became a doctor and specialized in radiology. After graduation she worked in Hong Kong before returning to England, where she married a pathologist. Her sister Jennifer, too, got married and settled down in England. Both their brothers, David and Arthur, wanted to be doctors, too. However, Koon-chun felt that there should not be too many doctors in the family and advised David to follow in his father's footsteps and become an accountant. Arthur could not be persuaded. Since childhood he had wanted to be a doctor, and so he did, becoming one of the best surgeons of his day.

Their grandfather, Koon-chun, after the reconciliation with Kan Tong-po in 1958, diligently involved himself in the work of the bank, attending all board meetings until 1962. That March, he took ill. An earthquake of unusual intensity struck Hong Kong on 19 March and, although it did little damage, he developed a fever from the shock, which turned into pneumonia and then into pleurisy. Doctors dosed Koon-chun with antibiotics and his condition improved somewhat, but he never recovered.

During his long illness, Koon-chun was cared for by his daughter Fanny. A devout Christian since her wartime conversion, she spoke to her parents often about Christianity. Due to her influence, Koon-chun and his wife were both baptized. When Kan Tong-po died in November 1963, F. S. told the board on behalf of his father that Koon-chun, next in line in seniority, could not serve as chairman because of his health. F. S. proposed Y. K. Kan succeed his father, Kan Tong-po. This was seconded by Kenneth Fung and approved unanimously. The next generation had taken over.

The 1960s differed from the early 1950s in that life's basic necessities were assured for the vast majority of people. There was almost no unemployment, as the economy was constantly expanding. However, it was a no-frills existence. There was no such thing as free education for children, no old-age pensions or retirement benefits, precious little in the way of social welfare, and little time for leisure activities. The colony, by dint of hard work, was laying the groundwork for future expansion. The engine of growth was exports.

The colony sent trade delegations abroad and took part in trade exhibitions where it cold show off its wares. In 1964, at the Seventh World Trade Fair in San Francisco, Hong Kong had the largest of more than 800 stands. A wide variety of Hong Kong products was on display. The centrepiece was a Chinese pleasure junk with a dragon painted on it.

F. S. was asked to lead the Hong Kong delegation at the fair, so he flew to San Francisco with Daisy. The ten-day fair was a great success, with the Hong Kong pavilion one of the most popular display centres, attracting 8 per cent of the 250,000 visitors. The biggest money makers for Hong Kong manufacturers were ivory goods and wigs made of human hair. When F. S. returned to Hong Kong, he predicted that exports to the United States would soon exceed HK$1 billion.

In May 1966, F. S. was appointed to Hong Kong's highest

policy-making body, the Executive Council. Of ten members, only four were Chinese, and they met every Tuesday morning with the Governor. These were the colony's most powerful people. Members of the Executive Council, like those of the Legislative Council, were appointed, not elected, but they were deemed to represent the Hong Kong public. F. S. had clearly become the standard bearer of the Li family.

F. S. was also active in sports. In 1965, he became vice president of the Hong Kong Football Association, the governing body of soccer in the colony. He had been fond of the sport all his life and had played on the school team at St Joseph's. In 1966, he became president. The position was largely honorary, since the association's day-to-day affairs were managed by its chairman. But the president and vice president were men of prominence who could be counted on to help the association morally and financially.

One of the highlights of F. S.'s term as president was the arrival of the world famous Sparta Praha soccer team from Czechoslovakia in early 1967. The team arrived in Hong Kong after an unbeaten tour of Australia, New Zealand, and Singapore. As expected, they won all three matches in Hong Kong. But financially, the tour was less than victorious. Czechoslovakia, like other countries in Eastern Europe, suffered from a chronic shortage of hard currency. After the Czechoslovakians arrived in Hong Kong, F. S., as president of the football association, invited the entire group (about twenty people, including players, manager, and captain) to a seafood dinner in the fishing village of Aberdeen. To the surprise of the host, after dinner, the manager thanked him for arranging visits to tourist spots, but confessed sheepishly that the team had run out of money. F. S. ended up giving each man HK$500 out of his own pocket.

F. S.'s move up to the Executive Council enabled him to put forward his ideas forcefully at the weekly meetings. When

141

private persuasion did not work, F. S. would speak his mind publicly in the Legislative Council. At the time, Britain required that Hong Kong's reserves be held in pounds sterling in London. Other members of the British Commonwealth could diversify and hold gold or foreign currencies, but because Hong Kong was a colony, it had no choice. After Harold Wilson became prime minister, F. S. warned about the impact of a devaluation of the British pound. In spring 1967, in a budget speech, he questioned the wisdom of keeping all Hong Kong's reserves in sterling and asked what steps had been taken 'to protect our reserves in the event of a devaluation of the pound. I should also like to ask if it is the government's intention to retain the existing link between the Hong Kong dollar and sterling should the pound be devalued'.

In fact, Hong Kong's reserves at the time played a major role in supporting the sagging pound, accounting for between a quarter and a third of British gold and foreign currency reserves used for backing sterling. The financial secretary, John Cowperthwaite, responded to F. S.'s comments by saying: 'Our links with sterling are too strong to be lightly broken. In any event, Her Majesty's Government have repeatedly emphasized their firm resolve to maintain the exchange value of the pound.' Eight months later, the pound was devalued by 14.3 per cent, and one-seventh of Hong Kong's reserves was wiped out overnight. Eventually, Hong Kong revalued the dollar so that it was devalued, not by 14.3 but by 5.7 per cent. Still, the move cost Hong Kong HK$450 million.

In May 1967, a year after F. S. was appointed to the Executive Council, Hong Kong was struck by its worst crisis since the Japanese occupation. The upheaval of the Cultural Revolution in China spilled over into Hong Kong. Riots broke out as radical supporters of Chairman Mao Zedong in Hong Kong called for the overthrow of the British colonial government.

F. S. and other community leaders rallied to the defence of the government. The communists reacted violently to the open support F. S. gave to the British. China's official trading agency, China Resources, summoned him in and told him to issue a public apology to the Chinese government. Otherwise, officials told him, they would no longer sell rice to Nam Wo Hong. F. S. refused to apologize, saying the views he expressed were his own, not those of Nam Wo Hong, of which he was only a director and minor shareholder. As a result, China Resources broke its contract with Nam Wo Hong, 'temporarily' suspending supplies of rice. Officials at China Resources said they were acting on instructions from Beijing. By this time, China accounted for almost 20 per cent of Hong Kong's rice imports, and China Resources announced it would increase supplies to other importers in order to 'satisfy the need of our Hong Kong compatriots'. Only Nam Wo Hong, not the people of Hong Kong, was to suffer.

The Bank of China building, the tallest in Hong Kong, became the headquarters of the radicals. It stood, cheek by jowl, next to the Hongkong Bank. Both were solid, imposing granite structures. The Hongkong Bank had bronze lions guarding its entrance, while the Bank of China had stylized Chinese stone lions. Both were built by the same architectural firm. But while the Hongkong Bank was the quintessential symbol of colonial power, of British imperialism, and of conservative capitalism, its next door neighbour was the headquarters of the communist establishment in Hong Kong.

The exterior of the Bank of China was draped with anti-colonial slogans. Loudspeakers denounced the British. Bank officials placed barbed wire on the roof to prevent the police from staging a helicopter assault. A radio journalist, Lam Bun, known for his anti-communist stance, was killed when he was dragged from his car, doused with kerosene, and set afire.

In July, F. S., normally low-key and tolerant, openly

denounced the communists for stirring up trouble. 'I think the time has now come to warn all troublemakers in the plainest terms and to avoid any possibility of misunderstanding, that action against the law will not be tolerated,' he said. 'If any disregard this warning, they will have to face grave consequences.'

The communists wanted to disrupt mass transportation in the colony. The first target was the Star Ferry Company, whose ferryboats were idled on 6 June when all the seamen walked off their jobs. The Hong Kong Tramway Workers Union was also a hotbed of leftist agitation. Bombs went off inside the tram depot to intimidate workers who chose not to strike. One day, F. S., the only Chinese on the board of directors, got a call from its chairman, Michael Young-Herries. 'F. S.,' he said, 'I'd like you to come down and talk to the employees tomorrow morning because they are threatening to go on strike.'

F. S. agreed. The governor, who knew about this arrangement, sent for the commissioner of police, who offered fifty policemen as an escort. F. S. declined police protection. When he got to the tram depot, he saw several thousand disgruntled workers milling around. Before talking to the workers, he asked the company secretary, W. H. Paterson, and all the company's European executives to leave. He did not want any white faces around him. Then he walked in, alone and unarmed, to confront the horde of angry men. He heard one worker mutter, 'This man has guts.' Adopting the abusive language of the agitators, he swore at them: 'You [swearword], what do you think you're doing? If you strike, you'll be making trouble not for the white-skinned pigs or the yellow-haired dogs but for your fellow Chinese. Who rides trams anyway? Not Europeans. Only Chinese who cannot afford taxis. They are the ones you will be making trouble for.'

F. S. told them he had full authority to close down the depot. Then he said, 'Those who want to resign, raise your hands.' After a few seconds, one man put up his hand and said, 'I want to resign.' F. S. asked why, adding, 'If you don't want to give your reasons, just give me your name and I'll see that you get whatever is due you from the retirement fund, as well as your bonus.' The man said his wife was nervous and did not want him to go to work. 'All right,' F. S. said. 'Give me your name. I'll see that you get paid tomorrow. Anyone else want to resign?'

Some said yes, they were getting too old to work and wanted to retire. Then a man in his twenties put up his hand. 'You're not too old,' F. S. said to him. 'Don't you want to work?'

'It's not that I don't want to work, sir,' the young man replied. 'It's just that we live in a hut on a hill in North Point and my mother has to climb down the hill every day to fetch water. I want to help her.'

'You're a very good son,' F. S. said. 'Give me your name and I'll see you get all your benefits. Does anyone else want to quit?'

There was a rustle as the workers looked around at one another. There were no more resignations and there was no strike. The tram company was able to maintain service. Government guards were assigned to the drivers, some of whom were injured during the disturbances.

Leaders of the agitators were angered by F. S.'s defiance of the radicals. An underground mimeographed news sheet appeared carrying a death list of six marked men—all Chinese, not British. They were denounced as traitors. The news sheet hailed the killing of Lam Bun as a 'big achievement' for the 'anti-British atrocities' squad. It declared that the others would meet a similar fate. The six were F. S. and his colleague Y. K. Kan, who had also used strong words in the Legislative Council; Paul Tsui, the acting Secretary for Chinese Affairs; and three community leaders, including an editor and a publisher.

The day after this death threat appeared, the Executive Council met under police guard. Publicly, the government pooh-poohed the threat, but privately they took it seriously. Bodyguards were assigned to all six men. Governor Trench offered F. S. protection around the clock at both home and office; those who had regular access to him were investigated. His gardener was found to be a frequent attender of communist gatherings, and the police advised F. S. to let him go. Before long, F. S. recalls, 'twenty or thirty policemen were coming to have dinner with me in my house'. The cook said he could not possibly prepare food for that many people, so F. S. took them to a restaurant. As a result, he said, he had to spend almost HK$50,000 a month on the police.

F. S. asked the two policemen in charge, Lam Kong and Lui Lok, if they could really protect him. Lui Lok, who in later years was exposed as a seriously corrupt policeman, told him the best thing was for F. S. to protect himself: 'I only earn a few thousand dollars from the government. I have my family to look after. Every month, I have to pay informers a few hundred dollars. If there is an attack on you, we would be the first to run away.'

Lui Lok advised him to get a gun and practice shooting. F. S. took lessons at the Police Training School in Aberdeen twice a week. The policemen there showed him how to shoot a pistol—at a cost of HK$5 per bullet. After the shooting session, F. S. had to take all the policemen out to dinner. They filled two tables at the Luk Yu Teahouse. Police protection, F. S. thought to himself, was expensive.

The disturbances of 1967 convinced the government of the need for additional channels of communications with the public. City district offices were established in 1968, each with a district officer whose role was twofold: to create greater public understanding of the government's policies and to communicate the problems and feelings of the people to the government. The government also stepped up the creation of advisory boards and committees. The number rose from sixty-four in 1961 to 132 ten years later. The people, too, grew politically aware and mature. Debates on public issues became more frequent in the Legislative Council, and the government was pressed to release information and take action. Young people became involved in the community, tacit acknowledgement that, while they might have family ties elsewhere, Hong Kong was their real home.

In the legislature, F. S. proposed that a professional body for accountants be set up, one able to help students obtain proper qualifications without having to go abroad to become apprenticed. Accountants, unlike lawyers and architects, did not have their own professional body. F. S. approached the governor, who gave the project his blessing but no financial support. Leading accountants in Hong Kong then formed a working party, which F. S. was elected to chair. After several years of protracted meetings, legislation to establish the Hong Kong Society of Accountants was adopted in December 1972.

One day, F. S. was approached by the principal of St Joseph's College, who said the Christian Brothers wanted to open a primary school, preferably near the existing secondary school. F. S. approached the governor and obtained a piece of land in Wanchai. He became chairman of the Primary School Fund Raising Campaign and personally footed much of the bill. F. S. laid the foundation stone of St Joseph's College Primary School on 16 April 1968, after it was blessed by Bishop Francis Hsu. The school itself opened eight months later. F. S. arranged for a hall in the primary school to be dedicated to the memory of his father, Li Koon-chun, just as Koon-chun had honoured his father with a Li Shek-Pang Hall in St Joseph's College.

Meanwhile, F. S.'s relations with the government deteriorated. The government was unhappy with his blunt and unrestrained behaviour, characterized by the dispute over holding Hong Kong's reserves in London, as well as his scepticism of government plans to construct a tunnel under the harbour to link Hong Kong Island with the Kowloon peninsula. When his two-year term on the Executive Council expired in June 1968, F.S. was not reappointed. Governor Trench wrote him a letter saying that, in view of his stated unhappiness with the government and his frequent threats to resign, perhaps he would be happier if he were to step down. In July 1968, with another year of his term to serve, F. S. resigned from the Legislative Council, citing health reasons. The governor, in accepting his resignation, voiced appreciation for the services F. S. had rendered over the years.

Modern Hong Kong

Chapter 18

Simon Li: First Chinese High Court Judge

F S. was not the only Li family member to become embroiled in the communist-inspired riots of 1967. His brother Simon was confirmed as a district court judge in 1966, just as China plunged into the tumult of the Cultural Revolution, which inevitably spilled over into Hong Kong. In fact, it spilled into his courtroom.

One morning, arriving at Kowloon District Court, Simon saw a crowd of people milling about in the hall. When he entered the courtroom, after first donning the traditional red-lined robe and white wig of a district judge, he found people in the public gallery waving copies of the little red book of sayings of Chairman Mao Zedong and chanting 'Long live Chairman Mao! Down with the running dogs!' He did not know it then, but similar demonstrations were being staged all over Hong Kong. The commotion went on until noon, when suddenly there was an eerie silence. He stepped outside his courtroom and found the floor covered with orange peel and other rubbish, but not a soul in sight; the mob was taking a lunch break too.

Demonstrations continued outside the courthouse for weeks. At the government's behest, Simon changed his travel pattern daily, to avoid a possible attack by radicals wanting to make an example of a Chinese who had given his loyalty to the British legal system. It was a frightening time. Bombs, both real and fake, were planted all over the colony. Demonstrators daubed tomato sauce over themselves to simulate blood, then made loud accusations of police brutality. Tear gas used by the police wafted into the courtrooms through the airconditioning system, reducing Simon and other judges to tears.

At the height of the riots, a man accused of possession of home-made bombs and ammunition was brought before Simon. The incriminating evidence was found under his bed inside a hut. The courtroom was filled with people waving Chairman Mao's little red book of quotations. The man refused to recognize the jurisdiction of a colonial court and refused to plead, so Simon entered a plea of not guilty for him. After the prosecution presented its case, the man refused to defend himself. The judge said: 'I have no option but to convict you.' The defendant was sentenced to eight years. Months later, the police found that it was all a mistake, and the real culprit was apprehended. The judge immediately recommended a free pardon, but the man had already served an undeserved jail term of eight or nine months.

Most cases, of course, were not heard in such a highly charged political atmosphere. One case that gave Simon much satisfaction was a divorce petition. The wife, an Italian, asked the court for a decree of divorce from her husband, a Philippine national of Spanish ancestry, on the grounds of cruelty. She said that he ruled the family with an iron fist. One evening they had a quarrel and he struck her, but apologized immediately. His wife left him. The judge came to the conclusion that, even though the husband was wrong, he deserved another chance, especially since the couple had three young children. He refused to grant a divorce. Nine months later, he received a postcard from Rome sent by the couple, thanking him for not granting the petition because the two had made up and were quite happy. Then one day, while Simon was in a grocery store, the Philippine man came up to him and said, 'I'm grateful to have the opportunity to thank you in person. We are very happy. The children are very happy.'

Simon had lost seven years of his life to World War II, and so was not admitted to the English bar until 1951, after graduating from University College, London. At the age of thirty, he was ready to launch his legal career. Life as a barrister in England was very hard in the immediate post-war years. Being Chinese made it doubly difficult. His father advised Simon to return to Hong Kong to join the government, which was just beginning to employ Chinese lawyers. Simon was given the job of crown counsel in the legal department, becoming the second Chinese crown counsel in the history of the colony. Most lawyers in the legal department were expatriates who, in addition to their salary, received extra allowances, such as home leave, free travel, and, most importantly, spacious government housing at a very low cost. Simon keenly resented the discrimination and thought it ironic that expatriates, who did not know Chinese, received better terms than someone like himself, who was bilingual.

He found it most galling when a crown counsel, junior to him, one day gave him a stack of files and said: 'Simon, would you be kind enough to look after this now? I have to go on leave.' Simon thought of quitting but refrained because a friend, Arthur Garcia, urged him to remain in the government and fight for the rights of local civil servants. He did, and from that effort emerged the Senior Non-Expatriate Officers Association. Its slogan was 'equal pay for equal work and equal benefits on equal terms'.

Ironically, because he was a local rather than an expatriate, Simon was assigned to a major criminal case. A well-known doctor with friends in high places was accused of raping a twenty-four-year-old virgin, a seamstress who had gone to him because of a stomach ache. Popular feelings were so inflamed that even during committal proceedings there were demonstrations outside the courthouse and the defence lawyer received threatening letters.

All the senior prosecutors were expatriates, but the legal department felt that the Chinese public might suspect that expatriates were biased in favour of prominent people like the physician, Dr Ng Yuk-kin. To guard against such public suspicions, the attorney general assigned Simon to the case, despite his junior status. The doctor was duly convicted.

Soon after Simon began to work in the legal department, his mother asked him for advice. Doy-hing wanted to draw up a will and sought his opinion on how to divide her assets. Simon told her to treat all her husband's children equally, whether sons or daughters, and whether her children or her stepchildren, an almost revolutionary idea. She did as he suggested and divided her assets into eleven equal shares.

Doy-hing in later life enjoyed playing mahjongg at home during the week. She was also a keen follower of the horses, going to the races every weekend until she died. She liked racing so much that, even if ill during the week, by Friday she would be all right because the next day was racing day. Doy-hing was superstitious about her gambling and did not like to hear the sound *shu*, or 'lose', when she gambled. Her grandchildren were instructed never to tell her what they did on Saturday mornings. Each Saturday, Lillian, Simon's wife, would take her children to a bookstore to buy comic books. However, because the word for book (*shu*) sounded the same as the word for 'lose', they were not allowed to utter that word in Doy-hing's presence.

Doy-hing was diabetic but the doctors controlled the condition for a long time. One day she fell and broke her leg and had to be taken to a hospital. There, the doctors inserted small metal pins into the bone. She was uncomfortable with them and, without the family's knowledge, she went to the hospital to have the pins taken out. The surgery was successful and she was happy for a couple of years. Though she was confined to a wheelchair, she could go to the races, where servants wheeled her to the betting booth and back.

One day, at the end of a race, she spoke to Simon, her oldest son, addressing him as 'Number Eight', since he was Koon-chun's eighth child. 'Number Eight, Number Eight,' she said. 'I find it very tiring. Racing is no longer of any interest to me.' Simon's heart sank. He knew the end was near.

The diabetes caught up with her. She had chilblains, she scratched and, being diabetic, she healed slowly. For a whole year she suffered, with nurses looking after her day and night. An active woman, she was irritated and unhappy when confined to bed because of her legs. Her thighs were covered with pinpricks and she pleaded with the nurses not to give her injections.

As a result of the diabetes she developed gangrene and the doctor suggested amputation of both legs. She fought the idea for a long time, finally turning to Simon for advice. She was old and in pain and she wanted the decision left to her sons. She did have the amputation, a success for several days, but then she collapsed and died. Before her death, she told Simon about a packet she had put in the family safe. Inside he found a little bit of gold, a little bit of silver, and a pearl. These were to be put into her mouth when she was buried, so she would not want in the next world.

News of Doy-hing's death was withheld from her husband, Koon-chun, who by then was totally inactive in business and, in fact, was heavily sedated. Koon-chun himself died in 1966, two years after his wife, at the age of seventy-nine. His funeral service at St John's Cathedral was attended by the colony's most prominent personalities. Governor Trench sent a wreath and dispatched his aide-de-camp to attend the service. Koon-chun's pallbearers included his good friends and business associates, fellow bank founder Wong Yun-tong, the philanthropist Sir Shiu-kin Tang, Sir T. N. Chau, Thomas Tam, Li Yiu-cheung, and Noel Croucher. The Kan family was well represented, with three of Kan Tong-po's sons in attendance.

Koon-chun bequeathed HK$20,000 to each of his seven daughters and to each of his four daughters-in-law, but the bulk of his estate, amounting to over HK$3.25 million, was equally divided among his four sons. This was in addition to the assets already channelled into the Hong Kong Investment Company, of which his four sons were the only shareholders.

Koon-chun had a special affection for Fanny, his only daughter to spurn marriage. A 1963 codicil to his will left her all the money he had on deposit in an account in Singapore as well as one with the Chase Manhattan Bank in New York. Moreover, in his will, he directed that his two houses on Kennedy Terrace were to be held by his trustees 'as part of my residuary estate' for thirty years so that his wife, Doy-hing, and Fanny, would always have a place to live. Since his wife had already died, preservation of the houses was solely for the benefit of Fanny.

Meanwhile, the Hong Kong government, responding to pressure from local civil servants for housing, agreed to sell land cheaply, with a low-interest loan, to a cooperative society consisting of fourteen senior Chinese civil servants. On the site a high-rise, Victoria Heights, was built on Stubbs Road. Simon's family moved in shortly before the children left for England. They occupied a spacious apartment on the fifth floor, with a big verandah and a breathtaking view of the harbour.

To ensure that his children would never be subjected to discrimination, Simon decided to send them to schools that catered to the small expatriate community. He also decided to send them to England to make sure they would receive expatriate treatment should they ever work for the Hong Kong government, and to give them a choice of where to pursue their career.

And so, by the mid-1960s, only the two youngest children—Stephen, six, and Paul, two—emained at home. At the time, Hong Kong experienced one of the worst rainstorms in its history, with more than forty centimetres of rain falling in one day. On the morning of 12 June 1966, a Sunday, almost twelve centimetres of rain fell in a single hour. Simon was in the habit of going hiking with a group of friends on Sundays. He normally left home by six in the morning. That morning, he woke up at five to find the sky still pitch dark, even though it was early summer. A friend called up to say the hike was cancelled because of the rain, so Simon went back to sleep. A little later, his eldest son, Simon Jr., who was back in Hong Kong for the summer, woke him up and asked Simon to drive him to St Joseph's Church, where he served as a lay reader. Simon got into his car and set out but had to turn back because the ground was covered with debris. After calling the church to say his son would not be able to attend, Simon went back to bed.

Shortly before noon, Simon heard a sudden loud noise, like an explosion. The impact lifted him up from the bed and dropped him down again. Dashing out, he saw that half the slope on which the building stood was gone, washed away by the storm. He ran downstairs and saw that the door had burst open and the area was already covered with mud up to chest level. He flew up the stairs to his apartment and found Stephen and Paul being fed by the amah. 'Out!' he shouted. 'Right now!'

He led his wife, children, and two servants down to the lawn above Stubbs Road, which was covered with liquid mud. Part of Stubbs Road had been-broken by the gushing waters. Any minute another mudslide could rip apart the hillside, taking the Li family with it. Everyone shouted for help. A group of students directed a company of British soldiers to the site, and the family was rescued.

Simon was promoted in 1971 to a rank known as puisne judge, which meant that he was now a high court judge, the first Chinese in Hong Kong's history to reach that level. He served alongside six Caucasian judges. Because Simon was the first local judge to be elevated to the high court, there was much interest in his views. Simon said he favoured strict treatment of offenders and dubbed himself a 'reactionary'. He said: 'Putting young people in jail is negative. We don't want to take large chunks out of their lives. The detention centre, with hard labour and hard discipline, is an ideal short, sharp lesson to shock them back to their senses.'

His targets were not merely youthful offenders. At a time when Hong Kong was rapidly developing into an international financial centre, Simon wanted to widen the bribery law to cover directors of public companies and public bodies. 'Is there not room for directors of different companies to exchange information and obtain an advantage over and above an ordinary share investor?' he asked publicly. 'Are directors a class of persons so clean and serene that our law should leave them alone?'

In a move that may have caught the government by surprise, Simon continued his crusade against inequality between expatriates and Chinese. 'I only get twenty-seven days holiday a year, while my colleagues get forty-five,' he said, perhaps injudiciously. 'This is unfair. On top of that, expatriates are given air fares, while a local is not. I have been fighting the issue for more than twenty years, for housing and other benefits for the locals.'

As Simon rose within the judiciary, he moved up socially as well. When appointed to the Supreme Court, Chief Justice Sir Ivo Rigby arranged for him to join the elitist Hong Kong Club, which formerly excluded Chinese members. And in May 1975 he was elected a voting member of the Royal Hong Kong Jockey Club, a group of 200 people who elect the club's stewards each year.

One case Simon dealt with in the fall of 1976 was the focus of public attention. It concerned a policeman, Detective Constable Au Pui-kuen, who had shot and killed a civilian during an argument on a crowded street. When a coroner's inquest returned a verdict of excusable homicide, there was a public outcry. The attorney general took the unusual step of ordering Au's arrest on charges of murder and unlawful wounding, despite the coroner's finding.

The public gallery was packed during the trial. When it ended, Simon summed up the case before the jurors retired to consider the matter. With no verdict by evening, he went to dinner with friends at the Nautilus Club in Repulse Bay. At about ten o'clock, just after finishing the main course, he received a phone call telling him the jury had reached a verdict. He was warned not to enter by the front entrance of the Supreme Court because an ugly crowd had gathered there, milling around Statue Square. He managed to slip into the courthouse without attracting any attention.

The jurors filed into the courtroom and delivered the verdict: guilty. A guilty verdict meant a mandatory death sentence. Simon put on his black cap to pronounce sentence. The court proceedings were over in ten minutes.

The news was greeted outside by a cheering and clapping crowd that shouted: 'He deserves it, he deserves it.' Simon knew the sentence would be commuted to life imprisonment, because no executions had been carried out in Hong Kong since 1966, when Britain abolished the death penalty. Simon changed, slipped out of the courthouse, and went back to the Nautilus, just in time to join his guests for coffee. Had the jury acquitted Au, Simon thought, the mob would have lynched the judge.

His rise within the judiciary was steady, but he knew in 1978 that he would never reach the top. That year, Sir Denys Roberts, the chief secretary, was appointed chief justice. Because the new chief justice was nine months younger than him, Simon knew that, if Roberts served until retirement age, he would not have a chance to become chief justice.

In the spring of 1980, Simon was appointed a judge of the Court of Appeal, the highest court in the land. Moving up to the Court of Appeal meant sacrifices. His case load was heavy, with each case involving voluminous transcripts of earlier hearings. Simon stopped playing mahjongg. He dropped his Sunday morning hikes. Some weekends, he even forewent horse racing. And when he did go to the races, he would work the rest of Saturday and the whole of Sunday.

In mid-1984, while all of Hong Kong was in suspense awaiting the outcome of the Sino-British negotiations (see next chapter), Simon was approached in confidence by the Governor, Sir Edward Youde, and told that the two countries were close to an agreement and that an Assessment Office would be set up to see if its terms were acceptable to the Hong Kong public.

Two men, one from London and one from Hong Kong, would be appointed as monitors to see if the Assessment Office did its work properly. Sir Patrick Nairne would serve as the British monitor. Would Simon serve as the Hong Kong monitor?

'I will consider it my duty to serve,' the surprised judge responded. No doubt he was appointed because he was the most senior Chinese judge. In a sense, his appointment was necessary to legitimize Britain's decision to hand over Hong Kong to China.

The assessment procedure was criticized by some people (including at least one Member of Parliament) as a farce, since Britain had made it clear that the agreement on China's policy of 'one country, two systems' could not be changed in any way and that failure to approve the Joint Declaration would result not in a different agreement but in no agreement. Since the choice was between accepting this agreement and having no agreement, many felt the assessment and monitoring offices were simply a waste of public funds.

Simon disagreed. Although the agreement could not be amended, he said, Hong Kong people must not be deprived of a chance to react to it and voice their opinions. In the end, the Assessment Office asserted: 'After the most careful analysis and consideration of all the information received, the Office has concluded that most of the people of Hong Kong find the draft agreement acceptable.'

The Monitoring Team, in its report, endorsed the conclusions of the Assessment Office by saying that it had done its work impartially, accurately, faithfully, and properly. In the closing paragraphs of their report, the Monitors displayed the insight they had gained into the situation after two months of work:

> Nobody in Hong Kong can escape the uncertainties of the future; those who have, or can acquire, a 'right of abode' elsewhere will take personal precautions in the short term while hoping for the best in Hong Kong in the long term. The minority who reject the draft agreement do so either because they can never accept reunification with Communist China or because they are bitter about the consequences for themselves as British Dependent Territory Citizens. The majority who accept it do so chiefly because they regard reunification as inevitable and are relieved that the terms of the draft agreement are as good as they are. But the verdict of acceptance implies neither positive enthusiasm nor passive acquiescence. The response to the Assessment Office has demonstrated the realism of the people of Hong Kong. They know that their future now lies in their own hands.

In May 1986, eighteen months after his historic assignment as Monitor of the Sino-British agreement, Simon made legal history. He acted briefly as chief justice when both Sir Denys Roberts and his deputy, Sir Alan Huggins, were away. On 16 May, when he presided over the Court of Appeal, Gerard McCoy, senior crown counsel, stood up to congratulate Simon on behalf of the entire legal fraternity. McCoy called it 'an auspicious day in the development of local law'.

By this time, he was less than a year from his sixty-fifth birthday, the date of his retirement. Judges are supposed to keep a low profile, and Simon rarely expressed his views in public. On the eve of his retirement, however, when honoured by the Chinese University of Hong Kong with an honorary degree of doctor of law, Simon discussed his views on the legal system.

At the conferment ceremony, Justice Li spoke of the need for Hong Kong to have an impartial judicial system after 1997, when the colony would revert to Chinese sovereignty. The words had special significance because he was serving as a member of the China-appointed Basic Law Drafting Committee, helping to devise the post-1997 judicial system. He showed his essentially conservative bent when he made clear his support for corporal punishment of certain criminals, such as rapists and robbers, so that, in his words, 'violence is met with violence'.

On 20 March 1987, his last day in court, lawyers appearing before Justice Li paid tribute to him. Kemal Bokhary, a Queen's Counsel, said lawyers held Simon in very high esteem and said Justice Li's fairness was an example to everyone. In response, the judge thanked lawyers who had appeared before him over the years. 'They must have tolerated many of my shortcomings and mistakes without complaint,' he said. Judges, he observed, can never please both parties. To mark Simon's retirement, the Bar Association presented him with a printed compilation of several of his judgments that had been appealed to London and upheld by the Privy Council.

Retirement did not mark the end of active life for Simon. His career with the British colonial government was finished, but a new and far more exciting career with the Chinese government was about to begin. He had wanted to work for China as a student during the war and now, in his retirement, he was finally able to do so.

Chapter 19

Aubrey Li:
Negotiating Hong Kong's Future (1982–1984)

The 1970s were a time of rapid change for Hong Kong. Having survived the exigencies of the immediate postwar period, Hong Kong by the early 1970s had transformed itself into a major manufacturing centre whose exports of clothing, footwear, textile yarn, fabrics, and electrical appliances ranked it among the world's top trading nations. Sweatshop factories blossomed in every available space, in side alleys, and under stairways. In those years, the colony experienced the economic boom ushered in by the Vietnam War. The period also saw the creation of three new stock exchanges, whose rambunctious activities gave Hong Kong the air of a cowboy town. This was a time of change for the Bank of East Asia as well.

In 1972, Y. H. Kan retired as chief manager, two years after taking over from his brother-in-law, Kenneth Fung. Now it was time for Li—Tse-fong's son Aubrey—to run the bank, the first time in the bank's history for a Li to assume that post. Aubrey, deputy chief manager and member of the bank's board for fourteen years, was ready for the job. Michael Y. K. Kan, the capable younger brother of Y. H., succeeded Aubrey as deputy chief manager.

Aubrey was a meticulous man who constantly wrote notes to remind himself of things that had happened or things that had been said. A serious man who took all his roles seriously, whether banker, husband, or father, Aubrey mostly kept his thoughts to himself. He was the de facto heir to his father, Tse-fong, because his elder brother, Norman, lacked either the will or the interest to assume Tse-fong's mantle. Aubrey, not Norman, stepped into his father's shoes and served on the boards of many companies with which Tse-fong had been closely affiliated.

The Vietnam War was at its height, and the bank's branch in Saigon was feeling the consequences. Aubrey took repeated trips to Vietnam to assess the situation. Both the branch manager and deputy manager, Chinese from Hong Kong, were past retirement age. No one in Hong Kong was willing to relocate to war-torn Saigon, so Aubrey recommended closing down the branch. The board asked him to look into the situation again.

Aubrey flew to Saigon one last time in November 1974 and remained there for three days. Upon his return to Hong Kong, he told the board that the branch manager wished to retire at the end of 1975 and his deputy the following March. The progressive devaluations of the Vietnamese piastre and the government's raising of capital requirements for banks created additional strains. The board decided to scale down operations and close the branch by September 1975, before the retirement of the two managers.

Events on the battlefield outstripped decisions in the boardroom and, in April 1975, both Saigon managers were recalled to Hong Kong, ostensibly for consultations. The branch's Vietnamese accountant, Diep To, was left in charge. Saigon fell to the Communists on 30 April. All private banks were nationalized. Aubrey reported to the board that all communications between the bank and its Saigon branch had been cut off. (A few years later, tens of thousands of Vietnamese took to the seas to flee their country. One was Diep To, who ended up in a Philippine refugee camp. The bank granted him a special gratuity to begin a new life in America.) The bank itself returned to Vietnam in 1995, when it opened a representative office in Ho Chi Minh City, formerly known as Saigon.

Aubrey's career at the bank reached a peak in 1984. When Sir Y. K. Kan announced his intention to retire as chairman after the next annual general meeting, it was widely agreed that Aubrey would succeed him. But one morning, Aubrey received two surprise telephone calls from fellow board members, informing him that Kenneth Fung had emerged as an unexpected contender and that some directors who had expressed support for him had gone over to the Fung camp. A secret ballot was held on 22 March, from which Aubrey emerged as victor by a single vote. From then on, each year, Aubrey's re-election as chairman was proposed by Sir Kenneth Fung to show that no grudge was held.

Like his father, Aubrey was called upon to serve on government advisory bodies. In 1974, he became a member of the Legislative Council. Given his banking background, it was natural that he concentrated much of his energies on financial matters. Finance companies, also called deposit-taking companies, were a big headache in the 1970s. Unlike banks, they were not regulated, but were allowed to take deposits of HK$50,000 or more. When they went bankrupt, their depositors lost everything. The government argued that anyone who could deposit HK$50,000 should be sophisticated enough to look after his own interests.

Aubrey urged the government to subject finance companies to similar regulations as banks, including compulsory registration, payment of an annual fee, minimum paid-up capital, a minimum liquidity ratio, and the filing of monthly returns. Only in 1978 did the financial secretary say, 'we now accept we have a duty towards the larger depositor as well as the smaller', and begin to require the filing of monthly returns.

In 1978 Aubrey was appointed to the Executive Council. He was given a royal honour the following year, when he became a Commander of the British Empire. He retired from the Legislative Council in 1981, but continued to serve on the Executive Council.

During this time, concern over the future of Hong Kong was mounting. The British, through the governor, Sir Murray MacLehose, sounded out Chinese leader Deng Xiaoping in 1979 and were given the message, 'Investors should set their hearts at ease.' Investors, especially bankers, were concerned about the expiration of Britain's ninety-nine-year lease on the New Territories in 1997; this area made up 92 per cent of the colony. The rest of the colony—Hong Kong Island and the Kowloon peninsula—had been given to Britain 'in perpetuity'. By 1982, with only fifteen years of the lease to go, banks were faced with the question of whether to accept mortgages in the New Territories that extended beyond 1997.

Before Prime Minister Margaret Thatcher flew to Beijing for discussions with Chinese leaders in the fall of 1982, she was briefed in London by Sir Edward Youde, who had succeeded MacLehose as governor. He brought with him five of his most trusted advisers, including Aubrey Li. Youde told the sixty-six-year-old Aubrey that he was meant to represent Hong Kong's older generation, while the forty-two-year-old businesswoman Lydia Dunn would represent younger people. K. C. Chan, a legislative councillor, was meant to represent labour. Sir S. Y. Chung, executive councillor, and Sir Roger Lobo, the senior legislative councillor, made up the rest of the delegation.

Before leaving Hong Kong, Aubrey and the other members of the group met among themselves to work out a common position. It was a sombre session, since the future of Hong

Kong was at stake. In London, they had a luncheon meeting with the prime minister. Each person was given a chance to state his or her views. All asked Mrs Thatcher to try to get an agreement whereby British sovereignty in Hong Kong could be extended beyond 1997. As Aubrey recalls, the prime minister responded wryly: 'You want us to negotiate a deal with China? They are barbarians.'

In Beijing, Mrs Thatcher agreed to formal talks on the issue. China wanted to deal only with Britain. It did not want any role for Hong Kong, considering the negotiations to be between the Chinese and British governments. But Britain felt it could not impose an agreement on Hong Kong, and so used the Executive Council partly as sounding board and partly as putative voice of Hong Kong's people.

Great responsibility lay on the shoulders of Aubrey and his associates, who had been chosen by the British to represent Hong Kong. The job entrusted to them was well nigh impossible.

The Thatcher visit was followed by nine months of deadlock, as the Chinese insisted that the British first acknowledge Chinese sovereignty over Hong Kong. The British, feeling they would have little left with which to bargain if they conceded sovereignty at the outset, rejected any preconditions to the talks. The Chinese insisted their demand was non-negotiable.

The British then tried to draw the Chinese out on what they had in mind for Hong Kong, hinting, first obliquely, and later broadly, that a concession on sovereignty was possible, but the Chinese refused to talk about substantive issues unless the British first acknowledged Chinese sovereignty. The Chinese, too, dropped hints, saying that if Britain would only take this one step, a satisfactory solution could be reached to all problems and Britain's economic interests in Hong Kong would be safeguarded.

The diplomatic deadlock resulted in widespread unease in

Hong Kong, and the local currency fell to a record low of HK$7.1 to the US dollar on 28 May 1983. The impasse was finally broken through the personal intervention of Mrs Thatcher, who sent a private message to Premier Zhao Ziyang, in which she proposed that substantive negotiations could begin with the understanding that Britain was fully aware of China's position on sovereignty. The Chinese were informed that, if Hong Kong's stability and prosperity could be guaranteed, the prime minister 'would be prepared to recommend it to the British Parliament' and sovereignty would be conceded at that point.

And so, on 1 July 1983, exactly ten months after his first trip, Aubrey was in London again, this time with eight other members of the Executive Council. Again, they met with the prime minister, though this time they did not get lunch. That day, the following announcement was issued in Beijing: 'Following the discussions between the leaders of the two countries in September 1982, and subsequent useful exchanges, it has been agreed that a second phase of the talks on the future of Hong Kong will begin in Peking on 12 July 1983.'

Aubrey and his fellow executive councillors were housed in the Sheraton Park Tower, where a whole floor was reserved for their use. They met with Mrs Thatcher and Foreign Secretary Sir Geoffrey Howe on 4 July, and the next day with the minister with special responsibility for Hong Kong, Richard Luce, to discuss Britain's strategy.

Faced with Chinese intransigence and British nervousness, Aubrey and his colleagues accepted the futility of asking for continued British sovereignty in Hong Kong after 1997. But they did propose that, while conceding sovereignty, the British ask China to agree to the continuation of British administration for an additional twenty-five years after 1997. China was so opposed to any role for Hong Kong in the talks that it even protested against the Executive Council being briefed, terming that act a 'breach of confidentiality'. But the British insisted on the involvement of Aubrey and his colleagues, with Youde saying that, constitutionally, he was obliged to consult the Executive Council on all major matters.

The first round of the second phase of Sino-British talks was held on 12 and 13 July. It ended with a simple communiqué reporting that the session was 'useful and constructive'. The second round, also held in July, ended with an announcement by the two sides that it was 'useful'. After the third round in August, the two sides issued a statement merely saying that talks had been 'held'. The phrase 'useful and constructive' was again missing after the fourth round, held in September. Things were clearly not going well. The reason was simple. The Chinese would not accept the British proposal of conceding sovereignty to China while continuing British administration of Hong Kong, even if it was limited to twenty-five years. The Chinese insisted that sovereignty could not be separated from the governance of Hong Kong. Sovereignty without administrative rights, they said, was hollow.

The optimism of July gave way to anxiety. With growing fears and uncertainty about the talks, the Hong Kong dollar experienced the sharpest fall in its history and on 24 September 1983, the day after the fourth round ended, plunged to a new low of HK$9.5 to the US dollar. Some businesses in Hong Kong refused to accept payment in the local currency, insisting on US dollars. Overnight, supermarkets were cleaned out. People stocked up on everything from food to toilet paper. Hong Kong's trading partners became unwilling to have prices denominated in the local currency. Vegetable dealers reported that Taiwan had decided to halt all shipments to the colony because the Hong Kong dollar was no longer acceptable. In this atmosphere of crisis, Aubrey and other members of the Executive Council were summoned to London again.

They arrived on 5 October 1983 and, with the governor, met senior British officials. Referring to the meeting, a statement issued by the prime minister's press office said:

> There was a thorough review of developments since the Unofficials last visited London on July 4–5. This took place in a warm and positive atmosphere. It produced a valuable exchange of views and complete understanding on the issues involved. The Governor and the Unofficials expressed their appreciation of this further opportunity to meet the Prime Minister and other ministers and for the continuing commitment of Her Majesty's Government to Hong Kong.

'We knew every time there was a deadlock, we were banging our heads against a stone wall,' Aubrey recalled years later. 'We knew we were getting nowhere.'

While publicly professing continuing commitments to Hong Kong, privately the British capitulated. Prime Minister Thatcher informed Premier Zhao of Britain's willingness to sever all ties with Hong Kong after 1997 and said Britain would concede sovereignty over all of Hong Kong, including the ceded portions. This British concession marked the biggest breakthrough in the talks. From then on, Britain and China were able to work together relatively smoothly. When the fifth round of talks ended on 20 October, the phrase 'useful and constructive' reappeared.

The session of 7 and 8 December, the last round of 1983, reflected the changed atmosphere. That round concluded with the encouraging public announcement that the two sides had reviewed 'the progress made so far' in the negotiations. It was the first acknowledgement of progress.

While Aubrey and his colleagues in the Executive Council visited London with Governor Youde in January 1984, rioting broke out in Hong Kong. The riots were triggered by taxi drivers, but they reflected the colony's nervousness. While the small handful of Executive Council members was kept informed of developments, nobody else knew what was going on. Hong Kong people felt frustrated, afraid that Britain, to safeguard its relationship with China, might sacrifice Hong Kong.

On 3 April, Aubrey and his Executive Council colleagues were back in London once more with the governor and briefed the foreign secretary, Sir Geoffrey Howe, on the feelings in Hong Kong.

This was a time of deepening gloom. Jardine Matheson, the oldest and one of the most influential British companies in Hong Kong, had just announced its intention to relocate its international operations to Bermuda. The shocking announcement caused the stock market to plummet. Howe held discussions with Chinese leaders in Beijing, then flew to Hong Kong. On 20 April he held a press conference where, for the first time, he revealed that Britain was giving up Hong Kong and that 'it would not be realistic to think of an agreement that provides for continued British administration in Hong Kong after 1997'.

To meet the Chinese-imposed deadline of September 1984, the talks were speeded up. On 27 July, Howe arrived in Beijing on his second official visit in three months. Stopping in Hong Kong on his return to Britain, he announced on 1 August the outline of the agreement that was emerging. The provisions included:

> Preservation of the existing legal system;
> Continuation of Hong Kong's status as a free port and as a financial and manufacturing centre;
> The right of property ownership;
> Continuation of Hong Kong's status as a separate customs territory;
> Continuation of Hong Kong's management of its own financial affairs;
> Convertibility of the Hong Kong dollar and free movement of capital;

Retention of the existing system of shipping and port management;
Freedom of travel in and out of Hong Kong;
Maintenance of the existing education system, and
Preservation of existing rights and freedoms enjoyed by the people of Hong Kong.

Aubrey's term on the Executive Council was due to expire in August 1984, as the Sino-British negotiations entered their final phase. Though in his sixty-ninth year, Governor Youde wanted him to stay. 'Aubrey, don't leave before the thing is signed,' the governor said to him. 'Don't upset the boat. You concentrate on this and, after this agreement is signed and ratified and deposited at the United Nations, I'll let you go.'

Aubrey accepted a one-year extension of his appointment. After the last round of Sino-British negotiations was concluded in Beijing and a draft agreement agreed upon, Aubrey and the other Executive Councillors made a final visit to London on 17 September 1984. There, they discussed the agreement in detail in meetings with British officials. Afterwards, a press statement said that British officials and the Executive Council had 'a full identity of views'. After returning to Hong Kong on 21 September, the Executive Council publicly endorsed the agreement. Five days later, at noon on 26 September, the Sino-British Joint Declaration on the Question of Hong Kong was initialed in Beijing by Sir Richard Evans and Vice Foreign Minister Zhou Nan.

As a reward for their work on the Joint Declaration, Britain rewarded members of the Executive Council with full British passports so that, if things went wrong and the agreement was not honoured, they could leave. The move reflected the degree of confidence—or lack of confidence—that London and its advisors in Hong Kong had in the agreement.

Aubrey stepped down from the Executive Council three months after the Joint Declaration came into effect but he did not retire. He was still chairman of the bank. His older brother Norman had died in Canada the previous year, leaving Aubrey the patriarch of the Li Tse-fong branch of the family.

His interest in racing was as keen as ever; in 1981 he became the first Chinese to be deputy chairman of the Jockey Club. In October 1986, a month after his seventieth birthday, Aubrey and Laura were accorded a signal honour when Governor Youde asked them to host a community luncheon in honour of Queen Elizabeth and her husband, Prince Philip. At the luncheon, the queen talked about nothing but racing. Aubrey introduced her to leading trainers and jockeys. Prince Philip, however, had other interests, as Laura discovered. He declined a copy of the day's racing programme, but talked with her at length about his work with the World Wide Fund for Nature.

By now in his seventies, Aubrey was still in good health. However, one morning in February 1988, he got up and discovered he could not speak. He picked up a pen and wrote, 'I've lost my voice.' Quickly, the family called his physician nephew Donald, who lived nearby. Aubrey was taken to hospital, and remained there for eight days. When he regained his voice, he could not speak normally, but only babble like a baby in nonsensical syllables. The doctor said the stroke had been brought on by a small blood clot. It took Aubrey months to recover.

This episode spurred Aubrey to organize the first major family get-together for all the descendants of Li Tse-fong, with 103 people attending a five-day cruise from Los Angeles to Mexico. In a family book prepared for the occasion, Aubrey wrote:

> Having passed the venerable age of 70, life has brought a new meaning and clarity for us. We are most thankful to God for his many blessings, chief among which is the love and concern of our children and grandchildren, and of our relatives and

friends. We have slowed down and are more relaxed about everything, taking each day as it comes. We look back at all the glad and sad events in our lives, and remember only the happy and humorous times. We look forward to whatever God has planned for us in the future.

One thing that lay in the future was his fiftieth wedding anniversary in 1990. He and Laura celebrated that by taking a trip to the United States to see their children. Another thing, just as exhilarating, was the offer by his alma mater, Boston University, of an honorary Doctor of Laws degree, fifty-four years after his graduation.

Chapter 20

David Li: Banker and Politician

In 1985, the year after the Sino-British Joint Declaration was signed, China began drafting a Basic Law, the mini-constitution for post-1997 Hong Kong, which was meant to put into legal terms the provisions of the Sino-British agreement. In recruiting members for the drafting committee, the Chinese approached two members of the Li family, Court of Appeal Judge Simon Li and Simon's nephew David Li, chief manager of the Bank of East Asia.

David, oldest son of F. S., was tall like like his father and shrewd as well, with an entrepreneurial flair. A sophisticated man of the world, he travelled widely and had a profound understanding of business and business practices in Britain, Europe, and the United States. He entertained lavishly and maintained a network of professional and personal contacts across the globe; he maintained a high profile and was involved in numerous charities.

Though only in his mid-forties, his hair was thinning and a bald spot spread on the back on his head. An unfailingly courteous man, he accommodated almost everyone, including members of the media. He regularly set aside time to compose handwritten notes, both in English and in Chinese, to individuals he met during the course of the day, offering his compliments. He spoke in rapid-fire fashion, usually in a low voice, as though his vocal chords were struggling to keep up with his fast-flowing thoughts.

Able to function with only four hours' sleep a night, David drove himself hard, regularly working until one or two o'clock in the morning before going to bed, only to rise at six o'clock in the morning. Often, he would have two breakfasts, one at home while he scanned the newspapers and another with business associates, during which he would discuss proposals and scan documents. He arrived at his office at eight o'clock for the first of a series of meetings with the bank's various executives and work through the day and into the night, busy holding meetings, giving speeches, and attending lunches, cocktails, and dinners, almost always for business.

His wife was Penny Poon, a gracious, California-educated hostess whose brother, Dickson Poon, was one of Hong Kong's youngest and most successful entrepreneurs. Penny, herself descended from a wealthy family in the jewellery business, had a nimble mind and was a great source of support for David. A strong, purposeful woman, she read widely to understand her husband's business and political activities and exercised each morning to keep fit. She was never obtrusive, content to play the demure wife, remaining in the background when necessary, chatting with the wives of his business contacts. Meanwhile, David would discuss business or politics with the men, injecting a note of humour every so often, for David loved both to hear and to tell a good story.

Even when a student at Cambridge, he enjoyed a good prank, and later wrote satirical songs, which he sang in a night club that he operated. One of them, written to the tune of a popular church hymn and titled 'Guide Me O Thou Hang Seng Index', ran like this:

> Guide me o thou Hang Seng Index
> Put more dollars in my hand,
> Script and bonds and soya futures
> And some shares in Hong Kong Land,
> Krugerrand and fixed deposits are the symbol of success,
> Let my checkbook buy my happiness.
> When my time on earth is over
> Let my soul depart on high
> Let me dwell forever in the Stock Exchange up in the sky
> Where the index never falters and returns are never low
> Let me take it with me when I go.

David was in Geneva on business in early 1985 when he received a long-distance call from his office telling him that Li Chuwen, deputy director of the New China News Agency, China's de facto consulate in Hong Kong, wanted to talk to him urgently. When he called back, Li Chuwen explained that China was setting up a drafting committee and wanted to invite him to be a member. David demurred, but the two men agreed to talk again the next day.

David then called his father for advice. F. S. told him to decline. In politics, F. S. said, you are used by others and when your usefulness is over you are discarded like an old shoe. But David's interest was piqued and, while he had great regard for his father's views, he was not sure he should brush aside China's offer to play a role in drafting a document that would be so vital to Hong Kong's future.

When David called Li Chuwen again, he was still of two minds. The Chinese official spent twenty minutes persuading him and in the end David decided to disregard his father's advice and said yes. The banker was venturing into politics.

David was one of eight vice chairmen, four from the

Mainland and four from Hong Kong, to make up the drafting committee. His unexpected appointment to such a high position—equivalent in rank to that of a vice minister—sparked speculation that the Chinese were grooming him to become the first chief executive, or governor, of post-1997 Hong Kong. David was the youngest of the vice chairmen and the only one who could legitimately claim to be a fourth-generation Hong Kong native. When asked if he was interested in becoming chief executive, he would always demur, saying: 'I am a banker, not a politician.'

That same year, David took another plunge into politics. To prepare Hong Kong for greater democracy, the government announced that nine seats in the Legislative Council would be allocated, through elections, to functional constituencies or occupational groupings such as lawyers, teachers, and social workers. One seat was reserved for bankers. David decided to run. He was nominated by Standard Chartered Bank and seconded by the Bank of China, showing that his support spanned both British and Chinese banking institutions.

There were reports of the Hang Seng Bank sponsoring a candidate, but David wound up unopposed. In September, he took his seat in the Legislative Council, becoming the third generation of the Li family to do so. But he was the first to be elected, not appointed, a sign of the changing times. With his election, David continued the close relationship between the Bank of East Asia and the Hong Kong government.

When David took his seat in the Legislative Council, it was a time of ferment and optimism in the aftermath of the ratification of the Sino-British Joint Declaration. As he said in one of his first speeches, 'Hong Kong looks to the future with renewed confidence and hope.'

David played a curious role in the Legislative Council. A conservative banker who represented the financial establishment, he often assumed the role of social critic, calling for greater assistance for the aged and the needy, and improved educational facilities. When the government introduced a bill making it a crime to publish 'false news', David called the bill 'a threat to press freedom' and to 'the freedom of expression of the people of Hong Kong'.

But he was no political liberal. Indeed, he frequently adopted a cautious, often neutral, stance. After the government proposed political reforms, David cautioned against 'change merely for the sake of making changes'. He warned that 'if changes are to be made, they should be made gradually and prudently so as not to risk destroying the success we have worked so hard to build'. Moreover, he frequently abstained from controversial votes, either absenting himself from the discussion entirely or, often, suddenly visiting the bathroom just as the vote was about to be taken.

By the time David became a member of the Legislative Council, he had been with the Bank of East Asia for fifteen years, since 1970. Born in London when F. S. was studying to be an accountant, he was only a few months old when war broke out and his family returned to Hong Kong.

David's early years were characterized by frequent moves because of the war. His parents left Hong Kong because of the Japanese occupation and went to Macao, where he attended kindergarten. After the war, the family returned to Hong Kong, and David was sent to study at St Paul's, like so many other members of the Li family. When his father returned to England to finish his apprenticeship as a chartered accountant, David and his siblings were brought up by their mother, Daisy.

At the age of fifteen, David was sent to boarding school in England. He was the first Chinese to attend the élitist Uppingham School, during which time his mother made sure he remembered his Chinese by sending a tutor to coach him every weekend. After graduation, he attended the Imperial College of Science and Technology in London, earning a degree in mathematics.

His father, however, felt there was little future in a career in mathematics. So, at the urging of F. S., David spent a year learning accountancy with Cooper Brothers. David did not enjoy his work. Much of it was either mind-numbingly monotonous—going through columns and columns of figures—or involved physical drudgery, such as carrying large ledgers and taking stacks of letters to the post office to send to the firm's clients. But he did learn auditing, how to write reports, and office discipline. He also got to know many people, since he was sent out to various firms to perform audits.

At the end of the year, he told his father that accounting was not for him. He intended to continue in mathematics and so enrolled in Cambridge for a postgraduate degree. F. S. urged his son to at least take the intermediate examinations for a chartered accountant. He offered a financial incentive: he would give David £5,000 and a car if he passed. The exams were scheduled for November; the Cambridge term began in October. David decided to do both. He went to Cambridge but, for the first few weeks, attended no lectures. Instead, he crammed for his accounting exams and did very well in them.

David's entrepreneurial bent became obvious during his years at Cambridge. He noticed that every student had a bicycle to help him get around the sprawling campus. The first thing a new arrival did was to buy a bicycle. Upon leaving, graduates would sell them to a second-hand shop, which resold them at a 100 per cent markup. He decided to go into this business himself. So he put up the capital and cut in the college porter, who would repair the bicycles, and the man in charge of the college bicycle shed, so that bicycles could be kept there before they were resold, giving the two 50 per cent of the business. Before graduates left Cambridge, David would buy their bicycles. The college porter would repaint the bicycles and provide them with new brakes. The bicycles would then be stored in the college shed before being sold to new arrivals the following semester. This business, started by David at age twenty-one, was a resounding success.

David also started a night club. He rented the Masonic Hall in Cambridge from five in the afternoon to eleven at night on Saturdays. A pub owner paid him £125 for the right to serve drinks in the hall. David also hired a band with vocalist. The money he got from the pub owner covered the costs of the hall and the band. Whatever was paid in entrance fees, David pocketed. Men paid £1 to get in, but women got special treatment. David went around to language schools, where foreign girls were studying English, to give out discounted tickets to the young ladies; really attractive ones got in for free.

By the time David returned to Hong Kong to join the Bank of East Asia, he had already acquired considerable experience in business and accounting. When the bank's chief accountant died, David stepped into his shoes and, shortly after, was appointed assistant chief manager. He was sandwiched between two Kans. He reported directly to Sir Y. K. Kan's brother, Michael Kan, the deputy chief manager, while Tom Kan, Sir Y. K.'s son, worked under him.

While there was friction at work, David's domestic life blossomed. He courted Penny Poon and married her, and she gave him two sons, Adrian and Brian, within three years. Little more than a year after the birth of Brian, David's uncle, Aubrey, announced that he would be retiring as chief manager at the end of 1976. He proposed Michael Kan as chief manager and David as deputy chief manager.

Michael Kan and David did not get along. Working under Michael, David experienced some of the most difficult times of his life. But in 1981, Michael Kan announced his retirement, and the board chose David as his successor.

As chief manager, David drastically changed the bank's style. From the time of Kan Tong-po down to his son Michael Kan, the bank had been controlled by the leading families and was run autocratically. David adopted a different style, one of consensus and cooperation. He also opened up top management positions to people outside the main families. Ten years after David took over, not one member from the leading families, other than he himself, was in a management position.

The Bank of East Asia was attractive to foreign banks interested in establishing a foothold in Hong Kong. Chemical Bank, seeking to carve out a role for itself in the Hong Kong–China region, was interested in acquiring a substantial shareholding, and the Bank of East Asia, with its long relationship with China, seemed just the right vehicle.

Chemical Bank approached Sir Y. K. and Aubrey, heads of two families with major shareholdings. The matter was never formally discussed within the bank's board, though various family members were consulted. Sir Y. K. and Aubrey were interested and the discussions went on for several months; significant progress was made.

But the deal never went through. The Bank of China got wind of Chemical Bank's intentions and made clear its opposition to Hong Kong's largest local bank coming under foreign influence or control.

David, too, wanted the Bank of East Asia to remain a purely Hong Kong institution, at a time when virtually all other local banks were being taken over. His position as chief executive would have been compromised if there was a 'big brother', in the form of Chemical Bank, looking over his shoulder. From David's point of view, the Bank of China had helped him out of an uncomfortable situation.

Under David Li, the Bank of East Asia continued to capitalize on its position as the oldest and largest local bank. In television commercials, it identified itself as 'the bank of the Hong Kong people', differentiating itself from other, bigger banks. While the bank diversified outside Hong Kong, at the same time it showed its commitment to the territory. In May 1984, a month after Britain disclosed that British administration of the colony would terminate in 1997, the bank offered twenty-five-year home loans. Previously, Hong Kong mortgages had a maximum maturity period of twenty years. The bank's offer was widely seen as a demonstration of its commitment to Hong Kong and a move to bolster confidence in the future.

As representative of Hong Kong's bankers, David found himself involved in the problems of other banks, including on one occasion the carrying out of a secret mission. In late 1985 the Ka Wah Bank was in serious trouble and the Hong Kong government was looking for someone to take it over. Banking Commissioner Robert Fell asked David to approach the Bank of China. The Bank of China, which had its own network of twelve 'sister' banks, was not interested in acquiring Ka Wah Bank but arranged for David to talk to the China International Trust and Investment Company (CITIC). On 30 December 1985 a telegram arrived inviting him to Beijing. He called Fell and said: 'I'm only a broker. I have no authority. Either you come with me or have David Nendick accompany me. Otherwise I will have no credibility.'

On 2 January 1986 David and Nendick, Secretary for Monetary Affairs, slipped off quietly to Beijing. CITIC officials met them at the airport and gave them dinner. The next day was spent negotiating with Rong Yiren, the CITIC chairman, and other officials. 'Nendick was negotiating with them and I was the draftsman of the original letter of intent,' David recalled. 'Fortunately I had a little legal training. So I was drafting it and they were negotiating and Nendick had to go to the British Embassy to telephone [Financial Secretary] John Bremridge in Hong Kong on terms.' The negotiations lasted from 8.30am until 9pm, except for meal breaks. But agreement was reached. An announcement was made that CITIC would inject HK$350 million into Ka Wah to acquire a 95 per cent stake. For his troubles, David received a pat on the back from

Bremridge and a compliment: 'I never realized you have that sort of influence.'

In March 1989, David put aside his concerns about the Basic Law, the Legislative Council, and the Bank of East Asia when he gave two lavish parties on successive nights to celebrate his fiftieth birthday. The celebrations began Sunday night, 12 March, with a party for 100 people at Gaddi's, Hong Kong's most exclusive restaurant, with the guest list including many of the colony's luminaries. The following night, on his actual birthday, he held another bash, this time for 300 people, at the Overseas Bankers' Club. The guests that night included Chief Secretary Sir David Ford and members of the Executive and Legislative Councils. David explained that he needed two celebrations to accommodate his many overseas friends. More than sixty people flew in from around the world to take part in the celebrations. As part of the evening's events, his uncle Simon gave a speech in which he outlined the major highways in his favourite nephew's career. A band played popular songs, as well as special requests like 'Daisy, Daisy', in honour of David's mother. A close friend, Ian MacCallum, adopted a light-hearted vein in his speech, discussing what he called 'some of the lesser-known byways' in David's career, joshing both David and his wife, Penny.

When David was courting Penny, MacCallum joked, she had many other keen suitors. One day, David arrived at Penny's house to see another suitor leaving. Furious, he said to her: 'Look here, Penny, I am not prepared to play second fiddle.'

'Second fiddle indeed,' she replied. 'Let me tell you, David, you are very lucky to be in the band at all.'

After they married, MacCallum went on, they had the usual domestic spats. On one occasion, David lost his temper and said, 'I was an idiot when I married you.'

'I know,' said Penny. 'But I was too infatuated to notice.'

The gaiety of the occasion was in sombre contrast to the

tense atmosphere that characterized Hong Kong in the weeks following the party. Massive demonstrations erupted in Beijing in April; students called for democracy and an end to official corruption. After martial law was proclaimed in Beijing, hundreds of thousands of people took to the streets in Hong Kong, in spite of a typhoon, to stage a peaceful demonstration to show their solidarity with the Beijing students. When tanks and machine guns crushed the student activists on 4 June, a million people in Hong Kong, on two successive weekends, mourned the dead and called for the overthrow of China's top leaders.

The outpouring of emotions in Hong Kong led David to ponder just how close its people were to China. At the same time, he felt, it also showed how different Hong Kong was from China and how lucky its people were to have the freedom to express themselves.

In a speech in the legislature, David showed that he, too, now agreed that democracy was vital to Hong Kong's future. 'Today there is a totally new situation in Hong Kong,' he said. 'We must accelerate the pace of democracy. We must protect civil liberties with a bill of rights. We must expand civic education so that the people of Hong Kong fully understand the rights and responsibilities of citizenship. Hong Kong is our home. We are united. We must remain united to protect our past, our present and our future.'

Ironically, the Tiananmen Square military crackdown provided an opportunity for David to return a favour to the Bank of China. The incident triggered off massive anti-China hysteria in Hong Kong and precipitated a run on the Bank of China and its sister banks. David telephoned officials there and offered to help. 'We were a much smaller bank,' David recalled, 'but we sent them cartloads of cash.'

The good relationship between David and Chinese officials helped the Bank of East Asia over the years. Whereas in 1985 the bank had only one branch in China, in Shanghai, eleven years later it had branches in Shenzhen, Xiamen, Guangzhou, Zhuhai, and Dalian, and representative offices in Fuzhou, Beijing, Qingdao, and Wuhan.

But there was a price to pay. Friends in high places in Beijing helped the bank in China, but had the opposite effect elsewhere. For example, it took the bank an inordinately long time to get permission to set up a representative office in Taiwan. And, when the bank tried to upgrade this office to a branch, it had to wait more years, during which both the bank and David himself were apparently investigated for communist affiliations. David was also upset to discover that Canadian authorities, too, delayed the Bank of East Asia's application to expand its banking business into Canada, presumbly because of the bank's closeness to China.

Through the years, David has maintained a high profile through his public speeches and travels, but as a businessman, not a politician. While he continued to be included in virtually all of China's advisory bodies for Hong Kong, he adopted a low political profile. He has learned that 'you really don't get anywhere by just being vocal'. Rather, he discovered the effectiveness of acting behind the scenes, talking directly to decision-makers, whether they be Chinese, British, or American.

'I find that if people know your political views, they don't talk to you that much because they know where you stand already,' he said. 'But if you are low-profile and appear to be neutral, to be issue-oriented rather than party-oriented, it's much more effective. I'm trying to assist Hong Kong in the best possible way as a financial trading and business centre in the future. I've been pushing for the preservation of the rule of law and press freedom, and I've also been pressing for China to open up more.'

Chapter 21

Ronald Li:
Father of the Stock Exchange

On 2 April 1986, a day deemed auspicious for 'trading and fishing' by the Chinese almanac, the Unified Stock Exchange of Hong Kong was launched, with Ronald Li, youngest son of Koon-chun and the brother of Simon, as its first chairman. This was a landmark event in the development of Hong Kong as an international financial centre and marked an end to a chaotic period in Hong Kong's financial history, when four stock exchanges operated side by side. Ronald, founder of the Far East Stock Exchange, had helped the government set up the unified institution. His strong personality helped push through many provisions resisted by one or the other of the old exchanges.

The founding of the unified exchange reflected a turning point in Hong Kong's history, as financial services gradually became a pillar of the economy, replacing manufacturing. The opening up of China since 1979 had seen a steady stream of Hong Kong companies shift manufacturing facilities across the border, to take advantage of cheap land and labour in Guangdong Province.

The stock exchange occupied new, streamlined, high-tech premises in one of two circular forty-nine-storey buildings, aptly named Exchange Square, which stood on reclaimed land. The stock exchange provided facilities for up to 2,000 floor traders, and each broker had his own computer terminal. Six hundred and seventy-eight brokers took part in the first day's trading, with a turnover of more than HK$226 million in the half-day session.

The new exchange was an instant success. The first company to apply for a listing was the colony's own airline, Cathay Pacific. The application was considered by the listings subcommittee, of which Ronald was convenor, on 10 April, eight days after the exchange first opened its doors. Five days later, the exchange wrote to Cathay Pacific and its advisors to say that approval was given in principle. This first issue on the exchange was massively oversubscribed.

Although Beijing promised that capitalist practices, such as horse racing and dancing, could continue in Hong Kong after 1997, the prospect of communist rule gave pause to anyone running the colony's stock exchange. In 1983, during the negotiations on Hong Kong's future, Ronald publicly asserted: 'I have no illusion about it. As long as I am useful to China they will keep me. If I outlive my usefulness I will be immediately slaughtered.'

With such a pragmatic outlook, he took steps to improve his relationship with Chinese officials and to enhance his usefulness to them. In 1984, when Club Volvo, a huge nightclub boasting a thousand hostesses, was launched, Ronald and the other backers were careful to invite the vice director of the New China News Agency, China's de facto consulate in Hong Kong, to officiate at the opening ceremony. When the unified exchange was formally launched, Ji Pengfei, a senior official in Beijing responsible for Hong Kong affairs, contributed a handwritten inscription.

187

The formal inauguration of the exchange was presided over by the governor, Sir Edward Youde, who in his speech paid tribute to Ronald for his 'seminal contribution' to Hong Kong's securities industry. Ronald invited chairmen of stock exchanges from around the world to attend a gala celebration at the Hong Kong Coliseum.

In his opening speech, Ronald said:

> In the midst of our celebrations we have not lost sight of the central purpose of our service—to act as a bridge between the creators of wealth in the economy and the investment required to give them strength. So we look to the future with confidence. We live in times of far-reaching and speedy changes. Hong Kong has thrived by fast-moving reaction to such changes in the past. We in the Stock Exchange of Hong Kong have every confidence that we shall be able to exploit every new opportunity offered by the extraordinary growth of technology and ingenuity in the securities industry which we serve.

By legislation, the exchange was independent of the government, with its management and control vested in the general committee, of which Ronald was chairman. Under Ronald's guidance, the Hong Kong stock market became one of the world's fastest growing, though not the most disciplined. Newly listed shares were frequently vastly oversubscribed, and shot up in value as soon as trading began. This was in part due to the exchange's ability to determine the pricing of new issues, unlike in other financial centres, where the company concerned and the issuing broker worked out the price. As the market grew, Ronald and his colleagues on the stock exchange grew with it. Not a single company that sought a public listing was turned away.

Ronald was on top of the world. At the age of fifty-seven, he had become chairman of the only stock exchange in a leading financial centre, wielding enormous power by being able to influence—if not decide—the terms under which companies would be listed on the exchange. His three children were grown up. He drank mostly tea or plain water, abstaining from anything alcoholic. He was an extremely successful man who relished his wealth and flaunted it. But in some ways he remained extremely frugal. When he and his wife, Irene, were in London for the annual meeting of the international federation of stock exchanges, Ronald complained about the hotel's charges and refused to eat breakfast in the hotel restaurant. He asked his wife to go out to buy doughnuts and coffee, which they then ate in their room.

Ronald's first love was business, and he constantly thought of new ways to make money. According to him, his father Koon-chun had explained to him in childhood such concepts as business partnerships and how to get a mortgage—even a second and third mortgage. His father also taught Ronald the workings of the stock market, how to buy shares and which shares to buy. Ronald would later boast that from the age of six he knew how to trade in shares. Koon-chun set up an account for Ronald, and the boy would tell his father what shares to buy and sell, and Koon-chun would execute his orders for him.

While he was in high school, Ronald again showed a flair for business, soliciting advertising for the school magazine. He was interested in chemistry and told his schoolmates that cosmetics were profitable. The ingredients, he said, cost little, yet women were willing to pay any amount of money for them.

When Ronald was eighteen, Koon-chun sent him to study in the United States and gave him the phenomenal sum of US$50,000, an indication of his love for his youngest son. After graduating from Wittenberg College and the Wharton School of Business, Ronald returned to Hong Kong where he soon became chairman of the Hong Kong and Kowloon Real Estate Association. He campaigned for ending, or at least limiting, rent control, especially of commercial premises. He said there was no reason for landlords to subsidize businessmen occupying pre-war premises, where rents were a small fraction of those of their next-door neighbours in post-war buildings.

The idea of setting up his own stock exchange dawned on Ronald when the Hong Kong Stock Exchange (which had rejected Ronald's application for membership) was temporarily shut down during the 1967 riots. He thought that if he created his own exchange, 'I won't be controlled by others and I won't have to pay commissions.' When the market was beginning to recover, he called his brother Fook-hing one day and said: 'The Hong Kong Stock Exchange is doing such a lousy job. Why don't we start a stock exchange ourselves?' Fook-hing thought it was a good idea.

Together with nine business associates, all Chinese, Ronald and Fook-hing set up the Far East Stock Exchange at the end of 1969, each putting up HK$50,000. This was a revolutionary move and a major breakthrough for local brokers. As one of Ronald's sons later recalled, many people involved in the stock market were asking, 'How can Chinese people establish a stock exchange?' Ronald answered that question through action. He became the first chairman of the Far East Exchange, while Fook-hing was a committee member. From this point on, Ronald's life revolved around stocks and shares. It was through the stock market that he accumulated immense wealth and became one of the world's wealthiest men.

At a press conference to launch the Far East Exchange, Ronald said there was 'an urgent demand within the economic structure of Hong Kong for the formation of an additional stock exchange'. He pointed out that there were only sixty-five public companies and, in the more than two decades since the end of the World War II, the Hong Kong Stock Exchange had added only an average of one new company per year to the public listings. Patently, this failed to reflect the rate of growth of the Hong Kong economy. Smaller entrepreneurs, he pointed out, were compelled to rely heavily on borrowed money, a fact that affected the stability of the economy.

The launching of the Far East Stock Exchange removed the bottleneck that the Hong Kong Stock Exchange had become. The Western-dominated exchange traded in only a small handful of shares, blue-chip companies controlled by expatriate institutions such as Hongkong Bank, Hong Kong Electric, Butterfield and Swire, and China Light. A small number of British businessmen sat on interlocking boards and maintained a stranglehold on the economy.

The Far East Stock Exchange unleashed pent-up energies in Hong Kong and did much for the development of the colony's economy and its transformation over the next two decades into a major financial centre. In 1972 alone, forty-two companies were listed, more than the number of companies newly listed on the old Hong Kong Stock Exchange in the entire post-war period. One of Ronald's main achievements was to get such up-and-coming local companies as Cheung Kong and Sun Hung Kai listed on his stock exchange. Their chief backers, Li Ka-shing and Fung King-hey, were later to become household names. Those who ran the old Hong Kong Stock Exchange did not court Chinese entrepreneurs to persuade them to turn themselves into public companies. Ronald did so, successfully.

To help the public, Ronald emphasized the use of Chinese, unlike the old exchange, which used only English. He extended trading hours and, for the first time, admitted women brokers. He permitted brokers to advertise, believing that by so doing they rendered a service to investors. The visitors' lobby was separated from the trading hall only by a glass panel. 'We hope the public will come and see and understand how stocks and shares are being traded,' he said. 'This will eliminate mysteries and inhibitions.'

So successful was the Far East Stock Exchange that, before long, a third exchange, the Kam Ngan, entered the fray. And the following year, a fourth, the Kowloon Stock Exchange, commenced business. Hong Kong took on the air of a cowboy town. The bull market of the early 1970s encouraged plans for a fifth exchange. However, the government rushed through legislation to make it illegal for anyone else to set up a stock exchange.

Trading on all four exchanges regularly exceeded US$100 million a day, and turnover often was more than half that of London, even though the number of companies traded in Hong Kong was a tiny fraction of those traded in London. The Far East Stock Exchange was ahead of its three competitors in daily turnover, number of securities listed, and number of members.

The existence of four stock exchanges reflected the somewhat confused state of the financial community. Because the four exchanges operated independently, it was difficult even to obtain an agreed share quotation. This deterred overseas investors. From the mid-1970s on, there was talk of a merger, and in 1977 the government formed a working party to discuss forming a unified exchange.

Ronald was not keen on a unified exchange. He said that in principle he favoured unification, but he wanted it done step by step, with two exchanges merging first, rather than all four exchanges sitting down and discussing a common merger.

Ronald's brash and brassy style intimidated some and angered others. When frustrated by what he considered to be stupidity, he would resort to the Cantonese expletive, 'No brains!' with little regard for the other person's feelings. And when Wittenberg College, his alma mater, gave him an honorary doctorate, he immediately put the title on his calling cards, and his secretary began instructing visitors to address him as 'Dr Li'. Considering that the family had been wealthy for generations, Ronald behaved like a member of the nouveau riche.

Windows, shaped like the letter 'L' (for Li), decorated the exterior wall of his Deep Water Bay home.

The late 1970s saw the arrival of international brokers. The Far East Stock Exchange was the first to offer full membership to a foreign firm, Vickers da Costa & Co. Ronald explained that the presence of big foreign brokers would result in more business all around.

Despite opposition by the four individual exchanges, the government was determined to set up a new, unified exchange and was willing to ride roughshod over them if necessary. In July 1980, the Unified Stock Exchange of Hong Kong was formally incorporated as a company whose purpose was to bring about a union of the four existing exchanges. It would take six years for the new exchange to be born. In the mean time, the four exchanges continued to operate.

Ronald was seen by many as the investment adviser par excellence, the man who knew better than anyone else how to turn one dollar into ten, then into a thousand, then into a million. 'Do not fall in love with your investment,' he once admonished. 'If you fall in love with the investment, then you won't give it up. If you treat an investment as a love affair, you will lose for sure.'

It may have been this philosophy that precipitated a horrendous corporate and family row when he sold his considerable shares in Chinese Estates. The company was founded in the 1920s by friends of his father, one of whom was Fung Ping-shan. Koon-chun was a major shareholder and, after his death, his four sons all became major shareholders. F. S., Fook-hing and Ronald served on the board. The company chairman was Sir Kenneth Fung, son of Fung Ping-shan.

Board meetings of Chinese Estates were light-hearted affairs. In fact, when a dispute erupted in 1975 over the distribution of profits, Ronald said to the press: 'We are all either good friends or relatives and I am sure we can sit down and discuss the matter.'

This cosy situation ended in 1986. At the time, the board consisted of the chairman, Sir Kenneth Fung, his son Lawrence, and eight other board members, four of whom were members of the Li family: F. S., Fook-hing, Ronald, and David, F. S.'s older son. Chinese Estates was a valuable company, being cash rich and debt free. It was not traded much, its shareholders treating it as a long-term investment that yielded good dividends. It held a controlling interest in the company China Entertainment, which owned China Building in the heart of the business district. The building generated lucrative rental income.

Sir Kenneth and F. S. were lifelong friends. When the former was on holiday, the latter would act as chairman of Chinese Estates. All this changed in March 1986, when the Fung family suddenly made a move to gain control of the company. The move may have stemmed from the family's much publicized financial problems, which were so serious that it was on the verge of bankruptcy. Chinese Estates was a cash cow that could be the answer to the Fungs' problems.

On 17 March 1986—three weeks before the opening of the Unified Stock Exchange of Hong Kong—the Fung family and Bill Wyllie, an Australian entrepreneur, announced that they had, through a jointly owned company, Shimako Investments, acquired just under 35 per cent of the shares of Chinese Estates. This made Shimako the largest single shareholder, with a controlling interest. This corporate coup succeeded only through the cooperation of Ronald who, without the knowledge of his relatives, had secretly sold his share of the company, about 11 per cent.

Ronald's motive was unclear. Perhaps it was just the prospect of profit. He may have felt there was little point in leaving his assets in a company that was largely inactive. He had frequently berated his brothers for not having as good a business mind as himself. Whatever his reasons, Ronald's brothers were furious that he should have sold out to the Fungs, thus undermining the Li family's interests. Even Fook-hing, the brother to whom Ronald was closest, was outraged.

The battle for control widened the rift that already existed between Ronald and his brothers, especially with F. S. It also pitted the Li family against the Fungs. Divergent financial interests finally snapped bonds of friendship that had endured for almost seventy years, just as they had created a rupture between the Lis and the Kans in 1958.

Four days after the Fung–Wyllie announcement, Chinese Estates held its annual general meeting. This time the bonhomie was missing. Bouncers were stationed at the entrance to keep out anyone who could not prove his right to be present. The acrimonious meeting went on for two hours. F. S., Fook-hing, and David were unceremoniously ousted from the board, while new directors were named, all from the Fung–Wyllie camp.

The ouster of all the Lis from the board ensured a war. Three days later the Lis struck back. They teamed up with Sun Hung Kai International and others and set up Bassina Ltd., a company formed to make a hostile takeover bid of Chinese Estates. By 8 April Bassina had acquired shares amounting to 33.1 per cent of Chinese Estates, compared to just under 35 per cent for the Fung–Wyllie camp. Bassina offered to buy all outstanding shares at HK$16 a share. With the Li campaign making headway, the Fungs regrouped. In conjunction with Wyllie, they made a counter-offer of HK$17.2 for each share.

Events took a dramatic new turn when, on 19 April, a third party entered the fray. Evergo Industrial Enterprise, controlled by well-known corporate raider Joseph Lau and his brother Thomas, announced that it had purchased a large number of Chinese Estates shares at HK$18 a share. It announced that Bassina had agreed to sell its stake at the same price, giving Evergo 42.8 per cent of the company. The Li family decided to withdraw from the bidding. While they failed to gain control, they at least succeeded in selling out at a price to their liking.

The Fungs, meanwhile, were left as minority shareholders in a company controlled by Evergo. The friendship that had marked the relationship between the Li, Kan, and Fung families in the 1920s and 1930s was gone forever. At the same time, Ronald's relations with his siblings worsened.

But Ronald did not seem to care. Being chairman of the stock exchange put him in a position to make even more money than ever. Money-making for Ronald bordered on an obsession, and many who knew him were put off by it, especially since he went to great lengths to profit at every possible opportunity. 'At the stock exchange,' one person said, 'he monopolized everything. Little things like pencils and paper, you could only buy through him.' When the stock exchange held a celebration, Ronald saw to it that it was held in a restaurant of which he was part owner.

He was also accused of nepotism. His son Alfred became the exchange's legal representative. His son Lawrence became its medical consultant. His sister Viola's son, Wong Hong-sun, worked in the exchange's security department. His cousin Fook-tong, son of Siu-pang, worked for his private securities firm.

Ronald, one of the most visible men about town, pontificated on a wide range of subjects. At a conference held in mid-1987, ten years before the scheduled handover to China, he assured foreign investors about the future in these terms: 'Hong Kong is a colony. It is a dictatorship, although a benevolent one. It is and has been a British colony, and it's going to be a Chinese colony, and as such it will prosper. We do not need free elections here.'

In late 1987, when the Hong Kong government was consulting the public on the pace of political reforms, Ronald issued a circular to all members of the exchange asking them to voice their opposition to the introduction of direct elections to the Legislative Council. The circular also proposed that the securities industry be given a seat in the legislature. If this were done, Ronald would have been a logical choice to fill it. The circular said if direct elections were introduced, it would be easy for the unscrupulous to gain power.

Questioned about his position on democracy, Ronald likened the relationship of China and Hong Kong to that of husband and wife, and said that for Hong Kong to insist on universal franchise 'would be like a wife annoying her husband by making the house very untidy and only cooking two meals instead of three meals a day'. He said that Hong Kong should be run by businessmen and added that if ordinary people were given the vote, they would elect pop singers as legislators. Democracy, Ronald said, 'is a word that should be obliterated from the dictionary. That's just another word for a nose count.'

Ronald was unafraid of controversy and, in fact, seemed to thrive on it. Less than a year after the formal opening of the Stock Exchange, he was embroiled in another controversy as headlines screamed: 'Stock Exchange Chairman Backs Girlie Bar Listing.' Ronald vigorously defended his plan to allow the public listing of Club Volvo, a plush night club in which he had an interest, whose main assets were its 1,000 young women. The nightclub was so posh and so large that it provided a Rolls-Royce to convey patrons from the entrance to the dance floor. Critics said a public listing of such a company could bring the exchange into disrepute.

Questioned at a press conference as to whether it was respectable for the stock exchange to list such a company, he retorted: 'What has that got to do with the respectability of the stock exchange? I will list anything under the sun that is both profitable and within the law. If the government allows it to exist as a legitimate enterprise, I don't think the exchange should play the role of the church.' In the end, Club Volvo was not listed. In fact, because the German car-maker threatened to sue over use of the name 'Volvo', it changed its name to Club Bboss.

Chapter 22

The Fall of Ronald Li

The global market crashed on Black Monday, 26 October 1987. In Hong Kong, twelve hours ahead of New York, Ronald received a telephone call in the middle of the night from a committee member in Canada who told him that the New York Stock Exchange was suffering tremendous setbacks.

In a pre-dawn call to the Financial Secretary, Sir Piers Jacobs, Ronald apprised him of the situation and said the exchange might have to shut down. Jacobs told him any such decision was a matter for the exchange itself. At eight o'clock, an emergency meeting of the general committee, a body of local brokers, decided to close down the exchange.

The move badly damaged Hong Kong's reputation, as international brokers traded jibes about the colony's 'Mickey Mouse' stock exchange. Ronald, however, defended the move, saying: 'It's far better if you're in a typhoon to take shelter.' Privately, he gave a more biting explanation: 'Why should we Hong Kong patriots lose a lot of money because of a bunch of New York Jews?'

During the four-day closure, the government discovered just how precarious the financial markets were. The problem was not just the stock exchange but, more seriously, the futures exchange, whose collapse was imminent if the stock market plummeted, as everyone knew it would as soon as the market reopened. The government called in expert advisors from London. These consultants arrived Friday evening when, ironically, the stock exchange was holding a gala charity concert to celebrate its first anniversary. With the help of the consultants, the government put together a HK$2 billion rescue package for the futures exchange.

When the stock exchange reopened the following Monday, it dropped 44 per cent in one of the largest falls in the world, wiping HK$200 billion off the value of shares. Many people blamed the sharp drop on Ronald, saying that if the market had stayed open, it would not have fallen as steeply. The government, fearful that the HK$2 billion rescue package might be insufficient, doubled its size with the help of banks and international brokerage houses. The price for their cooperation was an ending of the monopoly on power enjoyed by Ronald and his fellow local brokers over the stock exchange.

Ronald held a news conference on 26 October, the day the stock exchange reopened its doors after a four-day closure. An Australian reporter, Eric Ellis, asked if the closing of the exchange was done to protect his personal interests. Ronald exploded. In a scene recorded by television cameras and subsequently telecast around the world, Ronald pounded the table and, eyes bulging, pointed an accusing finger, demanding that the reporter be immediately hauled off to prison.

'This is slanderous,' Ronald shouted. 'I am going to sue you for this. You said I have acted against the law and I have committed nothing against the law. You have gone too far. If you don't retract right now you are going to get a lawsuit right now.' Ronald than jumped to his feet and, as the reporter beat a quick retreat, screamed: 'What is your name? You have got to give me your name. I am going to give you a writ right now. Why are you so irresponsible? Why are journalists so irresponsible?'

Ronald's performance at the press conference confirmed a widely held view that his departure was necessary if Hong Kong was to regain its reputation as a serious financial centre. He was seen as part of a discredited past. In little more than a year Ronald had been transformed from the proud father of the stock exchange to an embarrassing liability.

Although the stock exchange was a private company, the government stepped in and appointed former Banking Commissioner Robert Fell to take over as senior chief executive officer, thus removing authority from Ronald's hands. A new system of representation on the committee was devised. At the Futures Exchange, both Kim Cham, its chairman, and Ronald, its vice chairman, stepped down. Fortunately for the government, Ronald's term as chairman of the stock exchange expired on 16 December, and the rules of the exchange did not permit another term.

The government intended to give international securities companies a larger role in running the stock exchange. Ronald was unhappy about these plans and, in an interview, accused big foreign firms of being 'more dirty' than their local counterparts. He said the foreign brokers were 'trying to harm the image of the exchange unnecessarily and bullying the small brokers'.

A few days later, he made an even stronger attack on foreign firms while in Taipei for a conference of Asian stock exchanges. In an interview, Ronald denounced international brokers as racists who used bullying tactics against their local counterparts. 'Maybe because the colour of their skin is white, they think they can have half the seats on the council,' he said. 'Is Hong Kong being bullied or is it not?'

Even though he had to step down as chairman of the exchange, the rules allowed him to remain on the general committee. In fact, when a new chairman, Charles Sin, was chosen,

Ronald was elected as one of five vice chairmen. Clearly, he was still a force to be reckoned with.

Ronald's world crashed around him, suddenly and dramatically, in the early hours of 2 January 1988. He was rudely awakened by agents of the Independent Commission Against Corruption (ICAC) during a pre-dawn raid on his palatial mansion, the day after his return from a trip to Europe. His home was searched and he was arrested, along with Jeffrey Sun, the exchange's chief executive officer, and Donald Tsang, head of its listing department. The news created a sensation. Immediately after the arrests, the government demanded that certain members of the Stock Exchange committee—including its new chairman and four of the five vice chairmen— 'distance themselves' from the management of the exchange while the ICAC conducted investigations.

Ronald was formally charged twelve days after his arrest on a single count of bribery involving a listing application by a Japanese-controlled construction concern, Kumagai Gumi (Hong Kong) Ltd. The government alleged that he had, 'without lawful authority or reasonable excuse, accepted an advantage' in May 1987 in the form of 1.1 million Kumagai Gumi shares, allotted to him at HK$2.50 each. He allegedly accepted the shares as 'an inducement or reward' for facilitating the company's listing on the exchange.

On 10 August, Ronald appeared in court and was charged with four more counts of accepting beneficial interests in shares of companies that applied for listing on the stock exchange. The following day five additional charges were laid against him. The new charges, similar to the original one, alleged that he had received preferential share allotments in companies that were applying for listing as 'an inducement to or reward for showing favour or forbearing to show disfavour' in relation to the listing of the companies in 1986 and 1987. Along with him in court were seven of his former colleagues, including the new chairman, and three vice chairmen.

Regardless of the outcome of the court case, Ronald's reputation was in tatters. He was dropped from the new edition of *Who's Who in Hong Kong*. His name had been listed between those of his brothers F. S. and Simon.

The actual trial began on 3 September 1990, two years and ten months after his initial arrest. Time had taken its toll on Ronald; in court, he looked haggard and what little hair he had left was mostly grey.

The prosecutor told the jury of seven—all Chinese—that Ronald had abused his position as chairman of the stock exchange for personal profit. 'His motive, in common with most people, high or low, who act corruptly, was basically one of personal greed,' the prosecutor said.

During the trial, the court learned of a tape recording that showed Ronald had lied to Fell and the general committee about Cathay Pacific shares. Ronald had said at a meeting of the exchange's general committee, attended by Fell, that none of its members could obtain a Cathay allotment, although he had already been allocated half a million shares. Records of Ronald's personal dealings were shown to the jury. He had made HK$50 million in 1986–88, in spite of the crash.

The court heard that in both the Cathay and Novel Enterprises cases, just one day after the stock exchange's listing subcommittee, of which Ronald was convenor, agreed in principle to the listing, he privately rang up the merchant bankers acting for the companies and solicited and obtained shares for himself.

The Cathay shares in particular were many times oversubscribed. Only a small number of designated investors and subunderwriters received big allotments. Others received only a fraction of what they applied for. If Ronald had wanted half a million shares in competition with the public, he would have had to apply for more than 40 million shares, sending in a check for more than HK$140 million. 'But,' the prosecution said, 'he did not have to do that. He arranged his shares privately.'

The Novel offering, too, was massively oversubscribed and to obtain 300,000 shares as an ordinary member of the public, Ronald would have had to apply for almost eight million shares and submitted a check for HK$15.8 million. In the actual transaction, the prosecution pointed out, he had paid no transaction levy, no brokerage fee, and no stamp duty.

Ronald, surprisingly, opted to give his court testimony in Cantonese, in spite of his degrees from American universities. He was assigned an interpreter, who translated into Chinese everything being said by the British prosecutor. In turn, his testimony in Cantonese had to be translated into English for the benefit of the court. This time-consuming process may have given Ronald more time to think before answering questions, but it may also have damaged his image in the eyes of the jurors, who knew that he was fluent in English. This point was accentuated when the prosecution played a tape of Ronald's conversation with Fell. The prosecutor quoted from the transcript and, as the interpreter began to translate, he interjected: 'Now, Mr Li, you don't need to wait for the interpretation. You understand because they were your words, spoken in English.'

Ronald attended the trial wearing well-tailored suits, his horn-rimmed glasses sometimes raised high, resting not on his ears but against his temples, with the glasses tilted to enable him to read documents placed in front of him. He was assertive, even aggressive, displaying a self-confidence that was surprising in the circumstances.

His business suits were in stark contrast to the traditional flowing robes worn in British courtrooms. Judge Bokhary sported a red robe and white wig, while the barristers, attired in black gowns with white clerical collars, sat before two rows of solicitors wearing ordinary suits. Seats in the public gallery were almost all taken by the press, but occasionally the faces of well-known personalities could be spotted as they dropped by to see for themselves what was going on. Ronald sat ramrod straight. Next to the witness stand sat a policeman whose job it was to change the tape cassette in the recorder whenever it ran out.

Ronald told the jury that, while he had made HK$2 million from share dealings as a sub-underwriter in 1986, he would have made several times that amount if he had invested in treasury bills. When asked whether he had bought the Cathay shares for his stockbroking firm or for himself, he said: 'I am the largest client of myself.'

The senior archdeacon of the Anglican diocese of Hong Kong and Macao, the Reverend John Cheung, testifying as a character witness, said he had known Ronald for more than twenty-three years as a regular churchgoer who had become a friend over the years. Ronald, he said, was a man of principle who could distinguish between right and wrong. In addition to donations to the church, he said, Ronald had once gone to Macao at the church's request to do unpaid accounting work.

On 17 October 1990, Ronald was found guilty of corruption by a jury that deliberated for more than ten hours and returned a split verdict, five to two. Under Hong Kong's system, a majority—not unanimous—verdict was enough to convict. The next day he was sentenced to four years in prison. Judge Bokhary sentenced Ronald to two years on each count, to run consecutively. The maximum sentence of seven years, Bokhary said, was not imposed because of Ronald's record of public service, his character, and his age. 'You are a very wealthy man by any standards, and you have long been a wealthy man, so you have even less excuse than a poor man for doing what you did,' the judge told him when pronouncing sentence. 'That being said, your fall is greater because it's from a greater height.' Ronald, the most powerful figure in the Hong Kong stock market for over a decade, became the most prominent businessman ever to go to prison.

In addition to the four-year prison term, Ronald was ordered to pay to the government the profits he gained from the two illegal transactions, as well as the legal costs of the prosecution, estimated at HK$10–15 million.

After the trial, Secretary for Monetary Affairs David Nendick said: 'Clearly if we are to hold our head up in the world we will have to make sure there are no abuses of the securities system.' Evidently, much more was riding on the case than the guilt or innocence of one man. Many felt that if the outcome had been seen as a whitewash, then the territory's image as a financial centre would have been further tarnished.

'The jailing of Ronald Li represents a watershed in Hong Kong's commercial affairs,' the *South China Morning Post* editorialized. 'A four-year prison term will go a long way towards removing the stain on the integrity of the exchange in overseas eyes. The jury is to be congratulated for having the courage to convict one of Hong Kong's most famous figures, thus showing the world that a blind eye will not be turned to corruption in high places.'

On 16 October 1993, sixty-three-year-old Ronald Li walked out of prison a free man, having been given time off for good behaviour. He had served thirty-two months in prison, or two-thirds of his four-year sentence. The finance editor of the *South China Morning Post* estimated that, while Ronald was in prison, his personal fortune had grown by more than US$500,000 a day. His total assets were unknown, but in 1988 he had been listed as the third richest man in Hong Kong by *Capital* magazine, with assets in excess of US$1 billion.

Ronald decided to leave Hong Kong and live abroad. He went to Canada, where he had investments. Despite being an honorary citizen of both Toronto and Calgary, the Canadian government decided he was not welcome as an immigrant and ordered his deportation on the grounds that he was a convicted felon. He left voluntarily to avoid the ignominy of a deportation. Subsequently, he decided to live in self-imposed exile in Bangkok, only returning to Hong Kong on rare occasions.

Chapter 23

Li Fook-kow: A Very Senior Civil Servant

In March 1987, the government announced that it would hold the largest opinion survey ever conducted in Hong Kong, on the direction of future political reforms. This move had been foreshadowed in 1984 when the government, after signing the Joint Declaration, announced that indirect elections to the Legislative Council would begin in 1985, with direct elections to follow. A White Paper setting out government policy at the time stated:

'With few exceptions the bulk of public response from all sources suggested a cautious approach with a gradual start by introducing a very small number of directly elected members in 1988 and building up to a significant number of directly elected members by 1997.' The government promised that a review would be held in 1987 to decide how legislators should be chosen in the 'second phase of development'.

Soon, however, China made known its opposition to what it considered the too-rapid pace of development of democracy. In particular, China objected to the introduction of direct elections in 1988.

The Hong Kong government was in a dilemma. China was adamantly opposed to direct elections in 1988, but the government had already said that public opinion favoured direct elections in that year. So, in May 1987, the government produced a Green Paper, setting out different approaches to the development of representative government, ostensibly to find out what the Hong Kong people wanted. At the same time, it set up a Survey Office (similar to the Assessment Office of 1984) to 'collect, collate and report on public response to the issues discussed in the Green Paper'.

In another parallel with 1984, the government appointed two monitors to oversee the work of the Survey Office. In 1984, one monitor was from England and the other, Judge Simon Li, was from Hong Kong; in 1987, both monitors were local. An official announcement declared that Acting Governor Sir David Akers-Jones had appointed 'Mr Li Fook-kow, CMG, JP, and Mr Andrew So, OBE, JP' to serve as monitors. It was their job to determine whether the Survey Office had done its work 'accurately and impartially'.

Li Fook-kow, son of Tse-fong, brother of Aubrey, and first cousin of Simon, was knowledgeable in the ways of government, having spent his career in the civil service and risen to positions never held before by Chinese. At the time he was appointed a monitor, he was serving as chairman of the Public Service Commission. It was no surprise, therefore, that when Britain needed a man of standing, they should turn to Fook-kow.

To British officials, Fook-kow and other members of the Li family were sterling members of the community whose involvement was deemed highly important. Even on the eve of the 1990s, the government continued to turn to members of a small handful of families, seen as pillars of the community, to provide legitimacy and popular support for its actions. The fact that Fook-kow was Simon's first cousin, and that members of one family had been entrusted by the government twice with such delicate political matters, did not escape the attention of the press.

The *South China Morning Post* ran a story with the headline, 'Survey Role Runs in Family', pointing out the curious coincidence of members of one family being appointed to the delicate political task of monitoring.

Months of heated political debate followed the publication of the Green Paper as proponents and opponents of direct elections in 1988 slugged it out in the media. Those opposed were frequently conservative businessmen who did not trust the public to elect the 'right' people, or who were eager to do business with China. Virtually all public opinion surveys commissioned by newspapers or conducted by academics showed a substantial majority favouring direct elections in 1988.

It came as a shock, therefore, when the Survey Office announced in October that the majority of the population did not favour direct elections. Those in support of direct elections had organized signature campaigns, garnering some 250,000 signatures. The Survey Office decided not to count these as separate submissions. Those opposing direct elections had conducted a direct-mail campaign using pre-printed form letters. The Survey Office counted these separately, as 70,000 individual submissions.

In addition, the Survey Office had commissioned two public opinion surveys, neither of which asked the simple question: 'Are you in favour of direct elections in 1988?' Instead, the questions were stated in convoluted fashion, apparently designed to obtain a negative response.

Fook-kow and his fellow monitor's report was issued the same day as the Survey Office report. Commenting on the Survey Office's opinion surveys, the monitors said they were 'satisfied that they were carried out in a systematic way and that the questionnaire used for both surveys covered all the major issues in the Green Paper'. As for other surveys that came to the opposite conclusion, the monitors said: 'The growing popularity of surveys these days might have led to a tendency to overlook the fact that adequate professional knowledge and experience are required in conducting surveys and that they, if not properly conducted, may not reflect true public sentiments or produce meaningful findings. . .'

The two monitors said in their concluding remarks: 'We judge that the Survey Office has properly, accurately and impartially carried out its duties and followed the procedures prescribed in its terms of reference.'

The release of the Survey Office's report unleashed a political storm, as many accused the government of manipulating the surveys to cancel direct elections. The government, on its part, announced that the holding of direct elections would be deferred for three years, to 1991.

While the Survey Office report engendered much public anger, it was not directed at Fook-kow and his fellow monitor. After all, their task had been very narrowly defined, and whatever fault there was probably lay with those who had drafted the Green Paper and laid down the terms of reference for the Survey Office, not with the monitors.

Fook-kow's career as a civil servant was every bit as successful as that of his brother Aubrey in the commercial world. Arguably, his success was even more impressive because he had to start at the bottom, while Aubrey, being the representative of the Li family within the bank, was destined to be a mover and shaker. Fook-kow, in fact, was a trailblazer, being one of a handful of Chinese to be admitted as a cadet officer, a title later changed to that of administrative officer. Cadets were an elite group, administrators at the apex of the civil service. They wielded such power that a British director of recruitment for the colonies explained, 'In most colonies the civil servant is the government, and not the servant of government.'

210

Chinese were not admitted into this exclusive club until after the war. Only two other Chinese, Paul Tsui and T. C. Cheng, were cadet officers before Fook-kow. Fook-kow, a brilliant man with great intellectual depth, became the third.

This did not happen until nine years after Fook-kow's return to Hong Kong from the United States, accompanied by his bride, Edith, and armed with a master's degree from the Massachusetts Institute of Technology (MIT). Edith had gone to the United States at the age of nine with her father, the Chinese consul general in San Francisco, and had remained there until her marriage; she was American in her attitudes, although she never became a US citizen. Edith was a warm, outgoing person, unlike Fook-kow, who was quiet and somewhat aloof.

Fook-kow's first job within the government was with the Resettlement Department, which was newly created to build and run housing estates for the tens of thousands of homeless people from China whose ramshackle huts covered the hills of Hong Kong. His cousin Simon was with the Legal Department, the only other Li family member working for the government. Simon and Fook-kow were the same age and spent much time together after work, having meals, playing mahjongg, and going to the races. But Simon, who stubbornly championed the rights of Chinese in the civil service, was seen by the government as something of a troublemaker, while Fook-kow, who was friendly with his British colleagues and socialized with them, was seen as one of the boys. After a couple of years as a resettlement officer, Fook-kow went to Cambridge to attend an overseas administrative course. On his return to Hong Kong, he was appointed a labour officer.

He rose rapidly, becoming acting deputy commissioner of labour two years later. At this time the name 'cadet' was replaced by the new term 'administrative officer' and, in August 1961, Fook-kow was promoted to senior administrative officer.

By the time Fook-kow joined the civil service, he was

already the father of four children, two girls, Carol and Elaine, and two boys, Andrew and Michael.

Edith, unlike other Li women, actually took a job, joining a major property company, Hongkong Land. Strangely enough, she did this on doctor's advice. Edith was getting frequent headaches, and the doctor suggested that a job might help. She became a letting agent and negotiator in Hongkong Land's residential real estate department and, sure enough, the headaches diminished. She quit when her children went to boarding school in England, and she had to travel regularly to see them. She imposed strict discipline on the children and pushed them hard, telling them not to disgrace their family or their race.

Fook-kow, on his part, offered fatherly admonitions to his children. He advised that it was much more important to go to funerals than to weddings. Weddings were such joyous occasions that the people involved would be happy anyway. But funerals were occasions when emotional support was needed. He impressed on his daughters the importance of bearing a son to continue their future husband's family line, comparing this task to finishing their homework. (Ironically, later on in life, he was to discover that while both his daughters dutifully produced male heirs, neither of his sons had any sons to continue his line.)

Fook-kow was active in church affairs, doing volunteer work as an usher for the Anglican Cathedral. He and his cousin Fook-hing, son of Koon-chun, who had attended the Chung Hwa Middle School, Wah Yan College, and MIT with him, both sat on the cathedral's council—two of the few Chinese who served alongside British religious, governmental, and civic leaders.

In 1969, Fook-kow again went to London on study leave. This time, he attended courses at the Imperial Defence College, the first Chinese civil servant to be sent there, itself an indication that he was a rising star. He returned to Hong Kong the following January and was appointed Deputy Director of

Commerce and Industry. Six months later, he became Deputy Secretary for Home Affairs. At a time when British officials were beginning to recognize the need to bring Chinese civil servants up the ladder, he was clearly on the fast track.

In 1972, the year Aubrey became chief manager of the bank, Fook-kow made history when he became the first Chinese to be named Director of Social Welfare. At a press conference, he pledged to 'consolidate and improve' social services. He said that, as a boy, he had always wanted to serve the community, and his new position would allow him to do so.

By temperament, Fook-kow was relaxed. He was fond of taking off his shoes at every opportunity, even at official functions. He spoke quietly but had an incisive mind and a prodigious memory, able to recall almost exactly where in a particular file he had come across a certain fact. He was often silent at meetings, preferring to give his views privately, views which were given great weight. He was highly regarded by the governor, Sir David Trench, with whom both Fook-kow and Edith were on friendly terms. His distinguished pedigree, perhaps more than anything else, made his contribution to the government loom larger in the eyes of senior British officials than those of the tiny handful of other Chinese civil servants without the right family connections.

One Sunday, he delighted several of his British colleagues by taking them to a Chinese bathhouse in Wanchai, a seedy, rundown district known for its bars. There, Fook-kow led them into a traditional bathhouse operated by refugees from Shanghai. The Westerners, along with Fook-kow, were immersed in very hot water, then worked over by an expert who, using a wash towel, slowly peeled off the entire layer of old skin. The whole process, including resting and cooling off, took well over an hour and, at the end, they felt thoroughly relaxed and clean.

Edith became involved in volunteer work after quitting

Hongkong Land, especially with the Hong Kong Red Cross, a branch of the British Red Cross. By tradition, its president was Hong Kong's first lady, the wife of the governor. Lady Trench invited her to 'volunteer' and she did, serving on the council alongside F. S.'s wife, Daisy, who was the director.

Five years after joining the Red Cross, Edith became its director and served in that capacity for six years. During that time, the influx of boat people from Vietnam emerged as a major problem, with the collapse of the South Vietnamese government. On 3 May 1975, Dr Gerald Choa, director of medical services, alerted the Red Cross that a shipload of thousands of refugees would arrive the next morning, aboard the Danish freighter *Clara Maersk*. The Hong Kong government decided to allow them to land and to house them, under guard, temporarily in the newly constructed Princess Margaret Hospital. Dr Choa asked Edith to organize Red Cross volunteers and to distribute clothing and other items to the refugees. Edith did, leading a team of fifty Red Cross workers, mostly volunteers, to the hospital, which was not yet open and lacked even toilet paper. She saw to it that basic amenities were provided, including sanitary napkins for women. They worked through the night, handing out paper cups of orange drink, and distributing to each refugee a welfare parcel that contained a shirt, a pair of trousers, a towel, and a cake of soap.

Edith did not leave until eight o'clock the following morning, when she was scheduled to be presented, along with her husband, to Queen Elizabeth, who just happened to be visiting. Governor Trench mentioned that Edith had been up working all night distributing relief parcels to the Vietnamese refugees. Edith bowed to the Queen and felt faint from lack of sleep. The Queen held her hand firmly and, sensing her weakness, helped her along. For her work with the Red Cross, Edith was awarded an MBE by the British government.

The 1970s was a decade of change. Up until then, the majority of people living in Hong Kong had been born elsewhere, mostly China. They did not think of Hong Kong as home. But by the 1970s, their children accounted for a majority of the Hong Kong population. They grew up with a sense of Hong Kong identity and, increasingly, assumed positions of importance as professionals, civil servants, and businessmen. They ushered in a period of unimagined prosperity for Hong Kong.

Fook-kow, unusual in that his family had been in Hong Kong for generations, remained director of the social welfare department only briefly. The following year, he was promoted to Secretary for Social Services. In an interview, Fook-kow acknowledged the importance of the job he was to fill, pointing out that social services accounted for one-third of the government budget. Fook-kow defined his task as 'to prepare an environment in the society so that the number of criminals could be reduced'.

As secretary, Fook-kow sat as an Official Member in both the Executive Council and the Legislative Council. The following year, his brother Aubrey was appointed an unofficial member of the Legislative Council. It was the first time in the colony's history that two brothers sat in the legislature. While Aubrey and other unofficial members occasionally criticized the government, Fook-kow and his official colleagues defended it.

Parliamentary convention called for members always to refer to each other as 'My Honourable Friend' but, when it came to the two brothers, this nicety was at times a cause for hilarity.

In February 1974, Aubrey rose to ask: 'In view of the steep increase in prices, what steps are being taken to assist subvented voluntary organisations to meet their current expenditure on salaries?'

Fook-kow gave a long and convoluted response, ending by saying that representations were carefully studied and 'I can assure my Honourable Friend and brother that replies will be sent as soon as possible.'

Aubrey immediately rose and asked, 'Will My Honourable Friend, the Secretary for Social Services, tell this council that if and when replies are being sent to these representatives favourably, salary adjustment will be backdated so that they will be treated like their government counterparts?' His words caused laughter through the chamber.

Fook-kow resorted to a common government dodge, declining to answer by saying the question was hypothetical. 'It assumes that there will be a favourable answer, which I am not in a position to commit myself,' he said.

Perhaps the most important decision made while Fook-kow was Secretary for Social Services was the provision of nine years of free and compulsory education. The decision was not his alone, but, as secretary, his voice carried the greatest weight.

In 1977 Fook-kow was serving as Secretary for Home Affairs, a highly influential post formerly called the Secretary for Chinese Affairs. The name change in the late 1970s reflected the dawning of a less colonial era in Hong Kong, as the term 'dependent territory' gradually replaced the word 'colony'.

Fook-kow faced the serious problem of syndicated corruption within the police force. The Anti-Corruption Bureau within the police force was totally ineffectual in coping with the problem and, in 1974, a separate agency, the Independent Commission Against Corruption (ICAC), was set up to deal with the problem of corrupt policemen.

The ICAC had its own investigators and did not rely on the police for help. It was phenomenally successful in uncovering syndicates within the police force that worked hand in glove with criminal organizations that were involved in everything from prostitution to drugs. The work of the ICAC led to widespread discontent within the police force.

Many policemen agitated for disbanding or curtailing the ICAC. In late October 1977, off-duty policemen demonstrating outside the ICAC offices smashed its plate glass window, creating a near riot. Then, on Friday, 4 November, policemen in plain clothes marched to the headquarters of the ICAC in broad daylight and broke into it, smashing windows and furniture. There was a clear danger of a breakdown in law and order if the police should go on strike or stage a revolt.

An emergency meeting of top officials, convened that night, lasted until three in the morning. Only five men were present: Chief Secretary Denys Roberts; Police Commissioner Brian Slevin; Attorney General John Hobley; ICAC Commissioner Jack Cater; and Secretary for Home Affairs Li Fook-kow.

The five men feared an escalation of violence and the possibility that on-duty policemen would refuse to perform law enforcement duties when off-duty policemen staged violent protests against the ICAC. They decided that the only solution was to declare an amnesty. The following evening, an amnesty for corrupt policemen was announced. There was no opposition within the government. Everyone accepted amnesty as a necessary evil.

By the late 1970s, the government decided to consider taking steps towards greater representative government. Fook-kow and his senior British colleagues contemplated putting in place a system whereby people could select their own leaders. However, nothing as revolutionary as allowing an elected government was being contemplated. Rather, the questions concerned administration at district level: Should advisory bodies known as district boards have executive responsibilities? Should members be elected and, if so, who would elect them? The pace of change envisioned was leisurely. The first step was not taken until 1982, when a third of the seats on district boards was opened to elections.

In 1980 Fook-kow retired from the civil service. At his last sitting in the Legislative Council, Chief Secretary Sir Jack Cater paid tribute to him and to another retiring officer, Director of Home Affairs John Walden. 'Both have made distinctive and considerable contributions to this council and indeed to the government and people of Hong Kong,' Cater said. In his eight years with the Legislative Council, he continued, Fook-kow's 'wise counsel and penetrating judgment have been of great benefit'.

Retirement from the civil service did not mean a severance of ties with the government. Fook-kow was immediately appointed chairman of the Public Service Commission. While the commission was independent of the civil service, it was customary for the government to pick its chairman from among the ranks of retired civil servants, on the theory that the chairman should understand how the government works.

He retired from the commission in June 1987, a few months after serving as monitor, upon reaching the age of sixty-five. However, because his wife Edith had family connections with the Kuomintang, Fook-kow did not intend to stay in Hong Kong, in view of the impending communist takeover. Instead, he and his wife emigrated to Toronto.

Into the Twenty-First Century

Chapter 24

Simon Li:
Drafting Hong Kong's Constitution (1985–1990)

The five-year process of drafting the Basic Law ended in April 1990, when the National People's Congress of the People's Republic of China promulgated the document, Hong Kong's post-1997 mini-constitution. Much attention was paid to fashioning a document that would be acceptable both to China and to Hong Kong. Two drafts were released for public comment in Hong Kong so that revisions could be made before the Basic Law was made final. Still, parts of the Basic Law were considered unsatisfactory by some Hong Kong legal experts.

The pro-democracy uprising in Beijing in May–June 1989, and the subsequent military crackdown in Tiananmen Square, substantially affected the law's final shape. Because Hong Kong people had supported the student demonstrators by sending money and supplies, and by holding marches at which up to a million people took part, the communist authorities in Beijing became fearful that the territory would become a base for subversion.

To prevent this from happening, they made more stringent a section of the Basic Law, known as Article 23. This outlaws 'any act of treason, secession, sedition, subversion against the Central People's Government, or theft of state secrets'. It also prohibits foreign political organizations or bodies from conducting political activities in Hong Kong and prohibits political organizations in Hong Kong from establishing ties with foreign political organizations or bodies. This provision of the Basic Law is viewed by many as a potential threat to civil liberties.

Simon Li, Hong Kong's most senior legal figure involved in the drafting of the Basic Law, played an intimate role in the entire process. At the first meeting of the Basic Law Drafting Committee in Beijing in mid-1985, Simon and the other drafters were told that their first job would be to form another body, the Basic Law Consultative Committee, in Hong Kong. That body was to solicit views from the Hong Kong public and pass them on to the Drafting Committee.

Simon told the Chinese that he was interested primarily in the legal system, the courts, and the preservation of the laws of Hong Kong. So they made him the Hong Kong convenor of the legal subgroup (each subgroup also had a mainland convenor). But they also wanted him to serve on another subgroup, that involving the rights and duties of residents of the future Special Administrative Region (SAR). Its task, in effect, was to provide legal safeguards for Hong Kong's people after 1997. The only other legally trained person on the subgroup was Wang Shuwen, a mainland Chinese lawyer. So Simon was co-convenor of two of the five subgroups.

Each subgroup set about drafting its section of the Basic Law, held discussions among its members, and then reported to the plenary session.

Simon, at the first meeting, presented an entire draft of the section of the Basic Law on rights and responsibilities, article by article. 'I knew it would be torn to pieces,' he said, 'because it is far more detailed than is necessary. But I felt it would be easier to delete and redraft rather than leave something outstanding. We used that draft as the basis.'

At the first plenary session, the subgroup had to respond to questions from members of other subgroups as to why each provision was necessary, and to defend its wording. One major decision was whether the two main United Nations human rights conventions—the International Covenant on Civil and Political Rights and the International Covenant on Economic, Social, and Cultural Rights—should be written into the Basic Law. Simon concluded that it was not necessary. Most of the covenants' provisions, he decided, were 'covered already in the common law or our present ordinances'. He felt the future legislature should be allowed some room for manoeuver. For example, he said, by incorporating the right to life into the Basic Law, one would be tying the hands of the future legislature so that it could not restore the death penalty even if it wanted to.

But he did want to put in a provision giving women equal treatment. This, he found out, was not easy. When he approached one member to seek his support, the man refused, saying that 'when women are young they have their period, when married they have children, why should they get equal pay as men?' (The Basic Law, as finalized, does provide for equality of the sexes.)

While Simon dedicated himself to ensuring that rule of law continued in post-1997 Hong Kong, he was much less interested in the development of democratic institutions. Simon felt that an independent judiciary provided a better bulwark for Hong Kong against possible Beijing interference than a popularly elected legislature.

'The only way to assert your independence is through the courts,' he said. 'No matter how well you've written your political structure, if Beijing applies pressure, and the Special Administrative Region government succumbs, it will be exactly like England putting pressure on Hong Kong. All would be swept under the carpet and the world wouldn't know at all. But when you have an independent judiciary, it can't be swept under the carpet because judgment has been pronounced.'

A draft Basic Law was published in April 1988, followed by a five-month consultation period. One provision Simon was particularly unhappy about was China's insistence that its National People's Congress, not the Hong Kong courts, be given responsibility for interpreting the Basic Law.

One day, Simon and his wife, Lillian, were invited to a dinner hosted by Ji Pengfei, director of the Hong Kong and Macau Affairs Office of the State Council, the most senior Chinese official responsible for Hong Kong affairs. Also present were Ji's assistants, Li Hou and Lu Ping, as well as Xu Jiatun, China's main man in Hong Kong, and one of his deputies, Mao Junnian. It was a signal honour, as no other guests from Hong Kong were present.

The dinner passed pleasantly, with small talk about family matters and the general situation in Hong Kong, such as liberals going on hunger strikes. It appeared to Simon to be only a social occasion. But then, at the end of dinner, Ji told Simon that, if there was anything he wanted to pass on, he could just tell Lu Ping. He did, and the worrying passages in the draft Basic Law were subsequently amended, not to Simon's full satisfaction, but at least they had been improved. The revised draft still said the Standing Committee of the National People's Congress was the supreme authority for interpreting the Basic

Law, but it empowered courts in Hong Kong to interpret anything within the area of Hong Kong's autonomy.

In February 1989, a second draft of the Basic Law was published for another round of consultations. While this second draft was generally considered superior to the first, Simon remained unhappy with several provisions, in particular, with an article that said: 'Courts of the Hong Kong Special Administrative Region shall have no jurisdiction over cases relating to the acts of state.'

That sentence, he felt, was 'utterly superfluous and it serves to confuse'. Under the British administration, he said, the courts determined whether something is an act of state. But if that sentence stayed in the Basic Law, then it would no longer be up to the courts to decide if something is an act of state. Simon proposed deleting that sentence. He needed a two-thirds majority within the drafting committee to carry the day, but he got less than 50 per cent of the votes. He realized that some Hong Kong members of the drafting committee had joined mainland members in voting against him.

He was so unhappy that he made his views public. He prepared a paper in which he stated his fear that the Basic Law might lead to departures from traditional legal practice as well as create human rights problems. He explained that under the British legal system, 'When acts in national defence, foreign affairs and/or political acts have caused damage to the personal liberty or property of its citizens, the courts are empowered to entertain applications for writs of habeas corpus and for compensation.' But, he said, 'if the HKSAR courts are to be precluded from hearing of these aforesaid applications, then it would be against the original legal system now in force and this law becomes contradictory to the spirit of the Joint Declaration.'

'Suppose a member of the Liberation Army stationed in the HKSAR arrests a Hong Kong resident,' he said. 'Under the existing legal system, the said resident may apply to the Hong

Kong court for a writ of habeas corpus and the court has the power to adjudicate in the said matter. But this matter may involve national act or national defence or Central People's Government and HKSAR relationship. When the Standing Committee of the National People's Congress (NPC) in their interpretation of the relevant provisions give an opinion that the act is an act of state, then the Court of Final Adjudication in the Region cannot question jurisdiction over the case. Under such circumstances, how are human rights to be protected?'

Simon was also troubled by Article 157, which vested the power of interpretation of the Basic Law in the Standing Committee of China's National People's Congress.

As a judge, he knew that interpretation and judgment were closely linked. 'If you have to seek their interpretation before giving judgment,' he said, 'you are losing your independence. You are asking them how to judge it.'

'I want Hong Kong courts to have the power to interpret all the provisions of the Basic Law,' he said, 'with the Standing Committee reserving its right to interpret certain provisions relating to foreign affairs, defence, and matters within their jurisdiction.'

Simon displayed much courage in voicing his criticisms of the draft Basic Law. But, despite his urging, the objectionable articles remained largely as they were.

On 4 April 1990, the National People's Congress officially promulgated the Basic Law of the Hong Kong Special Administrative Region. 'I'm glad it's over,' Simon said. 'I'm fairly satisfied with it but as you know I'm not completely satisfied with the two articles concerning jurisdiction and interpretation. But they have made a slight improvement.'

The promulgation of the Basic Law coincided with another event of significance in Simon's life: the appointment of his daughter Gladys as Queen's Counsel, or senior barrister. She and another lawyer, Jacqueline Leong, appointed at the same time, became the first women in Hong Kong's history to be so honoured.

Simon was extremely proud of her and gave a lavish dinner in her honour at the Hong Kong Club, inviting relatives and family friends. After most of the guests had left, he joined Gladys and a group of her friends, introducing himself jokingly as 'the father of Queen's Counsel Gladys Li', and regaling them with tales of the legal profession in the early days.

Chapter 25

Gladys Li: Chairman of the Bar

On the afternoon of 13 May 1995, Gladys Li, a few days shy of her forty-seventh birthday, led a delegation of the Council of the Hong Kong Bar Association, of which she was chairman, to a meeting with the legal subgroup of the Preliminary Working Committee (PWC), of which her father, Simon, was the Hong Kong convenor. The PWC had been formed by China to assist it in organizing the transition to Chinese sovereignty after Beijing decided it could not count on Governor Chris Patten to cooperate.

The meeting with the legal subgroup was difficult to arrange, even though her father was its Hong Kong convenor. Perhaps each side was wary of the other. To the PWC, it might have seemed that the Bar Association tended to side with the British establishment, while to the bar, the PWC was a body whose legitimacy was in doubt.

For some time, the Bar Association had been trying to find out exactly what the legal subgroup was doing. It knew, of course, that the legal subgroup was reviewing all existing Hong Kong laws to decide which ones would be kept and which ones repealed after 1997. But it did not know precisely which laws had been identified as ones that would have to go, except for those publicized in the press, such as the electoral laws passed under Governor Patten. The bar wanted this information so that it could study the laws earmarked for repeal, to see whether they really were in conflict with the Basic Law.

Even though Gladys knew all the Hong Kong members of the subgroup and had met some of the mainland members, the atmosphere in the meeting room inside the imposing New China News Agency building was somewhat strained as the two groups faced each other on opposite sides of a long conference table. Gladys, flanked by members of the bar, sat across from Shao Tianren and Simon, the two co-convenors.

After introductions were made, Shao invited Gladys to speak. The bar delegation had brought along an interpreter because some of its members, including Gladys, were less than fluent in Chinese. Gladys first produced a document containing proposed ground rules for meetings between the Bar Council and the legal subgroup. But Shao countered by saying that the ground rules were only being presented for the first time; besides, there was no decision for the two sides to conduct regular meetings. He said members of the Bar Council could speak in an individual capacity; any views expressed would not be considered those of the Bar Association. Simon then interposed by saying that the same applied to members of the legal subgroup. Each person would only be expressing an individual opinion.

Since the Bar Council's main interest was to find out which laws were slated for repeal, Gladys began with a gentle probe by asking how much of the work of the legal subgroup could be made public. She said if the bar did not know what the legal subgroup was working on, it would make discussion difficult. Choosing her words carefully, she pointed out that the issue of repealing existing laws was one of great concern 'both to lawyers and to all the people of Hong Kong.' She said unless the bar knew which laws were determined to be in contravention of the Basic Law and the reasons for this determination, then the bar could not be effective in advising clients.

Gladys cited Article 160 of the Basic Law, which says the Standing Committee of China's National People's Congress can declare laws in Hong Kong to be in contravention of the Basic Law. But, she pointed out, no procedure is prescribed. She said this lack of knowledge of any procedures whereby the National People's Congress could declare laws invalid without consultation with the Hong Kong public, in particular without the participation of the legal profession, was cause for concern. She pointed out that in Hong Kong, laws are repealed through a legislative process, including consultations with the public and lawyers in a process that was transparent.

Shao, in response, said that the legal subgroup's work was confined to scrutinizing Hong Kong laws and that it was up to the Standing Committee of the National People's Congress to declare which of those contravened the Basic Law. He added reassuringly that China's policy was that Hong Kong laws would remain basically unchanged and he could not understand the worries that the bar had expressed.

Simon jumped in and said that the Bar Association should not be misled by the media, adding that his remarks on the bill of rights had been distorted by the press. This precipitated a rare public clash between him and his daughter.

Gladys said the so-called 'misunderstanding with the press' reflected a lack of transparency in the work of the legal subgroup. She said if everything had been put down in writing there would not have been any room for misunderstanding.

Asked later if she felt she was humiliating her father, she said, 'Perhaps I'm being a bit insensitive. He appears there in his capacity as a member of the subgroup just as I am appearing there in my capacity as chairman of the bar. As far as I am concerned, the family aspect of the relationship is excluded from those kinds of meetings.'

The two-hour meeting ended with what members of the Bar Council considered a long propagandistic speech by Chen Ziying, an official of the Hong Kong and Macau Affairs Office and also deputy secretary general of the PWC. Although he said that 'very few laws' had been found that contravened the Basic Law, he did not provide the Bar Council with a list. He also voiced delight that the legal subgroup had had the chance to meet Gladys and other members of the bar delegation, and thanked the bar for the attention it had accorded to the legal subgroup, implying that the bar had recognized the legitimacy of the PWC by that meeting, precisely what Gladys and other members of the delegation had wanted to avoid doing. Emerging from the meeting, Gladys thought to herself that it had been a total waste of time, and that the bar had unwittingly provided the Chinese with a propaganda opportunity.

Gladys and her father, miles apart politically, had a tacit agreement not to discuss politics, to avoid fighting in the presence of her mother. One of the few occasions when tempers flared was when father and daughter arranged to have dinner together. Simon found his way to the car park blocked and arrived late. He explained his delay by saying that there was probably some pro-democracy demonstration going on. Gladys countered by saying that she thought parts of Central District had been cordoned off so people could walk around to see the the special lights on display to mark the anniversary of the power company. Her father, she said, blamed everything on democracy. On the way home, the two continued their argument in the car. He dropped her off at her apartment, drove home, then telephoned her to continue the argument. It was all very silly, Gladys thought, and her mother was right in saying they could not talk about the subject without getting worked up over it.

Simon, on his part, may occasionally feel that perhaps it was a mistake to have sent Gladys off to study in England at such a young age, before she had received a proper education in such things as Chinese language and culture. Gladys was born in England when Simon was a law student and, though Simon took her to Hong Kong at the age of five, she was sent to England again, to boarding school, at age eleven. There she lived until she was thirty-four years old, having spent ten years trying to build up a legal practice in an old-fashioned, male-dominated atmosphere. She uprooted herself from England in 1982 to start a new career in Hong Kong.

In Hong Kong, she quickly achieved professional recognition. A private person who socialized little, Gladys devoted herself to her professional work and family. She never married, but visited her parents once or twice every week. Gladys was a serious person who had little time for small talk. Her black hair, liberally streaked with gray, was cut short, almost like that of a boy. She eschewed makeup except on special occasions and kept her weight down by eating only one full meal a day.

Although the meeting between the Bar Association and the PWC was unsatisfactory to both sides, it at least established informal contact between them. The PWC went out of existence in December 1995 and was replaced by the Preparatory Committee, a somewhat larger body of 150 people, the following month. All members of the PWC became members of the Preparatory Committee. Simon was one of nine vice chairmen.

One of the Preparatory Committee's main tasks was to establish a Selection Committee which would, in turn, choose the first chief executive of the SAR. Since China had decided to set up a Provisional Legislature, the Preparatory Committee decided that the Selection Committee would also choose the members of the Provisional Legislature, a decision that aroused great controversy.

On 30 March, the Preparatory Committee invited the Bar Association to a meeting to discuss the method of forming the Selection Committee. The Bar Association was happy to give its views on the issue, but it did not want its presence at the meeting to be interpreted as an endorsement of the Provisional Legislature. Accordingly, Gladys, in the name of the Bar Council, first sent a letter to the Preparatory Committee setting out the bar's position on the Provisional Legislature.

'We recognize the legal validity' of the decision to set up the Preparatory Committee, the letter said, 'but we doubt the constitutionality of the decision of the Preparatory Committee on the establishment of a Provisional Legislature.'

The Bar Association's meeting with the Preparatory Committee was held in the five-star Grand Hyatt Hotel, along with other professional bodies, such as the Hong Kong Society of Accountants. There were about eighty people present, representing some ten or twelve groups. The meeting was presided over by Nellie Fong, a Preparatory Committee member from Hong Kong. After she declared the meeting open, there were a few seconds of silence as nobody seemed anxious to be the first to speak. Gladys volunteered herself as the first speaker and, for several minutes, explained the Bar Council's position on the setting up of a Selection Committee.

To Gladys's surprise, several judges were also present. They, too, seemed unsure of their role. Nellie Fong explained that the Local Judges Association was a professional body and so had been invited. Gladys then rose and said that it was inappropriate for judges to be present. She said that procedures for forming the Selection Committee could be challenged in court, and if judges had been involved in advising how the Selection Committee should be constituted, then it could potentially compromise the judiciary. Similarly, since the legality of the Provisional Legislature could be challenged in court, it would be inappropriate for judges to serve on the Selection Committee.

Shortly after the meeting, Gladys received a message that Lu Ping, who had succeeded Ji Pengfei as head of the Hong Kong

231

and Macau Affairs Office, wanted to meet with the members of the Bar Council. As a result, Gladys and three other council members had a breakfast meeting with him in a villa in Stanley owned by the New China News Agency. Lu began by asking a Chinese legal authority, Xiao Weiyun, to explain the Chinese position on the Provisional Legislature. Xiao, in his discourse, said that because Britain had unilaterally decided on the method to conduct the 1995 elections, the intended 'through train' for the legislature—under which legislators elected in 1995 would serve until 1999, straddling the change in sovereignty in 1997—had been derailed. The Chinese considered electoral laws adopted under Governor Patten to be contrary to the Basic Law and hence invalid beyond 1 July 1997. Without electoral laws, he said, no elections could be held. And, since there could not be a legislative vacuum, there was no alternative but to set up a Provisional Legislature.

When Gladys and her colleagues asked which provisions of the various electoral laws had violated which section of the Basic Law, they received no clear answer. The Chinese position, it seemed, was that all the electoral laws passed during the Patten administration would be repealed because they had all been adopted after the breakdown in talks between Britain and China.

After Xiao finished speaking, Lu Ping turned to Gladys and asked her to speak. She articulated the Bar Council's position on the legality, or lack thereof, of the Provisional Legislature. She pointed out that the Preparatory Committee was merely a subordinate body of the National People's Congress and had no authority to do anything beyond its remit. The Provisional Legislature would technically be the first legislature of the Hong Kong Special Administrative Region. Since the National People's Congress had prescribed how the first legislature was to be formed, any departure from the NPC decision, such as the setting up of a Provisional Legislature, would have no legal or constitutional basis.

Obviously, a wide gulf existed between the Bar Council and the Preparatory Committee. Neither was able to convince the other, but both saw the need to continue the dialogue. As a result, Gladys and her associates were invited to Beijing to meet with various Chinese bodies.

Gladys had never been to Beijing before. The trip was, in a sense, a lobbying exercise. Gladys had been involved in political lobbying before, but her orientation was towards Britain. Now, with Britain about to withdraw from Hong Kong, Gladys shifted her lobbying efforts towards China. On Sunday, 14 July, she and the rest of the bar delegation arrived in Beijing and checked into the Holiday Inn Crowne Plaza.

Their busy three-day programme included meetings with representatives of the Hong Kong and Macau Affairs Office, the legal subgroup of the Preparatory Committee, the Legislative Affairs Commission of the Standing Committee of the National People's Congress, the Ministry of Foreign Affairs, the Ministry of Justice, the All-China Lawyers Association, the Supreme People's Court, and the Supreme People's Procuratorate.

Their first session was at the Hong Kong and Macau Affairs Office, with Director Lu Ping. Gladys found it encouraging that Director Lu seemed willing to consider a suggestion by the Bar Council that the Preparatory Committee make public its tentative recommendations regarding which laws should be repealed before sending them to the National People's Congress, so that Hong Kong's public and professional bodies, like the Bar Association, could comment on them.

On the whole, the meeting with the legal subgroup of the Preparatory Committee was the most substantive during the three days of discussions. The Hong Kong visitors felt they had at least had an opportunity to present their views. But they felt they had achieved little beyond that, apart from being told that further views would also be welcome. The standpoint of the legal subgroup, they felt, was very different from their own.

233

'When we were discussing the Bill of Rights Ordinance and electoral laws,' Gladys recalled later, 'what we were told about the Chinese objections appeared all to be based on political considerations and not legal considerations. Because we felt the gap was so substantial, we felt we hadn't achieved very much.'

When the Hong Kong lawyers asked which provision in a specific law destined for repeal appeared to contravene the Basic Law, they were told that their approach was too technical. But, in Gladys's mind, 'we regard that as legitimate and the only proper approach to take'.

Everywhere they went, they were fêted. At one lunch, Madam Liu Yang, Deputy Minister of Justice, remarked on the fact that both the bar chairman, Gladys, and the vice chairman, Audrey Eu, were women. The two then told her that the association's honorary secretary was also a woman.

'Don't the men mind having the association run by women?' asked Madam Liu in surprise. She was assured that male barristers did not seem to mind and, in fact, people in Hong Kong did not think there was anything particularly noteworthy about the chairman and vice chairman being women.

The moments of levity during the Hong Kong lawyers' sojourn in Beijing contrasted with the serious nature of their discussions. There were some encouraging signs of progress, such as on the knotty issue of the right to interpret the Basic Law.

A senior Chinese official with the Legislative Affairs Commission of the National People's Congress suggested that the question of interpretation of the Basic Law need not be such a serious problem. He said that it was up to Hong Kong's Court of Final Appeal to decide whether a particular question required an interpretation from the Standing Committee of the National People's Congress. And if the court decided it was not necessary, the Standing Committee would not step in.

Political differences did not diminish Simon's affection for his daughter. He exhibited clear parental pride in Gladys's achievements. After she led the Bar Council's visit to Beijing, Simon reported, he received 'many good comments about my daughter' as he met Chinese friends and acquaintances who had seen Gladys. They said that she did not try to stir up trouble, but sought to persuade through reasoning. The biggest compliment came from a man who said 'meeting Gladys and having discussions with her is like reading a new book'.

Chapter 26

Arthur Li: Doctor and Educator

On 6th September 1996, Professor Arthur Li, vice chancellor of the Chinese University of Hong Kong and one of the world's leading surgeons, returned to Hong Kong from Beijing, where he had taken part in a two-day session of the Chief Executive Subgroup of the Preparatory Committee. This momentous meeting had adopted recommendations on how to nominate the first Chief Executive of the Hong Kong Special Administrative Region.

Arthur and his colleagues had decided on procedures that were open and transparent, at a time when many people in Hong Kong believed that they would have little say on the subject because, they suspected, China had secretly decided who the chief executive would be.

Arthur, brother of David and nephew of Simon, had been invited to the New China News Agency the previous year and asked if he was interested in joining the Preparatory Committee. At the time, he was the president of the Hong Kong College of Surgeons.

Arthur was not inexperienced in Hong Kong politics. From 1985 to 1990, he had served on the Basic Law Consultative

Committee, which advised the Basic Law Drafting Committee. For four years, he had spent every Saturday holding meetings, with Chinese officials and people from Hong Kong. 'It was a very interesting exercise,' he recalled, 'and I learned a lot.' And in 1994, he was appointed a Hong Kong affairs adviser by China. After thinking over China's latest offer, he accepted. He was assigned to the Chief Executive Subgroup, which was to decide on how the Chief Executive should be chosen.

The twenty or so members of the Chief Executive Subgroup held a series of meetings in Beijing, culminating in the session on 4–5 September. The Basic Law provided that the first chief executive, instead of being elected through universal suffrage, would be chosen by a 400-member selection committee. Many people in Hong Kong were concerned that the committee would merely be a rubber stamp, endorsing whomever China might choose. For this reason, the subgroup members felt, it was important that the work of the selection committee be open and fair, and that the procedures for choosing members of the selection committee, as well as the procedures by which candidates for chief executive were to be nominated, should be transparent. If candidates were subjected to political vetting, then the legitimacy of the whole procedure would be open to question.

The subgroup's decision to make the nomination process as open as possible was widely applauded. The *South China Morning Post* reported the news on the front page under the headline 'New rules to make choice of first chief more open.' The subgroup decided that would-be candidates should submit themselves to questioning by selection committee members in the presence of the media so that the public would know where each candidate stood on major issues.

The subgroup also decided that candidates would have to disclose if they had a criminal record, and whether they possessed a foreign passport. Arthur, mindful of the situation in

Russia after the election of President Boris Yeltsin in 1996, suggested that a candidate should also disclose the state of his health. The suggestion was adopted. Arthur was pleased at the role he played in decisions so vital to Hong Kong's future.

Being vice chancellor, or head, of the Chinese University made Arthur one of Hong Kong's top educators. He was almost as surprised in landing this job as he was in being asked to become a member of the Preparatory Committee, which happened at almost the same time.

Arthur was dean of the university's medical school when it became known that the eminent physicist Charles Kao, called the father of fibre optics, who had served as vice chancellor since 1987, would be retiring. The university decided to launch a worldwide search for a successor and advertisements were placed overseas in January 1995.

In mid-April, Sir Q. W. Lee, a leading banker who chaired the Chinese University council, telephoned to inform Arthur that his name had been put forward for the job. Was he prepared to stand? Arthur had become an internationally known physician and educator since he returned to Hong Kong in 1982 to take charge of the department of surgery of a new medical college being set up by the Chinese University. He had quickly become a pillar of the medical establishment, serving as chairman of surgical services of the Prince of Wales Hospital, the teaching hospital of the Chinese University. He was president of the Hong Kong Surgical Society and a professor of surgery. His pioneering surgical procedures had helped to put Hong Kong on the world map. But becoming head of a major educational institution would present new challenges and opportunities. He allowed his name to stand.

Two months later he was interviewed by a headhunting firm in New York that had been hired by the university's search committee. He was grilled for four hours, with questions, he said, going back to what he had done in kindergarten. After that, he was interviewed for three hours by the search committee.

The next thing he knew, he was conducting an operation in Australia in mid-August, 'elbow-deep in blood, when someone came in and said there was an urgent call from Hong Kong'. It was Sir Q. W., who told Arthur that he had been chosen as the next vice chancellor in a unanimous decision. Arthur decided to continue to practice medicine while serving as head of the Chinese University. In the previous few years, he had scored a number of breakthroughs in the surgical world. In 1993, for example, he had successfully transplanted half of a man's liver into his three-year-old daughter, who was in danger of dying from liver disease. The procedure had only been performed before in Brisbane, Kyoto, and Chicago, never in Hong Kong or elsewhere in South-East Asia.

Even before this operation, the team at the Chinese University under Arthur's direction was recognized as leading international experts in the field of liver cancer treatment. At a symposium in 1991, attended by over 400 doctors, Arthur explained how inoperable liver cancer could be treated and thus prolong the lives of liver cancer patients. One procedure developed in Hong Kong, Arthur explained, involved targeting and concentrating radioactive isotopes specifically in the liver tumor. He compared this to the use of 'smart' missiles in the Gulf War. 'The missiles are directed to the tumour in the liver and the warhead will then destroy it while the surrounding normal liver tissue is spared,' he explained. The procedure developed by Arthur became known as the Li technique.

Arthur's enquiring mind was evident at a young age. When about four years old, he went downstairs to his Aunt Fanny's apartment when she was out to admire her tank of tropical fish. They were of different colours and sizes and Arthur wondered whether they could survive outside of the tank, and for how long. In quest of scientific data, the boy scooped the fish out one by one, placing some in the sun and others in the shade.

He soon found that the ones in the sun did not survive for long. He also wondered whether there was a correlation between the differently coloured fish and their ability to survive. He would keep one fish out for a couple of minutes and return it to the water. If it survived, he scooped it out again and, this time, kept it out a little longer. In the course of the afternoon, he killed off all his aunt's tropical fish.

This crude experiment was not encouraged by Aunt Fanny, or by his father. F. S. gave him such a spanking that he would remember it for the rest of his life. But it did not snuff out Arthur's inquiring mind. He loved to go into the kitchen and watch live chickens being cut up by the cook. As the boy grew up, he decided to become a doctor. His grandfather, Koon-chun, thought the nimble-minded lad should study law, but Arthur knew what he wanted and stuck to it.

At the age of sixteen, Arthur was sent, like his brother David, to Uppingham School. David had already graduated and Arthur found himself the only Chinese student there. Worse, Arthur found himself the object of much curiosity. Since he was the only Chinese the other students knew, everything he did was interpreted not as the acts of Arthur Li, but as Chinese acts. He was no longer an individual. He felt like the representative of the entire Chinese nation. Likewise, his views were seen as the views of one billion Chinese. It was a heavy responsibility, and it made him more competitive because he felt he had to uphold the honour of the Chinese race. It was greater pressure than he had ever encountered, and it made him apply himself that much more.

After Uppingham he was admitted to Cambridge University where, at last, he was able to study medicine, his life-long ambition. He enjoyed university life immensely, and did well. For the next three years, he lived like a proper young Englishman, rowing for King's College, and won first class honours. He spent the following three years in London, where he did his clinical training at Middlesex Hospital Medical School.

After he qualified, Arthur entered the real world. In Britain, a medical student was expected to work for six months in a medical job and another six months at a surgical job before registering to be an independent practitioner. Arthur had to get a job as a house officer, or intern, for six months. Having graduated with first class honours and won prizes in medical school, he considered himself eminently employable. He applied to seventeen hospitals in and around London. He was turned down by all of them.

He could not believe what he was experiencing. He would sit in an interview room and watch his classmates who had done much more poorly get jobs while he was rejected. Sometimes he was told that he had no experience. At other times he was told he was too good and that the hospital was looking for someone quite ordinary.

Desperate, Arthur wrote to a professor who had examined him on kidney disease. Later, during the interview, the professor asked if he had applied for other jobs and Arthur answered yes, he had applied for seventeen other jobs. 'Why didn't you get any of them?' the professor asked. 'I think it is racial prejudice,' Arthur answered candidly. 'Why don't you think I'll be prejudiced too?' the professor continued. 'Because you're an academic,' said Arthur disarmingly. He got the job.

After this six-month stint, his professor advised him to return to Middlesex for six months of surgery training. He took his advice and, after six months, decided to be a surgeon. He worked at various small hospitals on a rotational basis before going in 1973 to St Mary's Hospital in London as a registrar, the equivalent of a senior resident in the United States. Two years later he moved to Royal Free Hospital as senior registrar, just one rung below consultant, the highest surgical post. He was, at the age of twenty-nine, one of the youngest senior registrars in England.

Perhaps surprisingly, in view of his experience of racial prejudice, Arthur ended up marrying an English girl. He met Diana Chester when she was a nurse and he was a student at Middlesex Hospital. They found a strong mental rapport with each other. She was planning to do a doctorate in epidemiology when Arthur proposed marriage. Their first son, Alexander, arrived in 1975.

In 1977, Arthur was given a one-year research fellowship in the United States. He was associated with three institutions: Harvard Medical School, Massachusetts General Hospital, and Shriners Burns Institute. He did much research, taught external medicine, and enjoyed the experience tremendously. In 1979, he was put on the surgical staff of Mass General and made instructor in surgery at Harvard. His talents were being recognized. At this time, his second son, Peter, was born, and Arthur thought he would make his life in the United States.

But Diana became homesick for England. Their two sons, too, needed to begin schooling. Arthur decided to return to England.

Before long, however, he became restless. England was beset by trade unionism, and Arthur found the atmosphere stifling. In 1981, at the age of thirty-five, he started to look for other pastures. He heard that the Chinese University in Hong Kong was setting up the colony's second medical school, and wanted someone to take charge of the department of surgery. After being interviewed, he was told the job was his; he thus returned to Hong Kong to work and to make a home.

Chapter 27

One Family, Four Nationalities

The impending takeover of Hong Kong by China was extremely worrying to the vast majority of people in the British colony when it was first announced in 1984. Most Hong Kong residents were refugees from the Communists, or the children of such refugees. They had fled China in earlier decades and found refuge in Hong Kong, but now their refuge was to be handed back to China. In this situation, many decided they would have to flee once more.

Some applied to join family members abroad, mainly in Canada, the United States, Australia, or New Zealand. Others invested large sums of money to be eligible for business migration programmes. Still others simply purchased passports of convenience from island states such as Tonga, not intending to live there, but simply wanting security in the knowledge that if they ever had to leave Hong Kong, they would have the means to do so. Many who left intended to return to Hong Kong after obtaining an 'insurance policy' in the form of a foreign passport.

The number of those leaving annually rose to 30,000 by the mid-1980s and to over 45,000 in the late 1980s. After the Tiananmen Square massacre, the number of people leaving soared to over 60,000 a year. To keep people from leaving Hong Kong, Britain launched a so-called nationality scheme, under which 50,000 key families would be given British passports so that they would have the confidence to remain in Hong Kong, secure in the knowledge that they could leave if worst came to worst.

Even though members of the Li family were very much involved on both the British and Chinese sides in drawing up the rules for the post-1997 dispensation, the Lis themselves were not exempt from apprehensions about the future. One example was the children of the horse lover Li Lan-sang, who sought in various ways to protect themselves and their families.

After the death of racing enthusiast Lan-sang in 1969 (at the race course, watching his horse coming in), his principal wife went to live in the United States with her children. But his concubine and her children—Eric, Helena, Alan, and Cornel—remained in Hong Kong. Eric was a businessman, Alan a chartered accountant, Cornel a dentist, and Helena a housewife. All the brothers had returned to Hong Kong to work after studying abroad.

Justifiably or not, they felt they had been mistreated by the senior branches of the Li family, perhaps because their mother was a concubine and because their father's mother, too, had been a concubine. Since Lan-sang had been on the board of directors of the Bank of East Asia for almost four decades and was one of the bank's largest shareholders, his family expected his seat on the board to go to one of his sons. To their surprise and chagrin, it went to their cousin, Dr Henry Li, the brother of Aubrey and Fook-kow.

The hot-tempered Eric, eldest son, considered himself head of the family. He wrote a blistering letter to his cousin F. S., senior member of the Li family serving on the bank's board, to complain. F. S. sought to pacify him by pointing out that there was no provision for seats on the board to be passed on from father to son. F. S. recalled that when his own father, Koon-chun, died, his seat had gone to someone outside the family. He pointed out that Henry had served as the bank's medical adviser for eighteen years and was the person most acceptable to the other parties. Eric and his brothers were not placated by this reply and, for years, refused to speak with F. S. It would be twelve years before Lan-sang's family was able to fight their way on to the board again, when Alan, like his father an avid racing enthusiast, joined in 1982.

Eric devoted his life to business, working first for Sonca Industries, a wholly-owned subsidiary of Union Carbide that manufactured flashlights. After ten years, he joined the Hong Kong Trade Development Council, subsequently becoming their United States representative, based in New York. But, by the time of the Joint Declaration, Eric had been running the family company, Kowloon Dairy, which Lan-sang had helped to finance, for a decade. His brother Alan, a chartered accountant with a French wife, helped him run the company. Their brother, Cornel, while a member of the board, concentrated on being a dentist. His wife, like himself, was a British citizen.

The family of Eric's wife, Jean, lived in San Francisco and, because of this, she returned there to give birth each time she was pregnant. Being a United States citizen herself, she wanted to be sure her children were born on American soil. So Evan and Erica, like their mother, were American citizens. As a result, Eric's entire family was American. But Eric was not. He carried a British Dependent Territory Citizen passport which, while allowing him to travel, did not give him the right to live anywhere outside Hong Kong.

Soon after the Joint Declaration was made public, Eric decided that he would have to leave Hong Kong. 'I don't think I can live under Communist rule,' he explained. He did not trust the Communists. 'They say the governor is going to be a Hong Kong person,' he said. 'I don't think so. When the time comes, somebody from the central government will be sitting right on top. I don't mind losing everything else, but my freedom, that's one thing I don't want to lose.'

Eric believed China's promise to keep Hong Kong as a capitalist society. 'No doubt they probably will run Hong Kong like a capitalist system,' he said. 'But they will be running it, not you.'

Eric uttered those words in 1991. At the time, he said he planned to leave Hong Kong in 1995. In late 1996, however, he was still in Hong Kong. 'I've changed my mind,' he said candidly. 'I'm staying.' In the intervening years, he explained, China had changed a great deal. His company, Kowloon Dairy, now had a joint venture operating in Guangzhou, and he was going to Shanghai to look for another joint venture partner there.

No one thing made him change his mind. 'My mind changed gradually,' he explained. 'I don't know anything about politics. I'm not a politician. I don't worry about it. As long as I'm left to live my way of life and do my business, then I'm fine, and I can see that it'll continue, probably for my lifetime.'

'I cannot see any reason why the Chinese government would want to put Hong Kong in a situation where it would die economically,' he continued. 'In 1991, I wasn't sure which way China was going. But I've been back to China and I really don't see any difference between Hong Kong and cities like Beijing and Shanghai.'

But while his view of Hong Kong's future had changed drastically in five years, he still wanted to take precautions. Eric applied for and was granted a full British passport under Britain's nationality scheme. Since Eric's wife and children were all American citizens, he would have little trouble settling down in the United States. But, with a British passport, he felt doubly secure.

Eric's siblings, too, were protected. His brothers, Alan and Cornel, qualified for British passports because they had spent many years studying in Britain. His sister, Helena, emigrated to

Canada with her husband in the late 1980s and returned to Hong Kong in 1991, a month after acquiring Canadian citizenship. So, on the eve of the handover of Hong Kong to China, Eric had become British, while his wife and children were American citizens; Alan, too, was British, with a French wife and French children. Cornel was British, with a British wife and British children, and their sister Helena and her husband and their children were Canadians. It was, in a sense, a typical Hong Kong family. Only in Hong Kong would a family with four nationalities be unremarkable.

Chapter 28

Andrew Li: The First Chief Justice

June 30, 1997, a date anticipated by some and dreaded by many, dawned under leaden skies. This was the last day of British administration in Hong Kong. At midnight, sovereignty would return to China after more than 150 years. It was a day full of emotion: anticipation, sadness, fear, and hope.

Crowds of people mobbed Government House in the afternoon to wave goodbye and to catch a final glimpse of its occupant, Chris Patten, the twenty-eighth and last governor of Hong Kong, as he left it for the last time to attend an open-air farewell ceremony. The ceremony, presided over by Prince Charles, heir to the British throne, was a grand affair, but it was boycotted by the Chinese as well as by the incoming chief executive, Tung Chee-hwa. The Sino-British bickering went on until the very last minute.

The highlight of the day was the handover ceremony, in the just completed annex to the Convention Centre. The British team included Prince Charles, Prime Minister Tony Blair, and Foreign Secretary Robin Cook. The Chinese team, headed by President Jiang Zemin, included Premier Li Peng and Foreign Minister Qian Qichen.

Just before midnight, Prince Charles, wearing a blue, double-breasted jacket, stood behind a rostrum decorated with his coat of arms and delivered a sobering speech in which he hailed Hong Kong's 'triumphal success' under British administration. Voicing affection and good wishes to the people of Hong Kong, he concluded: 'We shall not forget you.'

It was then the turn of President Jiang Zemin to speak. The Chinese leader, wearing a business suit, was equally solemn, noting that people all over the world were watching Hong Kong. Then the Union Jack and the Hong Kong flag were lowered to the strains of 'God Save the Queen'. This was followed by the raising of the five-starred Chinese flag and the bauhinia flower regional emblem of the SAR, as a Chinese military band played the stirring 'March of the Volunteers'—the Chinese national anthem. Those were the most emotional moments of an emotion-packed night.

As soon as the Chinese flag reached the top of the specially designed flagpole, a jet of artificially generated wind emanating from the hollow flagpole caught the flag and sent it billowing out. This led to a round of spontaneous applause on the part of Chinese in the hall. The British were silent.

With the change in flags, the transition was complete. The British were no longer masters over Hong Kong. Chris Patten boarded the royal yacht *Britannia* and sent his last message to London: 'I have relinquished the administration of this government. God Save the Queen.'

The departure of the British cleared the way for the Chinese to do the work they were impatient to do: the setting up of the government of the newly born Special Administrative Region. President Jiang, in a brief ceremony, pronounced the establishment of the SAR. Then came the inauguration ceremony, beginning with the swearing in of Chief Executive Tung Chee-hwa and his principal officials, presided over by Premier Li Peng. This was followed by the chief executive presiding over the swearing in of his government: the Executive Council, the Provisional Legislative Council, and the judiciary.

This last ceremony, the most colourful, was led by Andrew Li, the first chief justice of the Hong Kong Special Administrative Region. Andrew himself, in flowing black robes, led the other members of the newly constituted Court of Final Appeal and the bewigged judges of the High Court, in rich red robes, in reciting the oath of office.

In heavily Cantonese-accented Mandarin, Andrew uttered these words: 'I will uphold the Basic Law of the Hong Kong Special Administrative Region of the People's Republic of China, bear allegiance to the HKSAR of the PRC, serve the HKSAR conscientiously, dutifully, in full accordance with the law, honestly and with integrity, safeguard the law and administer it without fear or favour, self-interest or deceit.'

In deference to the many Western judges who knew no Chinese, but who would continue to serve in the SAR judiciary, the oath was repeated in English, at which point the Western judges chimed in.

In a few minutes, the entire ceremony was over. The SAR was in existence, as were all three branches of its government. For many, the sight of so many non-Chinese judges, resplendent in red robes, appeared jarring, but somehow reassuring, providing as they did a sign that, even though sovereignty was changing, much of what was familiar would remain.

Tung Chee-hwa's choice of Andrew as the first chief justice was particularly welcomed in the weeks before the handover. In the thirteen years since the Joint Declaration was signed, the feeling had grown within Hong Kong that the preservation of an independent judiciary was vital to the territory's future. Everyone knew that the chief executive would be appointed by China, and that the legislature would not be wholly elected by universal suffrage. So hopes were pinned on the judiciary.

Andrew was one of Hong Kong's most eminent barristers, and his family had had close ties with the British colonial government. His father, Fook-kow, had been a senior official in the government. And he himself had served as a member of Chris Patten's inner cabinet, the Executive Council. So Andrew was seen as someone who could by no stretch of the imagination be deemed as pro-China. His decisions, it was felt, would be based purely on the law rather than on politics.

The fear that China would put political pressure on Chinese judges inspired a great effort to get as many overseas judges as possible to serve on the top court, the Court of Final Appeal. This fear was enhanced after China vetoed Britain's proposal that two of the five judges could come from overseas, insisting that the number be limited to one.

Still, the Chinese did not insist that local judges be Chinese nationals, except for the chief justice. Traditionally, few Chinese were interested in joining the judiciary, whose ranks were filled with judges from Britain, Australia, and other parts of the Commonwealth. In fact, when Andrew was sworn in, he was the only Chinese national among the SAR's top judges. And even he had to give up his British passport to qualify for the post.

Andrew's willingness to forego his British passport showed how much had changed in Hong Kong as 1997 approached. China's willingness to accept Andrew's nomination as Chief Justice, even though he had served as one of Chris Patten's closest advisers, also showed to what extent China had changed. As the date of the handover approached, both sides had the same objective: to preserve Hong Kong's stability and prosperity after 1997, without regard to ideological concerns.

Andrew was dedicated to the law and was not interested in political involvement. Patten's predecessor, Sir David Wilson, had offered him a seat on the Legislative Council in 1988, but Andrew had turned it down.

After the arrival of the new governor, Andrew was again

approached, this time to see if he would be willing to accept a seat on the Executive Council. Patten was not an expert on China, unlike his immediate predecessors, all knowledgeable in Chinese history, politics, and culture, and who could speak and read Chinese with ease. It was generally felt that Patten would be heavily dependent on his advisers.

Andrew was sounded out in August, a month after Patten's arrival, by Baroness Lydia Dunn, the senior member of the Executive Council, who called one day to invite him to lunch. Andrew had an inkling that this was a special occasion. Lydia had invited him for lunches and dinners before, but always with other people, and always the invitation came from her secretary to his secretary. This time, the baroness called him personally.

Turning things over in his mind, Andrew decided that, if invited to join the Executive Council, he would accept, since this was an opportunity to serve Hong Kong at a critical moment in history. 'I regard myself as being in public service,' Andrew explained. 'I distinguish that from being in politics, or being a politician, let alone being an opportunist.'

Andrew had a vision of Hong Kong and its future under Deng Xiaoping's concept of 'one country, two systems'. Hong Kong, he felt, 'will be the most modern city of China, and it has a definite role to play in China's modernization as China developed into a world power in the Pacific Century'. And, he thought, he would approach his work in the Executive Council with that vision in mind. Long before he arrived for lunch at the Garden Lounge, on the fourth floor of the Hong Kong Club, his mind was made up.

It did not take the baroness long to broach the subject. 'Andrew,' she said to him, 'the governor is thinking of appointing you to the Executive Council. If he approaches you, will you accept?'

'Yes, sure,' Andrew responded with alacrity. Lydia Dunn was a little surprised that he did not ask for time to think over the offer. But Andrew had already given the matter considerable thought. As a member of the Executive Council, he would be involved in all major decisions affecting Hong Kong, but he would not have to be accountable to any constituents. In fact, he would not be allowed to talk about his work, since he would have to swear an oath of secrecy.

Andrew suffered a personal tragedy in late 1992, when his mother, Edith, died suddenly of a heart attack in Toronto. This was a big blow to Andrew, who felt that his mother had been a strong influence in his life. 'She was a person of very strong principles and conviction and she, I think, instilled in us that integrity and hard work are really the most important things,' he recalled. He was particularly sad that she did not live to see him awarded a CBE a few months later for his work on the Executive Council and other community work.

Andrew had been close to his mother all his life. She had accompanied him to London, stopping over in Rome for sightseeing, when he went to boarding school in England at the age of fourteen to attend Repton School in Derbyshire, the first Chinese boy to do so. Edith impressed on her son what a privilege it was for someone from Hong Kong to be able to attend such an elite prep school in England. 'You must really do your very best not to disgrace your people,' she told him. During his years in England, she wrote to Andrew every week. She saved Andrew's letters and, many years later, returned them to him so he would have a record of this period of his life. Andrew did not let her down. He skipped a class after half a term and did well throughout his years at Repton.

After graduating from Repton, Andrew won a place at Cambridge University. However, he had almost a year before term started. Fook-kow gave him a round-the-world ticket, and the eighteen-year-old Andrew went to the United States, where he traveled across the country, doing the grand tour: New York, Washington, the Grand Canyon, Los Angeles, and San Francisco.

Before leaving on his holiday, he conceived the idea of working as a reporter in Hong Kong and so wrote to the *Far Eastern Economic Review*. The *Review* took him on, paying him by the article. Getting a job was unusual because Andrew, unlike other students, did not need to work. Becoming a journalist was more unusual because reporters, in Hong Kong's money-conscious society, did not enjoy a high social status. Andrew obviously enjoyed journalistic work because, the following summer, he was back at the *Review* again.

Despite two stints as a reporter, Andrew did not consider a career in journalism. Ever since his early teens, he had wanted to be a lawyer. Fook-kow therefore arranged for him to have a talk with his Uncle Simon. Simon took him on a long walk on the hillside and explained to him the differences between the two branches of the legal profession under the British system, solicitors and barristers. At the end of the walk, Andrew knew what it was he wanted to be. He wanted to fight cases, and to argue in court. He would become a barrister.

He studied law at Cambridge, where he was chairman of the Chinese Society. Its members were largely from Malaysia and Singapore as well as Hong Kong. After finishing the bachelor's degree, he did a year of post-graduate work. He returned to Hong Kong at the age of twenty-four and threw himself into his work, accepting all clients who came along, trying to establish a reputation for himself. He handled criminal cases and divorces and traffic accidents. For the next fifteen years, he set himself such a hectic pace, working Saturdays and Sundays as well, that he had little leisure time.

But he did find time to get married. His wife, Judy Mo Ying Woo, had attended university in Hong Kong, and after her graduation she worked for her father, who was in the property business. A quiet person who eschewed mahjongg and concerts, she devoted herself to her family, especially after the children started to arrive. The first child was a girl, Andrea Yen-kei, who was named after Andrew. A second child arrived three years later, another girl, named April Yen-eu. Unlike many traditional Chinese, Andrew and Judy stopped having children after the two girls were born, content not to have a son.

Having spent so much of his early life in England, Andrew's Chinese was weak, even though he grew up speaking Cantonese at home. At work, and in court, he only spoke English. He decided to train himself by reading Chinese newspapers every day. While unable to write a speech in Chinese, he could handle interviews with the press. He also felt it was important for his children to know Chinese. During the holidays, his wife would tell them Chinese folk tales. They were both sent to England to study as teenagers.

Andrew continued the Li family tradition of serving on the Hong Kong government's network of advisory boards and committees. His first appointment was to the Lands Tribunal, after which he served on a variety on bodies, including the Securities Commission, the Inland Revenue Board of Review, the Law Reform Commission, and the Judicial Services Commission. He was also active in the Bar Association, serving for a year as its secretary.

Aside from law, his other area of interest was education and he served as a member of the Council of the University of Hong Kong. In September 1986, the Government appointed him to a panel to map out plans for creating a new university that would emphasize science, technology, management, and business studies. It took five years, but in 1991 the Hong Kong University of Science and Technology accepted its first students.

Like his father and grandfather, Andrew was an ardent racing fan. In the summer of 1988, he decided to run for the vacant position when one of the Jockey Club's twelve stewards stepped down. His uncle Simon was a steward, as was his uncle Alan, son of Lan-sang. Inevitably, there were people who muttered that there were already 'too many Lis, why should we have another one?' Andrew Li and Dr Robert Fung, son of Sir Kenneth Fung, contested the vacancy. Andrew won.

Andrew became chairman of the Universities and Polytechnics Grants Committee (UPGC) in January 1989. The committee was a buffer between the government and universities which, while receiving government funding, were meant to remain independent. Its members consisted of laymen and academics whose job it was to ensure that the institutions' autonomy was protected, while the committee decided how much public funds to allocate to them. Thus, it played a key role in advising the government on the facilities, development, and financial needs of institutions of higher learning.

Only months after Andrew became chairman of the UPGC, the Tiananmen Square crackdown occurred, a event that affected millions of people in Hong Kong. Andrew joined a group of people who published a full-page 'Appeal to the Citizens of Hong Kong' in the newspapers. It said:

> In the wake of the bloody suppression of the patriotic democratic movement in China by the Chinese government, confidence in Hong Kong has completely collapsed, thereby seriously damaging the stability and prosperity of Hong Kong. We therefore think it right to start a Hong Kong People Saving Hong Kong Campaign, in order to unite all the people of Hong Kong and to encourage them to stay here and work out a future for Hong Kong.

The group called on Britain to allow 'all the people of Hong Kong to enter and live in the United Kingdom'. It also urged Britain set up 'a fully democratic government in Hong Kong before 1997'.

The Tiananmen Square incident accelerated the exodus from Hong Kong, as people looked for an insurance policy in the form of a foreign passport. Andrew was safe, since he already had a full British passport, acquired in the early 1980s. Anxious about the future, he had written to Repton School and to Cambridge University for supporting documents to show he had lived in England from 1963 to 1972, and so was eligible for a British passport. His application was approved. Armed with a British passport, he could move to England whenever he wanted.

The post-Tiananmen exodus caused the Hong Kong government to sharply increase the number of places in tertiary institutions, so that there would be enough highly educated people to replace those who left. The UPGC, under Andrew's leadership, was asked to increase the provision of first-year, first-degree places from 7,000 in 1990 to 15,000 in 1995. That meant that tertiary education would be provided for 18 per cent of the relevant age group, up from 13 per cent.

Andrew agreed with the government's policy of creating enough university graduates to replace those who left Hong Kong for fear of political uncertainty. He also urged former Hong Kong residents who had emigrated to return. In March 1990, Andrew, in a video conference between Hong Kong's Baptist College and the University of Western Sydney, made an impassioned appeal to academics in Australia to return to Hong Kong. 'To those Australians whose roots were in Hong Kong,' he said in a keynote speech, 'I wish to say simply and as forcefully as I can: Come home, Hong Kong needs you.'

His interest in education continued during his years on the Executive Council. In 1996, he became vice chairman of the Hong Kong University of Science and Technology. He also became vice chairman of St Paul's Co-Educational College, the secondary school he had attended, along with many other members of the Li family.

But, perhaps more significantly, he was approached by Tsinghua (Qinghua) University in Beijing for help to restart its law school, which had been shut down since the Communists took power in 1949. Tsinghua approached Andrew both for his legal and educational background as well as his connections with businessmen; the university wanted him to help raise funds to build a new law school. 'I feel very strongly it's a worthwhile project,' Andrew said, 'because law, the legal system, rule of law, is very important to the future of China, and Tsinghua of course is one of the very top universities in China.' Andrew set up a fund, called the Friends of Tsinghua University Law School Charitable Trust. So successful was he that Tsinghua honoured him by appointing him a visiting professor.

His relationship with Tsinghua indicated that Beijing did not view him with hostility, despite his serving as one of Patten's closest advisers. 'Whether service on the Executive Council will affect my future after 1997, I don't know for certain, but I do not believe so,' he declared. 'I don't believe that this will prejudice my future. But even if it does, it doesn't matter to me because I have a clear conscience. I've tried to do my best. I have tried to contribute to the transition bearing in mind my vision of the future of Hong Kong as part of China.'

In fact, so confident had he become of the future that, even before he was offered the position of chief justice, Andrew had made it clear that he was willing to give up his British passport. Even if things did not work out well for him after 1997, he insisted, he would not leave Hong Kong. 'Hong Kong is my home,' he affirmed strongly, 'and if—as I don't think will happen—I find conditions here not to my liking, I would try to continue to work here. If not, I would simply retire. I would not practice law anywhere else.'

Fortunately, Andrew did not have to retire. Instead, he became the first Chief Justice of the Hong Kong Special Administrative Region, an appointment that provided much reassurance that rule of law would remain in Hong Kong.

The first test of the independence of the new Court of Final Appeal came in early 1999, when the court heard a case relating to the right of abode in Hong Kong of mainland children with a parent who is a Hong Kong permanent resident. The case stemmed from the earliest days of the Special Administrative Region. The Provisional Legislature had passed immigration legislation that came into effect on 10 July 1997, but that was made retroactive to 1 July. It set up a Certificate of Entitlement scheme, under which mainland Chinese who claimed the right of abode in Hong Kong were issued with a certificate after their claim had been verified. Then, with the certificate attached to an exit permit issued by the Chinese authorities, they would be permitted to enter Hong Kong.

The legislation excluded children who were born out of wedlock, as well as those born before their parents became Hong Kong permanent residents.

The validity of the legislation was tested in the courts, with test cases wending their way through the judicial system. Finally, in mid-January, the case came before the Court of Final Appeal. At issue were two articles in the Basic Law that had to be interpreted. Article 24, in the chapter on rights and responsibilities of Hong Kong residents, did not provide a definition of 'children'. Article 22, in the chapter on the relationship between the central authorities and the region, described the procedures under which mainland Chinese (or 'people from other parts of China') could apply to leave the mainland and enter Hong Kong for settlement.

The Special Administrative Region government argued that the Court could not interpret Article 22, since it bore on the relationship between the central government and Hong Kong, an area that was excluded from the Court's jurisdiction by the Basic Law. It argued that the Court should refer the case to China's National People's Congress for an interpretation first. Lawyers for the children, however, argued that the substantive issue was Article 24, which was an immigration matter and hence within the area of autonomy of the Special

259

Administrative Region. Interpretation by the National People's Congress would presumably have resulted in a victory by the Special Administrative Region government, since the National People's Congress is widely perceived to be nothing more than a rubber-stamp body that carries out the wishes of the Chinese government, which had already made clear its support for the Special Administrative Region government's position.

On 29 January 1999, the Court of Final Appeal handed down a landmark judgment. The court decided that it was not necessary to refer the case to the National People's Congress. In fact, it declared that 'it is for the Court of Final Appeal and for it alone to decide, in adjudicating a case' whether it is necessary to refer the case to the National People's Congress. It went on to say that it had the jurisdiction to examine legislative acts of the National People's Congress and 'declare them to be invalid if found to be inconsistent' with the Basic Law.

As for Article 22, the court decided that the phrase 'people from other parts of China' does not 'include permanent residents of the Region upon whom the Basic Law confers the right of abode in the region. Persons with permanent resident status under the Basic Law are not, as a matter of ordinary language, people from other parts of China'.

The Court struck down as unconstitutional the retrospective provisions of the immigration ordinance, thus granting immediate right of abode to those who had arrived in Hong Kong before 10 July 1997, whose status as children of Hong Kong permanent residents was not contested by the government.

As for the definition of 'children', the court decided that it includes those born out of wedlock as well as those born before their parents became Hong Kong permanent residents. In one fell swoop, it opened the doors of Hong Kong to countless thousands of people from the mainland, a development that both the Special Administrative Region and Beijing governments had tried to avoid. However, the Court did uphold the

Certificate of Entitlement scheme, saying that those claiming the right of abode have to make that claim on the mainland, not in Hong Kong. Anyone in Hong Kong making that claim must first return to the mainland.

The court's landmark judgment was immediately hailed by constitutional scholars as a major blow for the rule of law. While the Special Administrative Region government moaned about pressures on social services in Hong Kong such as housing, education, and hospitals, it indicated that it would do its best to make plans and accommodate the expected influx.

Beijing was even more unhappy. On the weekend of 6–7 February, the Xinhua News Agency reported that four Chinese legal experts, all of whom had been involved in the drafting of the Basic Law, had voiced criticism of the judgment. They pointed out that the Preparatory Committee, which was set up in 1996 by the National People's Congress to prepare Hong Kong for the change in sovereignty, had, in fact, decided on the definition of 'children'—a definition that did not include those born out of wedlock or born before their parents acquired Hong Kong permanent residency. Moreover, the Preparatory Committee's work report had been endorsed by the National People's Congress. Thus, they said, the National People's Congress had already made a decision, and the Court of Final Appeal should not overturn a National People's Congress decision.

The legal experts strongly criticized the court's pronouncement that it could invalidate legal decisions of the National People's Congress, pointing out that, under the Chinese constitution, the National People's Congress was 'the highest organ of state power'. Not even the Supreme People's Court can invalidate National Peopl's Congress decisions, they said. How could a Hong Kong court claim this authority? In effect, they accused the court of violating Chinese sovereignty.

On the evening of 7 February, a Chinese official, Zhao Qizheng, head of the information office of the State Council, told journalists that the views of the legal experts reflected those of the Chinese government. Meanwhile, editorials in the communist press in Hong Kong daily excoriated the court's judgment. Pro-China figures in Hong Kong made public statements condemning the Court of Final Appeal. One of them compared Chief Justice Andrew Li to a little boy who had not asked his mother, China, for permission before making an improper decision.

The Special Administrative Region government tried to contain the damage. The Chief Executive issued a statement saying that, while an independent judiciary was important, the Special Administrative Region was giving great weight to the views of the mainland legal experts and was studying them in detail. This was followed by an announcement that the Secretary for Justice would go to Beijing to discuss the situation with mainland officials.

Secretary of Justice Elsie Leung went to Beijing on 12 February, returning to Hong Kong the next day after meeting with officials from the Hong Kong and Macao Affairs Office of the State Council, members of the legal affairs committee of the National People's Congress, as well as the legal experts themselves. Upon her return, she said that China believed that the court had made a mistake, which had to be rectified.

Inevitably, the controversy aroused international interest, since it was the first time in nineteen months that there was a confrontation between Hong Kong and mainland China. Britain's consulate general in Hong Kong said any moves to restrict the powers of Hong Kong's highest court would raise 'serious concern'. In Washington, too, voices were raised warning Beijing against taking any action to undo the Court of Final Appeal's ruling. The Chinese Foreign Ministry reacted, predictably, by warning foreigners not to stick their noses into China's internal affairs.

On 24 February, the Special Administrative Region government took action to defuse the issue. It submitted legal documents to the court asking it to 'clarify' its judgment, primarily relating to the relationship between the Court of Final Appeal and the National People's Congress. The unprecedented move created an outcry within the legal community, with many saying there was nothing to clarify, since the judgment was already quite clear, and neither party to the dispute had sought clarification. Some legal authorities called on the court to reject the proposal.

However, on 26 February, the court did hold hearings and, in the afternoon, issued a new judgment. It did not change any of its original decisions, but it did attempt to clarify its relationship with the National People's Congress by saying: 'The Court's judgment on 29 January 1999 did not question the authority of the Standing Committee to make an interpretation under Article 158 [of the Basic Law], which would have to be followed by the courts of the Region. The Court accepts that it cannot question that authority.'

The following evening, the Xinhua News Agency reported that a spokesman for the Commission of Legislative Affairs of the National People's Congress had called the new court statement a 'necessary step' to clarify the 29 January judgment. He emphasized that the National People's Congress is the highest organ of state power in China and added: 'The National People's Congress and its Standing Committee will perform its duties according to the principles of "one country, two systems" and the Basic Law of the HKSAR.'

The clarification sought by the Special Administrative Region government, in a sense, saved face for all parties concerned, including the Court, the Special Administrative Region government, and the Chinese authorities. If Andrew and his fellow judges had refused to issue a clarification, the rift between Hong Kong and China would have widened, and the crisis would have deepened. While many in the legal community deplored the government's action, and the court's willingness to cooperate with the government, this course of action was the most pragmatic in terms of damage limitation. The issuance of the clarification resolved the first constitutional crisis between Hong Kong and the Chinese government without serious damage to the Court's integrity.

Andrew no doubt foresaw, when he accepted the position of Chief Justice, the possibility of confrontations with the Chinese legal or political systems. But, as Hong Kong entered its new life, he and other members of the Li family seemed fully committed to the SAR, with the fortunes of the Li family inextricably tied to those of Hong Kong itself.

CONCLUSION

As this book goes to press in mid 1999, Hong Kong has experienced twenty-two months as a Special Administrative Region of the People's Republic of China. Predictions of gloom and doom, so prevalent before the change in sovereignty, have failed to come true. China has lived up to its promise not to interfere in Hong Kong's internal affairs, and to let Hong Kong people run Hong Kong.

Many of the half million people who left Hong Kong in the years after signing of the Joint Declaration have returned. Most of them have secured an insurance policy in the form of a foreign passport, so they can leave again if, for any reason, things should go drastically wrong. But, by and large, fears of a loss of rights and freedoms have receded.

This chronicle of the Li family will help to show how Hong Kong has developed over the last century and a half, being transformed from a small trading post on the China coast into one of the world's most vibrant financial centres, how its colonial status permitted economic growth while handicapping political development, and how its people have, slowly but surely, gained in self-confidence and are now taking part in the grand experiment of governing themselves.

No one knows what the future holds but, for now at least, there is little reason to be pessimistic. The whole world is positively disposed towards Hong Kong. The countries in North America and the European Union wish to anchor Hong Kong in the West. China itself clearly wants the experiment of 'one country, two systems' to succeed. Even Taiwan, which does not want to become another special administrative region itself, wants Hong Kong to succeed.

And, if the past is any guide, Hong Kong will succeed. True, its future is inextricably linked with that of China. But its people are now more in control of their destiny than they have ever been. And, as in previous generations, Hong Kong is likely to benefit from an infusion of fresh blood, as many people from mainland China, including some of the country's best and brightest, seek to make their homes in Hong Kong, and, in time, to identify themselves as Hong Kong people.

THE LI FAMILY TREE

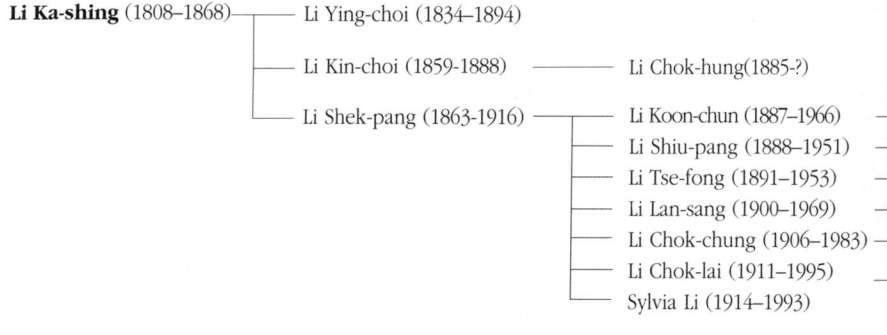

Li **Ka-shing** (1808–1868) ── Li Ying-choi (1834–1894)
                            ├── Li Kin-choi (1859-1888) ──── Li Chok-hung(1885-?)
                            └── Li Shek-pang (1863-1916) ──┬── Li Koon-chun (1887–1966)
                                                           ├── Li Shiu-pang (1888–1951)
                                                           ├── Li Tse-fong (1891–1953)
                                                           ├── Li Lan-sang (1900–1969)
                                                           ├── Li Chok-chung (1906–1983)
                                                           ├── Li Chok-lai (1911–1995)
                                                           └── Sylvia Li (1914–1993)

The Li Family Tree

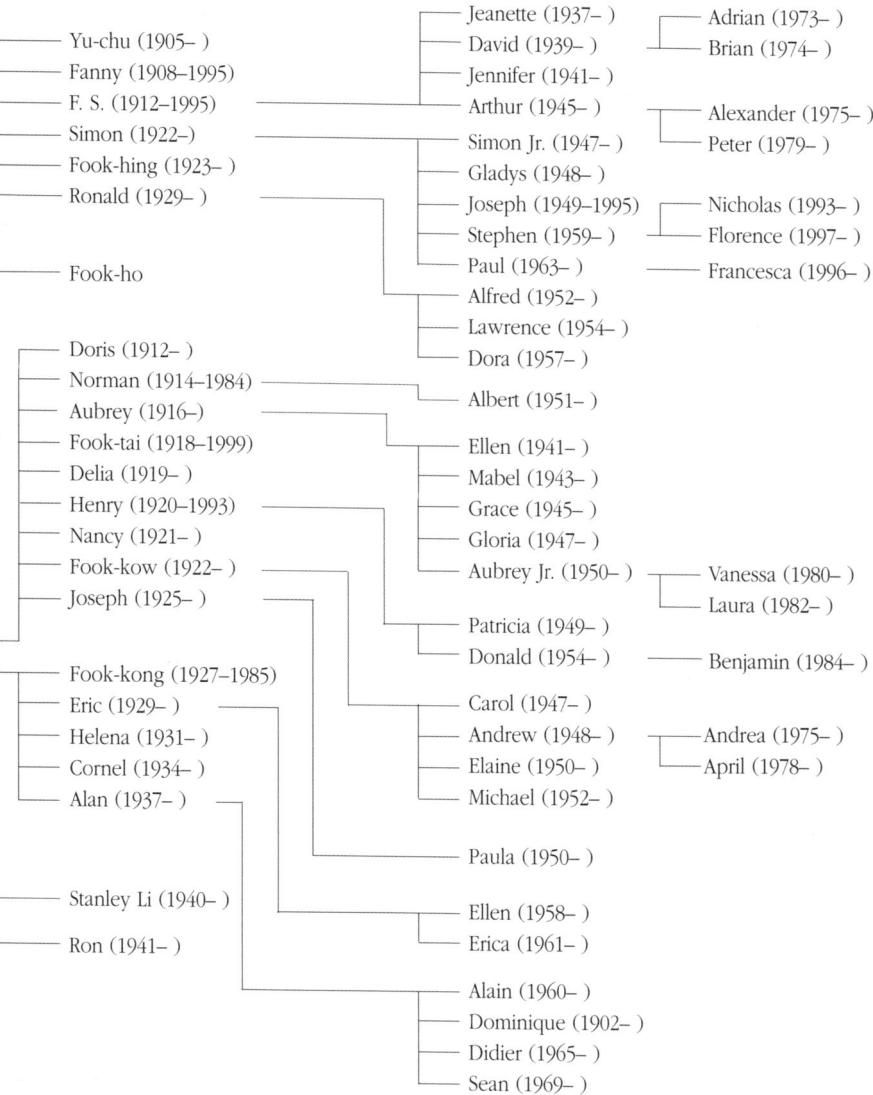